A Guide to
THE PROPHETS

by

STEPHEN F. WINWARD

JOHN KNOX PRESS
ATLANTA

Originally published in Great Britain by
Hodder and Stoughton Limited, 1968,
and in the United States by John Knox Press, 1969

Paperback edition, 1976,
John Knox Press
Third printing 1983

ISBN: 0-8042-0131-5
Library of Congress Catalog Card Number: 68-55819
Copyright   1968 by Stephen F. Winward

Printed in the United States of America

Contents

Preface and Acknowledgments

An Ethiopian, returning from Jerusalem in his chariot, was reading aloud from a scroll of the prophet Isaiah. Overtaking and overhearing him, Philip the evangelist enquired, 'Do you understand what you are reading?' The African replied, 'How can I, unless someone guides me?' Now, as then, the reader is in need of a guide, if he is to understand the words of the prophets. I know from my own pastoral experience that the last third of the Old Testament is a closed book to many Christians. With the exception of the interesting stories, and the great passages about the Messiah, the Servant, and the Spirit, read at Christmas, Passiontide, and Pentecost, much of the material in the books of the prophets is unintelligible. Martin Luther's description of the impression made by the recorded words of the prophets on the average man, still holds good. 'They have a queer way of talking, like people who, instead of proceeding in an orderly manner, ramble off from one thing to the next, so that you cannot make head or tail of them or see what they are getting at.'

On one occasion, a prophet was commanded by God to write a message in large characters, so that even a runner might read it without difficulty. It is often hard to do what God requires, but the prophets certainly did not intend that the divine messages should be difficult to understand. It is the responsibility of the teacher and guide to make the meaning clear and plain. This book attempts to give a straightforward account of the prophets in chronological order. The problems which rightly and necessarily concern biblical scholars—the original text, the date, authorship, composition, and unity of the various books—are not dealt with at length; for the general conclusions reached by the scholars are accepted with gratitude and taken as the starting point.

This book is concerned with four things—with the history of Israel, with the lives of the prophets, with the writings which bear their names, and above all with their teaching. It tells the story of Israel from the time of the first to the time of the last of 'the writing prophets'. Some knowledge of this history is necessary, for the ministry of each prophet must be set in its historical context if the messages are to be rightly understood. The lives of the prophets fall within this history. The auto-biographical and biographical material found in the books is used to tell the story of each prophet—in so far as it can be known. The literature itself has come down to us from prophets known and unknown, through disciples and collectors, editors and scribes. Each book is introduced and outlined, and questions of authorship, date, and composition are briefly discussed. The primary concern of this book, however, is with the teaching of the prophets, and with the relevance and application of their message to our situation today. It is written in the belief that the God who 'in many and various ways spoke of old to our fathers by the prophets', still continues to speak to men today through their recorded and transmitted words.

Unless otherwise indicated, all scripture quotations are taken from the *Revised Standard Version of the Bible*, copyrighted 1946 and 1952, and used by permission.

I acknowledge with gratitude my indebtedness to many biblical scholars, as indicated in the footnotes. Factual information has been gathered from the four volumes of *The Interpreter's Dictionary of the Bible* (Abingdon Press). For the interpretation of the text of the various prophets, help has been received from several of the contributors to volumes V and VI of *The Interpreter's Bible* (Abingdon Press). I am especially indebted to the authors of the following books:

The Relevance of the Prophets, R. B. Y. Scott (Collier–Macmillan, Ltd.)
Prophecy in Ancient Israel, J. Lindblom (Blackwell)
Old Testament Theology, Volume II, Gerhard von Rad (Oliver and Boyd, Ltd.)
The Living World of the Old Testament, Bernhard W. Anderson (Longmans, Green and Co., Ltd.)
Inspiration and Revelation in the Old Testament, H. Wheeler Robinson (Clarendon Press)
The Latter Prophets, T. Henshaw (George Allen and Unwin, Ltd.)
Prophecy and Religion, John Skinner (Cambridge University Press)
The History of Israel, Martin Noth (Adam and Charles Black, Ltd.)

I desire most of all to acknowledge the constant and invaluable help of my wife in the preparation of the script.

Chronological Table

The names of the kings of Israel (Northern Kingdom) are on the left, and the names of the kings of Judah (Southern Kingdom) on the right hand side. The exact dates of their reigns cannot always be determined, and the figures given should be taken as approximate. References to the canonical prophets are in italics.

	The Disruption—the division of the one kingdom into Israel and Judah, 931	
931–910 JEROBOAM I		931–913 REHOBOAM
		913–911 ABIJAH
		911–870 ASA
910–909 NADAB		
909–886 BAASHA		
886–885 ELAH		
885 ZIMRI		
885–874 OMRI	Omri founds city of Samaria, 879	
874–853 AHAB	Ministry of Elijah	870–848 JEHOSHAPHAT
853–852 AHAZIAH		
852–841 JEHORAM	Ministry of Elisha	848–841 JEHORAM
		841 AHAZIAH
841–814 JEHU	Jehu pays tribute to Shalmaneser III, 841	841–835 ATHALIAH
814–798 JEHOAHAZ		835–796 JOASH
798–783 JOASH		796–781 AMAZIAH

783–743
JEROBOAM II   *Ministry of Amos*—between 760 and
750

781–740
UZZIAH

750–740
JOTHAM
(as regent)

Reign of Tiglath-pileser III: 745–727
Ministry of Hosea—between 743 and
734

743 ZECHARIAH

743 SHALLUM

743–738
MENAHEM

Call of Isaiah, 740
First appearance of Micah
Menahem pays tribute to Tiglath-
pileser, 738

740–736
JOTHAM
(as sole ruler)

738–737
PEKAHIAH

737–732
PEKAH

Syro-Ephraimite War, 734
Ministry of Isaiah
Tiglath-pileser subdues Israel and
annexes Galilee, Transjordan, Jezreel, and the Sea Plain, 733

736–716
AHAZ

732–724
HOSHEA

Death of Tiglath-pileser, accession of
Shalmaneser V, 727
Hoshea withholds tribute from Assy-
ria, 727
Shalmaneser V invades Israel, cap-
tures Hoshea, and besieges Samaria,
724
Siege of Samaria by Shalmaneser V
and Sargon II, 724–721
Capture of Samaria and deportation
of inhabitants, 721
End of Northern Kingdom, 721

716–687
HEZEKIAH

Establishment of Ethiopian dynasty
in Egypt, 714
Anti-Assyrian revolt in Ashdod, 714–
713
Ministry of Isaiah
Ministry of Micah
Sargon II captures Ashdod, 711
Reign of Pharaoh Shabaka: 710–
696

Accession of Sennacherib, 705
Judah's alliance with Egypt, 705–701
Ministry of Isaiah
Ministry of Micah
Sennacherib invades Judea, Hezekiah pays tribute, 701
Second campaign of Sennacherib, *c.* 688
Ministry of Isaiah
Retreat of Sennacherib from Jerusalem and Judea, 688

687–642
MANASSEH

Death of Sennacherib, accession of Esarhaddon, 681
Pagan worship under Manasseh
Death of Isaiah
Esarhaddon captures Lower Egypt, 671
Ashurbanipal captures Thebes, 661
Assyrians driven from Egypt, 650

642–640
AMON

640–609
JOSIAH

Scythian invasions
Ministry of Zephaniah—between 630 and 625
Call of Jeremiah, 626
Discovery of 'The Book of the Law' and Josiah's Reformation, 621
Ministry of Jeremiah
The Medes capture Ashhur, 614
The destruction of Nineveh by the Medes and Babylonians, 612
Ministry of Nahum—shortly before or after 612
Capture of Harran, 611
Reign of Pharaoh Necho: 609–593
Battle of Megiddo, and death of Josiah, 609

609 JEHOAHAZ

Ministry of Jeremiah
Pharaoh Necho replaces Jehoahaz by Jehoiakim, 609

609–598
JEHOIAKIM

Temple Sermon of Jeremiah
Judah subject to Egypt, 609–605
Battle of Carchemish, Jehoiakim becomes subject to Babylon, 605

Ministry of Habakkuk—between 605
and 598
Jeremiah dictates his oracles to Baruch, 605
Ministry of Jeremiah
Jehoiakim revolts against Babylon,
602
Judea raided by bands of Babylonians
and Arameans, 602
Babylonian army besieges Jerusalem,
598
Death of Jehoiakim and accession of
Jehoiachin, 598

598 JEHOIACHIN

Jehoiachin capitulates to Nebuchadrezzar. First deportation of exiles,
598

598–587
ZEDEKIAH

Death of Pharaoh Necho, and acces-
sion of Psammeticus II, 594
Ministry of Jeremiah
Call of Ezekiel, 593
Zedekiah renounces his allegiance to
Babylon, 589
The siege of Jerusalem, 589–587
Accession of Pharaoh Hophra, 588
Ministry of Ezekiel
Ministry of Jeremiah
The capture of Jerusalem, the des-
truction of the city and the temple,
and second deportation of exiles, 587
End of Southern Kingdom, 587
Gedeliah governor of Judea
Jeremiah taken to Egypt, 587
The Babylonian Exile, from 598 and
587 to 538
Ministry of Ezekiel
Cyrus of Anshan revolts against
Astyges of Media, 553
Cyrus overthrows Median Empire,
550
Cyrus overthrows Kingdom of
Lydia, 546
Ministry of Second Isaiah between 550
and 539
Cyrus enters Babylon, end of Baby-
lonian and beginning of Persian
Empire, 539
Return of exiles under Sheshbazzar,
538

Restoration of altar, 538, and foundation of Second Temple, 537

Restoration of Second Temple interrupted for 18 years, 538–520

Death of Cyrus, accession of Cambyses II, 530

Reign of Darius the Great, 522–486

Widespread disturbances in Persian Empire, 522–521

Zerubbabel governor in Jerusalem

Ministry of Haggai, 520

Ministry of Zechariah, 520–518

The building of the Second Temple, 520–516

Third Isaiah

Battle of Marathon, 490

Xerxes I captures Athens. Battle of Salamis, 480

Ministry of Obadiah—about 460

Reign of Artaxerxes I: 456–423

Ministry of Malachi—about 450

Nehemiah rebuilds the walls of Jerusalem, 444

Ministry of Joel—between 440 and 400

The mission of Ezra the Scribe, 397

The Book of Jonah

Birth of Alexander the Great, 356

Battles of Granicus, 334, Issus, 333, and Arbela, 331. End of Persian and beginning of Hellenistic period

Foundation of the city of Alexandria, 331

Death of Alexander the Great, 323

Judea under the Ptolemys of Egypt, 323–198

Second Zechariah

I

General Introduction

The twenty-four books of the Hebrew Bible are arranged in three divisions, known as the Law, the Prophets, and the Writings. The second of these divisions is itself sub-divided into the Former Prophets and the Latter Prophets. The four books Joshua, Judges, Samuel, and Kings are grouped under the title the Former Prophets, and the four books Isaiah, Jeremiah, Ezekiel, and the Twelve are grouped under the title the Latter Prophets. This may come as a surprise, for in our Christian Bibles Joshua, Judges, Samuel, and Kings are separated from the prophetic literature, and are regarded by us as history books. According to Jewish theory, these books are known as the Former Prophets because Joshua wrote the book which bears his name, Samuel wrote the books of Judges and Samuel, and Jeremiah wrote the book of Kings. While discarding this theory as fanciful, we need not question the wisdom of the Jewish classification of these four books. It is true that they record the history of Israel from the death of Moses to the fall of Jerusalem in 587 B.C., yet they tell and interpret the story from the prophetic standpoint. In their present form, these four books are the product of writers profoundly influenced by the book of Deuteronomy, the nucleus of which was discovered in the Temple in 621 B.C., and was the basis of the great reformation of religion under King Josiah.[1] In the form of exhortation and legislation, 'Deuteronomy is an attempt to translate the spiritual and moral principles on which the eighth-century prophets (Amos, Hosea, Micah, Isaiah) had insisted, into the actual social and political life of Israel'.[2] Under the influence of the ancient Mosaic tradition and the teaching of the great prophets, the Deuteronomic school of writers told the story of Israel from a religious standpoint. They made use of the historical material

[1] See page 127.
[2] T. H. Robinson, *Decline and Fall of the Hebrew Kingdoms*, 241.

at their disposal to illustrate the prophetic doctrine of retribution. Whenever leaders and judges, kings and people worship the Lord, keep his covenant, obey his commandments, they are rewarded with prosperity and peace. Whenever they turn aside to other gods and do that which is evil in the sight of the Lord, retribution overtakes them, disaster comes upon them. For this reason, the Jewish custom of calling these four books 'the Former Prophets' and setting them alongside the Latter Prophets, has much to commend it.

During the last two and a half centuries before Christ, the Hebrew Bible was translated into Greek at Alexandria in Egypt—a version known as the Septuagint. In that version the books were arranged according to chronology and subject matter, and the Latin Bible, the Vulgate, adopted (with some modifications) the same arrangement, now familiar to us in our English Bibles. The third division of the Hebrew Bible, the Writings, was inserted between the Former and the Latter Prophets, and the order of the books within that third division was altered. The books of Samuel and Kings were each divided into two, and the two books, Lamentations and Daniel, were taken out of the Writings and put with the Latter Prophets. For it was believed that Jeremiah was the author of Lamentations, and that Daniel was one of the prophets. Since Jeremiah was not in fact the author of Lamentations, and the book of Daniel is not prophecy but apocalyptic, these two books which belong to the Writings are not included in this study of the prophets. With these two exceptions, this book is a study of all the material to be found from Isaiah to Malachi in our English Bibles.

The arrangement of these books in our English versions follows the Hebrew Bible, in which the Latter Prophets are comprised in four rolls—Isaiah, Jeremiah, Ezekiel, and the book of the Twelve. The Twelve Prophets on the fourth roll are commonly known as the Minor Prophets—an unfortunate title if it conveys the impression that they are of minor importance. While the three great prophets Isaiah, Jeremiah, Ezekiel, were arranged in the proper sequence, the oracles of the Twelve Prophets were not. They were collected on one scroll as a matter of convenience, and the Twelve Prophets were not arranged in chronological order, either with reference to one another or to Isaiah, Jeremiah, and Ezekiel. In this book the prophets are studied not in the order in which they now appear in the Bible, but in chronological order. This is essential to a right understanding of the historical background of each prophet and of the development of prophecy as a whole. In so far as it can be discovered, the sequence of the Latter Prophets is —Amos, Hosea, Micah, Isaiah, Zephaniah, Nahum, Habakkuk, Jeremiah, Ezekiel, Second Isaiah, Haggai, Zechariah, Third Isaiah, Obadiah, Malachi, Joel, Jonah, Second Zechariah.

THE PROPHETS BEFORE AMOS

The prophets whose names have just been mentioned are known as the canonical prophets because their words have been preserved, collected, and included in the library of sacred writings recognized as inspired and authoritative. But these men of God were not at the head of the procession, for there were prophets in Israel long before the canonical prophets. To see the latter in perspective, we must first glance at this earlier prophetic movement. The origin of prophecy is shrouded in mystery. 'The earliest Old Testament evidence for its appearance are the accounts of the Dervish-like enthusiasts who from time to time emerged up and down the land, probably to be eyed askance by the settled Israelite farmers.'[1] On his way home from Ramah, where he had been anointed king by Samuel, Saul met a company of wild ecstatics 'coming down from the high place with harp, tambourine, flute, and lyre before them, prophesying' (I Samuel 10: 5). Infected by their frenzy, Saul was 'turned into another man'. The ecstasy of the group could be communicated by direct contagion. On one occasion, three bands of messengers sent by Saul to arrest David were all in turn infected by the uninhibited emotion and fervour (I Samuel 19: 20, 21). Four hundred ecstatics of this kind were consulted by King Ahab before he set out to recover Ramoth-Gilead (I Kings 22: 5–12). It is recorded that during the days of Elijah, the faithful Obadiah hid a hundred prophets of the Lord in a cave, lest they should be destroyed by the pagan Queen Jezebel (I Kings 18: 4). From the narratives about Elijah and Elisha, it may be inferred that 'the sons of the prophets' were united in guilds or associations. They had a leader, shared meals, and lived together (II Kings 2:1–8; 4: 38–41).

In addition to these groups of ecstatics and prophetic confraternities, sometimes associated with them (e.g. Samuel and Elisha), usually in entire independence of them, there were

[1] G. von Rad, *Old Testament Theology*, Vol. II, 8.

B

many individual prophets, some of outstanding importance. 'The Lord your God will raise up for you a prophet like me from among you' (Deuteronomy 18: 15). Later writers, looking back to the origin of the nation in the wilderness, recognized Moses, Aaron, and Miriam as prophets, for God had spoken to them and transmitted his word through them. The patriot Deborah is called a prophetess, and Samuel is described both as a seer and as a prophet (Judges 4: 4; I Samuel 3: 20; 9: 9). Through Nathan the prophet, David was assured of the permanence of his dynasty, and through Gad the seer he was directed to purchase the site of the future Temple (II Samuel 7: 12–17; 24: 18). During the reign of his son Solomon, Ahijah the prophet, tearing his mantle into twelve pieces, and handing ten of them to Jeroboam, foretold and enacted the disruption of the kingdom; during the reign of Ahab, Micaiah the prophet, contradicting the 400 prophets who had been enticed by a lying spirit, predicted the defeat of the king and his death in battle (I Kings 11: 29–31; 22: 5–28). With the possible exception of Samuel, more is known about Elijah and Elisha than any of the other prophets who preceded Amos. Powerful in speech and action, austere and zealous, 'the prophet Elijah arose like a fire, and his word burned like a torch' (Sirach 48: 1). Fed by ravens, raising to life the widow's son, challenging the nation on Mount Carmel to choose between the God of Israel and the Syrian Baal, listening to the still small voice on Horeb, rebuking King Ahab for the murder of Naboth, taken up to heaven in a chariot of fire—the stories of Elijah are among the best-known and best-loved in the Bible (I Kings 17; 18; 19; 21; II Kings 1; 2: 1–12). In the New Testament he appears as the representative of the prophets (Mark 9: 4). His successor Elisha, who was associated with the prophetic confraternities and to whom a number of miraculous deeds are attributed, played a prominent part in the affairs of Israel and of neighbouring states (II Kings 2: 1 to 13: 20). In contrast to these prophets about whom much or something is known, there are others, such as Jehu son of Hanani and Jonah son of Amittai, about whom little or nothing is known beyond their names.

This short account of the earlier prophetic movement will serve to indicate that the canonical prophets had many predecessors. Like the earlier prophetic groups, they too were subject to ecstasy. There are important differences between the earlier

ecstatics and the canonical prophets, but it would be misleading to contrast them in terms of the ecstatic and the non-
ecstatic. God *sometimes* revealed himself to some of the canonical
prophets when they were in a state of ecstasy. There is a second
resemblance. Some of the canonical, like the earlier prophets
were figures of national importance, rebuking, encouraging, or
advising kings, and influencing the affairs of state. In this
respect Isaiah and Jeremiah bear some resemblance to Samuel
and Elisha. Furthermore, the moral demands of a righteous
God were not affirmed for the first time by the eighth-century
prophets. Nathan, who rebuked David for adultery with
Bathsheba, lived long before the days of Amos, who rebuked
the magnates of Samaria for the oppression of the needy.
Elijah, who denounced the murder of Naboth by the wicked
Jezebel, lived a century before Isaiah, who denounced the
selfish luxury of the ladies of Jerusalem. The word of the Lord
was spoken to the earlier as well as to the later prophets. The
canonical prophets cannot be rightly understood, apart from
the received religious tradition. They were not isolated from
the community and the past; they were grounded in a living
tradition which went back to Moses and to which many of
their prophetic predecessors, known and unknown, had contributed. This is not to detract in any way from the greatness of
the canonical prophets, or to question the unique contribution
they made to the life of Israel, the Christian Church, and mankind. It is simply to recognize that they were members of a
community with a past, heirs and intepreters of a tradition
to which they were deeply indebted.

THE RECEPTION OF REVELATION

In picture language, the vocation of the canonical prophets
may be understood in terms of the ears and the mouth. They
were called to listen to the word of God and to speak that word
to men. Their two-fold task was the reception and the transmission of the revelation. The role of the true prophet is clearly
expressed in a well-known incident. Moses attempts to evade
the task to which he is being called, on the ground that he is
not an eloquent man. God says to him, 'See, I make you as
God to Pharaoh; and Aaron your brother shall be your
prophet' (Exodus 7: 1). Moses was God to Aaron; Aaron was
a mouth for Moses. As the task of Aaron was to listen to what
Moses said and pass it on to Pharaoh, so the task of the prophet

was to receive the words of God and to speak those same words to men. These two functions will be illustrated again and again in the chapters which follow. First comes the reception of revelation. Having been encountered and called by the Lord, the ears of the prophet were opened, i.e. his mind and heart were receptive to the divine word. The relationship between the Lord and the prophet was not impersonal and external, but direct and intimate. For 'the prophet who is properly so called was a man who knew God in the intimacy of experience'.[1] The relationship was like that of a friend confiding in a friend, and not like that of a commander issuing an order to a soldier.[2] The prophets were the king's friends or counsellors.[3] They were the men to whom he confided his plans and purposes. 'Surely the Lord God does nothing, without revealing his secret (Hebrew *Sodh*) to his servants the prophets' (Amos 3: 7).

The word *Sodh* used by Amos is employed elsewhere to describe the assembly for consultation between the Lord and the beings who surround and serve him in heaven. One such meeting of the heavenly council is described by the prophet Micaiah. 'I saw the Lord sitting on his throne and all the host of heaven standing beside him on his right hand and on his left.' The prophet overhears the discussion between God and the heavenly beings and the decisions reached, and can for that reason understand what is happening or is about to happen on earth (I Kings 22: 19–23). That which God decides in the council in heaven, he discloses to his servants the prophets on earth (Isaiah 6: 8). Of the false prophets God says—'If they had stood in my council, then they would have proclaimed my words to my people' (Jeremiah 23: 22). This highly suggestive conception of the heavenly council enables us to appreciate the great privilege and responsibility of the prophets as the confidants of God, and also the objective nature of the word which was given to them from heaven. The words of the true prophet were not self-produced, were not the product of human reflection; they did not have their source and origin in the prophet. They were given to him by God. Touching the lips of Jeremiah, God said 'Behold, I have put my words in your mouth' (Jeremiah 1: 9). Offering Ezekiel a scroll on which his

---

[1] *The Old Testament and Modern Study*, edited by H. H. Rowley, 143.
[2] In the Book of Wisdom (7: 27) we find the phrase 'friends of God and prophets'; cf. John 15: 15.
[3] I Kings 4: 5.

messages were written, God said 'Son of man . . . eat this scroll, and go, speak to the house of Israel' (Ezekiel 3: 1). The message was received and inwardly digested before it was transmitted and spoken.

ECSTASY, VISION, AND AUDITION

The messages of God were received by the prophets when they were in a condition of mental and spiritual exaltation. On some occasions this exaltation of spirit was of such intensity that the prophets were in a state of ecstasy when they received revelation from God. This has been defined as 'a mental state in which human consciousness is so concentrated on a particular idea or feeling that the normal current of thoughts and perceptions is broken off and the senses temporarily cease to function in a normal way'.[1] In this condition the prophet ceased to be aware of the ordinary circumstances and relationships of life and became intensely aware of God. The personality of the prophet was not set aside; it was raised to a new intensity through encounter with God, and became the medium of divine revelation. It would be contrary to the evidence to deny the importance of ecstasy in the experience of some of the canonical prophets, but it would also be an error to exaggerate it. 'Unlike their predecessors, the great prophets did not experience ecstasy of a wild and orgiastic type. Their revelatory states were of a more moral and personal character, with the tranquillity of sublime inspiration.'[2] There are degrees of concentration and excitation, of enlightenment and exaltation, and the prophets were not always—and the evidence suggests not usually—in a state of ecstasy when they received revelation from God. But they were in a condition of exaltation; it was to a mind elevated and a heart profoundly moved by encounter with God, that revelation was imparted. For it was not abstract and impersonal knowledge that the Lord disclosed to the prophets, but himself, the living God—his mind and his will, his plans and purposes, his indignation and compassion. In receiving revelation, the prophet felt as well as understood. 'It was not only the knowledge of God's designs in history that was communicated to him, but also the feelings in God's heart, wrath, love, sorrow, revulsion, even the doubt as to what to do or how to do it.'[3]

[1] J. Lindblom, *Prophecy in Ancient Israel*, 106.   [2] Ibid., 178.
[3] G. von Rad, *Old Testament Theology*, Vol. II, 631.

Revelation was received by the prophet as something seen (vision) or as something heard (audition) or as a combination of both. In the account of the call of Isaiah, for example, we have a combination of vision and audition—he sees the throne, the robes of God, the seraphim, the smoke, the live coal; he hears the song of the seraphim, the declaration of pardon, the question put by God to the heavenly council (Isaiah 6: 1–8). On the other hand, the call of Jeremiah is described largely in terms of things heard, and only at the conclusion of the dialogue does he *see* the hand of God outstretched to touch his lips (Jeremiah 1: 4–10). In the prophecy of Ezekiel, things seen predominate. Neither with visions or auditions are the physical eyes or ears involved. The vision is seen with the inner eye, the voice is heard with the inner ear. On some occasions, however, that which is seen is also seen with the physical eyes of the prophet. Jeremiah sees (literally) a sprig of blossom, a boiling cauldron, a basket of figs, a potter at his wheel. As he attends to these common objects of his natural or social environment, that which he sees becomes a channel of divine revelation. The prophets also received revelation in a way more closely akin to poetic inspiration. The mind and creative imagination of the prophet expressed in literary form the revelation imparted by God. The essential content of the message was given by God; the form was supplied by the prophet. Many examples of these literary visions will be given in the chapters which follow—but at this stage we are passing from the reception to the transmission of revelation. Not in one way, but 'in many and various ways God spoke of old to our fathers by the prophets' (Hebrews 1: 1).

Yet whatever the way chosen by God, the prophets were aware both of the objectivity or givenness of the word, and also of the obligation to communicate it to men. The obligation, the sense of compulsion, the inner moral constraint felt by the prophets to declare God's word, is expressed in terms of the hand and Spirit of God. Isaiah, Jeremiah, and especially Ezekiel, refer to the hand of God. The personal experience of compulsion is described in terms of physical force. The prophets feel the grip or the pressure of the hand of God, impelling them to speak or to act (Isaiah 8: 11; Jeremiah 15: 17). 'The Spirit lifted me up . . . the hand of the Lord being strong upon me' (Ezekiel 3: 14). As indicated in this quotation, the experience of constraint is also attributed to the inspiration of the Spirit of God (Hosea 9: 7; Isaiah 61: 1). Micah tells us why he feels compelled to declare the word of God, however unacceptable it may be to the people. 'But as for me, I am filled with power, with the Spirit of the Lord' (Micah 3: 8). This emphasis on the Spirit, however, as the source of prophetic inspiration and constraint is less prominent than might have been expected. This may be due to the fact that the wild ecstatics and false prophets attributed their inspiration to that source. These two conceptions give expression to the objectivity of the word of God as well as to the obligation to declare it. The hand presses from without, the Spirit comes upon the prophet from without. The word comes not out of but to the prophet from the Lord. It is this awareness which enables the prophet to preface his messages with 'Thus says the Lord'.

THE SPOKEN WORD

The task of the prophet was to pass on to men the revelation and message he had received from God. This transmission took place originally through the spoken word. It is customary to refer to the canonical prophets as the 'writing prophets' because their words were preserved and collected in books. The phrase is misleading, however, if it conveys the impression that the great prophets were literary figures. They were preachers, not writers; heralds of God, not authors of books. They declared the word of God to individuals who came to enquire of them, or to whom they themselves were sent. Most of their messages, however, were delivered to the public—in the streets, the squares, the gates of cities, at the various sanctuaries, in the courts of the Temple. They preached wherever people had assembled or were to be found in large numbers. Because the word uttered by the prophet was not his own, but the word of God, it was believed to have effective power. We use words to convey information to others, but God does not speak to men simply in order to impart knowledge. He acts through his word, which 'runs swiftly' (Psalm 147: 15). It has vitality and potency; it is creative and quickening. The word is instrumental, as well as revelatory. Through it the Lord breaks down and he builds up. 'Is not my word like fire, says the Lord, and like a hammer which breaks the rock in pieces?' (Jeremiah 1: 10; 23: 29). Filled with divine energy, the word of God accomplishes the purpose for which it is sent. For as the descending rain and snow make the earth fertile and fruitful, 'so shall my word be that goes forth from my mouth; it shall not return to me empty, but it shall accomplish that which I purpose, and prosper in the thing for which I sent it' (Isaiah 55: 10, 11).

Like the spoken word, so also the enacted word of the prophet had effective power. Many examples of this will be given in the chapters following. Some of the prophets, especially Isaiah, Jeremiah, and Ezekiel, had recourse to symbolic actions. These were not simply visual aids, attempts to reinforce a message addressed to the ears by presenting it also to the eyes. For 'such an action served not only to represent and make evident a particular fact, but also to make this fact a reality'.[1] God himself was at work in and through the symbolic act of the prophet done in obedience to his command. These enacted words 'initiated the divine action in miniature, and thus helped towards the fulfilment of what was foretold'.[2] The spoken messages of the prophets, divinely inspired, are known as oracles. They are usually concise and rhythmical, and are frequently introduced by phrases such as 'thus says the Lord', 'hear the word of the Lord', 'thus said the Lord to me'. In the ancient East, when a servant or inferior delivered a message for his master or superior, in the presence of the recipient he would make himself nothing and speak in the name of the one who sent him—'thus says so and so' (e.g. Numbers 22: 16; Isaiah 37: 3). This 'messenger formula' was used by the prophets who spoke to men in the name of God. In order to convey to their hearers the oracles received from God, they selected and made use of a great variety of literary forms. For it was the responsible task of the prophet to choose *the form* which best expressed *the content* of the revealed message. The revelation might be transmitted as a song or a dirge, a hymn or a prayer, an argument or a dialogue, a parable or an allegory, an exhortation or a question, a vision or action. For the transmission, like the reception of revelation, took place 'in many and various ways'.

THE WRITTEN WORD

These messages, however, were not only transmitted to the contemporaries of the prophet through the spoken word; they have also been handed down to subsequent generations and to

[1] J. Lindblom, *Prophecy in Ancient Israel*, 172.
[2] H. Wheeler Robinson, *Inspiration and Revelation in the Old Testament*, 227.

us through the written word. In this process of transition from speech to writing we may discern four stages. First, there is evidence that *the prophets themselves* put some of their messages into writing—whether by the manual act of writing, or by dictating to a scribe. Isaiah, Jeremiah, Ezekiel, and Habakkuk are all said to have done this (Isaiah 8: 16; 30: 8; Jeremiah 30: 2; 36: 4; Ezekiel 43: 11; Habakkuk 2: 2). On two widely separated occasions in his life, Isaiah was commanded by God to commit oracles to writing (Isaiah 8: 16; 30: 8). Since his contemporaries had refused to heed his words, they were to be preserved 'for the time to come as a witness for ever'. At the dictation of Jeremiah, his scribe Baruch wrote down all the oracles the prophet had spoken up to that time (Jeremiah 30: 2; 36: 4). It is likely that the very first 'writing prophet', Amos, recorded his own visions, since they are in the first person singular (Amos 7: 1–7).

Secondly, the *disciples* of the prophets played an important part in the transmission of the oracles of their masters. It is known that Isaiah was accompanied and assisted by a band of disciples, and that Jeremiah had a faithful scribe called Baruch (Isaiah 8: 16; Jeremiah 36: 4). It may be assumed that others, perhaps all, of the great prophets, were likewise assisted by disciples—men who responded to the message, and who treasured and preserved it. A retentive memory was highly valued in the ancient East, and the concise, rhythmical utterances of the great masters were memorized by their pupils. The messages of the prophets were also transmitted by their disciples in writing, and for some considerable time the two processes, the oral and the written, went on side by side. The material transmitted in writing consisted of messages and narratives—the oracles of the prophets and the stories about the prophets. The latter, the narrative, was either autobiography or biography. In Isaiah, for example, there are stories told by the prophet (e.g. chapter 6) and there are stories told about the prophet (e.g. chapter 7: 1–9). In both cases the material comes from the prophet, but whereas the autobiographical passages were probably, although not necessarily, *written down* by the prophet, the biographical material was certainly written by the disciples. It is also possible to distinguish the oracles which have been transmitted verbatim (because they retain the concise, rhythmical, poetic form of the original), from the oracles which have been paraphrased by the disciples, who remembered the substance but not the exact words spoken by the prophet.

Thirdly, the *collectors* also played an important part in the transmission of the material. Oracles or narratives, written or oral, which had hitherto been transmitted separately or in small groups, were at this stage brought together and arranged in anthologies. Sometimes the collectors arranged the material in chronological order, sometimes according to subject matter, and sometimes according to catch-words. But for the most part, the oracles are not arranged according to chronology or topic. In the case of Isaiah and of Jeremiah it is indicated when, and for what reason, the original collection of oracles was made.[1] To these original collections of oracles, other collections were added. The prophetic books as we now have them, may be described as collections of collections of oracles, plus narratives.

Fourthly, the redactors and editors who followed the collectors, added dates and additional historical material, reinterpreted some oracles to fit the changed conditions of their own time, and included later messages of consolation and hope to counterbalance the earlier words of judgment and doom. They helped to make a collection of collections into a unified whole— to give to it the form of a book. It will be evident that for the material in the prophetic books, we are indebted not only to the great prophets, some of whose names are known, but also to a large number of unknown disciples, collectors, and editors. Without their devoted labours, the inspired words and stories of the prophets would never have reached us.

THE PAST: THE LIVING TRADITION

We turn now from the reception and the transmission to the content of the revelation. If it is to be rightly understood, the teaching of the prophets must be seen in relationship to the activity of God in the past, the present, and the future. The popular idea is that the prophets were concerned with the future only. According to this widespread assumption, they were entrusted by God with a mysterious knowledge of the future, and were therefore able to tell their contemporaries in advance exactly what was going to happen. To prophesy is to predict. Contemporary speech usages—phrases like 'weather prophets', expressions such as 'I wouldn't like to prophesy'— bear witness to this common misunderstanding. Given this

[1] See pages 74, 133.

assumption, the prophetical books become manuals for divining the future. Whereas the superstitious study the configuration of the stars, the pious 'study prophecy' to read the future course of events. 'Some Christians believe ardently—and many others vaguely—that the Bible foretells the course of events in the present and future ages, so that a skilled interpreter can learn from its pages the secrets of history as yet unwritten.'[1] In order to counteract this popular misunderstanding of the nature of prophecy, some writers have made use of the distinction—not foretellers, but forthtellers. The prophets were primarily concerned with the declaration of the word of God to their contemporaries, and not with the prediction of future events. Yet while this contrast between forthtelling and foretelling helps to counter the popular error by putting the emphasis in the right place, it is itself misleading. For the prophets *were* concerned with the future as well as with the present—and with both present and future seen in relationship to the past.

We look first at tradition, at that which has been handed down in the community, whether by the spoken or the written word, from the past. The prophets were not innovators; they were rooted and grounded in the past. They were not the originators of the faith of Israel, they were the heirs and interpreters of a tradition that went back to Moses. The revolutionary discovery made in the nineteenth century, that the Law did not precede the Prophets, but the Prophets preceded the Law, is true only in the sense that the Pentateuch as a whole (Genesis to Deuteronomy) did not reach its present form until after the time of the prophets. But some of the material contained in the Pentateuch *antedates* the time of the prophets, and embodies in story and commandment the ancient tradition of Israel, common to them and their hearers. The story, written and recited, told of the dealings of God with the patriarchs, of the Exodus from Egypt, of revelation and covenant at Sinai, of the wanderings in the wilderness, of the conquest of Canaan. Through these saving deeds, God had disclosed his own righteousness, holiness, and love, and in so doing had also made known the corresponding quality of life required of his people. That way of life was expressed in the commandments, the moral demands made by the Holy God upon the people with whom he had entered into a covenant.

[1] R. B. Y. Scott, *The Relevance of the Prophets*, 2.

This stream, of which Moses the prophet of God was the source, and to which many others had contributed from age to age, had been channelled through prophets and priests, through patriots and historians, through codes and rites. In this process of transmission the cult, the system of religious worship regulated by tradition and law, had played an important part. At the various sanctuaries and at the Temple in Jerusalem the recital of the story of Israel and of the commandments, of the saving deeds and the moral demands of the God of the covenant, took place at certain festivals. The view has been expressed that the prophets 'belonged to the cultic personnel of the different sanctuaries in as real a sense as did the priests'.[1] (See e.g. I Samuel 9: 13; I Kings 19: 10; Isaiah 6: 6.) It is possible that Isaiah, Nahum, Habakkuk, Haggai, Zechariah, Malachi, and Joel were cultic prophets, although in the case of the others, there is little or no evidence that they were 'on the staff' of the sanctuaries or the Temple. What *is* beyond question is that both prophets and people alike were familar with the ancient Mosaic tradition, as it was handed on through the recital of story and commandment in the cult. 'We thus see that in passing judgment on the great social, economic, and political problems of their own day the prophets made use of old norms derived from the cult.'[2] They also describe the future salvation largely in terms of the ancient tradition—there is to be a new Exodus, a new Covenant, a greater David, a new Jerusalem. The dependence of the prophets upon the past, and the relationship of their messages to the tradition, will be abundantly illustrated in the chapters which follow.

THE PRESENT: ASSYRIA, BABYLONIA, PERSIA

The appeal of the prophets to the past was motivated by their concern for the present. The Lord is the same today as yesterday. He who had made himself known in 'the former times' was also intensely active in current events. Through the historic tradition and their own encounter with God, the prophets were aware of his awesome presence and ceaseless activity in the world. They could see him at work in the contemporary situation. His voice was sounding in their ears through the world-shaking events. 'Ah, the thunder of many

---

[1] A. Jones, *The Old Testament and Modern Study*, 301.
[2] G. von Rad, *Old Testament Theology*, Vol. II, 400.

peoples, they thunder like the thunder of the sea! Ah, the roar of nations, they roar like the roaring of mighty waters!' (Isaiah 17: 12). God was speaking to Israel in the unknown language of contemporary events, and the prophets were sent to translate it. The message was event-plus-prophet; it was history interpreted. The revelation was for the contemporaries of the prophet who received it; it was communicated in their language and thought forms, related to their needs, relevant to the situation in which they lived. That is why it is always necessary to look at a given message against the background of the historical situation in which it was delivered. Only when it is studied in its original context can any message be rightly understood, and be rightly re-applied to the changed circumstances of our own times.

In setting the messages of the prophets in the context of world events, it will be helpful to keep in mind the three main periods during which they lived—the Assyrian, the Babylonian, and the Persian. The geographical centre of these three successive empires was the land of the two rivers, the Euphrates and the Tigris, the territory of the present-day state of Iraq. Many centuries before the time of the prophets, Palestine had been part of the Egyptian empire, but for the whole period from Amos to Malachi the seat of the dominant empire was in Mesopotamia. The original home of Assyria was in the upper part of that region. From Nineveh, the capital city, arrogant and aggressive kings and commanders with their cruel and ruthless soldiers set forth on the various campaigns which eventually extended the dominion of Assyria from Persia to Eygpt, and inflicted untold hardships and sufferings on the subject nations. As Assyria expanded towards the Mediterranean, Israel was forced to pay tribute, and in 734 B.C. much of her territory was annexed. With the capture of Samaria in 722 B.C. the Northern Kingdom was destroyed, and soon afterwards the Southern Kingdom became tributary. In 701 B.C. the territory of Judah was ravaged by the Assyrians, but Jerusalem was saved, and the Southern Kingdom preserved from destruction. For Amos, Assyria was a distant threat; for Hosea, a near and ever-present menace. Micah and Isaiah witnessed the invasion of Judah by the dreaded Assyrian armies. By the time Zephaniah and Jeremiah appeared, the dissolution of the empire had begun, and Nahum lived to rejoice over the fall of Nineveh.

As mistress of the world, Assyria was succeeded by Babylonia. After the fall of Nineveh (612 B.C.) and the defeat of the Egyptian forces at Carchemish (605 B.C.), Judah, which had survived the Assyrian threat, became subject to Nebuchadrezzar of Babylon. The revolt of his vassal, Jehoiakim, king of Judah, led to the first deportation of exiles in 598 B.C. The second attempt to throw off the Babylonian yoke under King Zedekiah resulted in the destruction of Jerusalem and the Southern Kingdom in 587 B.C. and a second deportation into exile. The Babylonian captivity lasted from 598 and 587 B.C. to 538 B.C., when the exiles began to return to Jerusalem. Habakkuk appeared at the beginning of the Babylonian period, and the long ministry of Jeremiah, which began before the collapse of Assyria, extended far into it—a little beyond the fall of Jerusalem in 587 B.C. The ministry of Ezekiel began after the first deportation into captivity, and continued long after the fall of Jerusalem. The anonymous prophet known as Second Isaiah who, like Ezekiel, lived among the exiles, was concerned with the downfall of Babylon and the rise of the Persian empire.

In contrast to the Babylonian empire which lasted for less than a century (612 to 538 B.C.), the Persian dominion established by Cyrus endured for over two centuries (538–333 B.C.). The cruel policy of the Assyrians and the Babylonians, who deported the upper classes of the nations they had conquered, was reversed by the humane and tolerant Persian. The exiles were allowed and encouraged to return, and the Temple and the city of Jerusalem were rebuilt. Judah did not, however, regain her independence. Haggai and Zechariah, Obadiah and Joel, together with the anonymous prophets to whom we owe the material in the books known as Third Isaiah, Malachi, and Jonah, all ministered in the discouraging period which followed the return from exile. It is probable that the messages collected in the book known as Second Zechariah, together with various oracles now scattered in other prophetic books, belong to the period following the conquest of the Persian empire by Alexander the Great. With the exception of these, all the oracles in the canonical prophets belong to one or other of the three periods outlined—the Assyrian, the Babylonian, and the Persian.

Another helpful way of dividing the whole period into three, is to take the beginning and the end of the Babylonian exile as key dates. All the messages delivered before 587 B.C., the date of the fall of Jerusalem and the destruction of the Hebrew state, are *pre-exilic*. The oracles which belong to the period of the Babylonian captivity (587–538 B.C.) are *exilic*. After 538 B.C. the material from the prophets of the Persian or Greek periods is *post-exilic*. An account of the historical situation in which each prophet delivered his messages will be given in the chapters that follow. To keep that information in the setting of the whole story, it will be useful to have in mind the three great and successive empires, and the periods before, during, and after the exile.

THE FUTURE: JUDGMENT AND SALVATION

In the thought of the Hebrews, the past and the future were not regarded as unrelated to or severed from the present, but as contained within it. The personality of a man in middle life includes much of what he was as a child and what he will be in later years. So it is with a nation. For the prophets, 'the former time' and 'the later time' were both present within the present time. They were able to predict what the Lord of history would do in the future, because they already knew him and his people in the present. This kind of prediction has nothing in common with the forecasts of those who make charts of the future course of world history. The prophets did not know *what* was coming, but they knew *who* was coming. Because they already knew the character of God through the living tradition and through personal experience, they knew what he would do when came to put things right.

The predictions of the prophets have four main characteristics.

First, they were concerned with the future as the outcome of the present. The events which they predicted were the consequence of the moral and spiritual condition of their contemporaries. The crop to be harvested was already growing in the field of the world. There was a nexus of cause and effect between the state of the nation and the impending events announced by the prophet. The 'not yet' was related to the 'now'; the coming event would be the response of God at work in history to the situation which already confronted the prophet. That is why the future, even that predicted by the prophet, was not predetermined. For if the people would respond to the message in repentance and faith (and why deliver it, otherwise?) God might also modify or change what he had planned to do.

Secondly, that which the prophets predicted as a consequence of the present moral and spiritual condition of the nation and of the nations, was the advent of God in judgment. This announcement of impending judgment, absent from the preaching of the false prophets,[1] was characteristic of the preaching of the true prophets. They announced the death and destruction of the nation. 'Then the Lord said to me, "The end has come upon my people Israel; I will never again pass by them"'(Amos 8: 2). The judgment might be inflicted through Assyrian or Chaldean invaders, through locust or earthquake, through drought or famine. Yet whatever the agency, it would be an act of God himself, punishing the sinner and the oppressor, and setting right that which was wrong. The prophets were the heralds of a catastrophe, and they startled and shocked their contemporaries with the unacceptable news that the victim was to be Israel.

Thirdly, the prophets predicted the advent of God in salvation. This announcement is scarcely heard in Amos and Zephaniah, for they are almost entirely preoccupied with the impending judgment; but even in these prophecies there is a hint that a small minority would survive the disaster. This conception of the remnant is developed by Isaiah. As the eight members of the family of Noah had escaped destruction by the waters of the flood, so when the judgment came, a remnant would survive. In the pre-exilic prophets, the messages of doom and deliverance, of destruction and redemption, of judgment and salvation, are found side by side. For Second Isaiah, during the exile, the advent of God in salvation was of such decisive importance that the Exodus, and the other mighty deeds of God in the past, could now be forgotten. What God was going to do, was what really mattered. 'Remember not the former things, nor consider the things of old. Behold, I am doing a new thing' (Isaiah 43: 18). Isaiah and Jeremiah, Ezekiel and some of the Twelve Prophets, depict the new age of salvation. Like dead men raised to life, the scattered exiles would return, and the reunited nation would live in peace and security. Jerusalem would be rebuilt and glorified and the land would be made astonishingly fertile. The people would be changed in heart. All alike would know God and live in obedience to

[1] See page 146.

his commandments. These two strands in the prophetic preaching go together. The deliverance would come after the judgment; the nation would go down to death and be raised up to life. 'The prophets were therefore the first men in Israel to proclaim over and over again and on an ever-widening basis that salvation comes in the shadow of judgment.'[1]

Fourthly, the advent of God in judgment and salvation would take place in history. The prophets envisaged the establishment of the kingdom of God on earth—although upon the earth transformed by the power of God. There would be continuity between 'the new thing' and 'the former things' which God had done here on earth. There would be a new Exodus, a new Covenant, a new Return from captivity, a new Jerusalem. This announcement of salvation to be achieved within history was, by some of the prophets, associated with a king, a vice-regent of God, his anointed One, the Messiah. There would be a new David in the coming kingdom. Like the son of Jesse, he would originate in Bethlehem, and on him the Spirit of the Lord with its manifold gifts would rest (Micah 5: 2; Isaiah 11: 1, 2). Bearing the noble titles 'Wonderful Counsellor, Mighty God, Everlasting Father, Prince of Peace', from David's throne he would rule over a wide dominion in justice and righteousness (Isaiah 9: 6, 7). Isaiah called him 'God with us', and Jeremiah, 'The Lord is our righteousness' (Isaiah 7: 14; Jeremiah 23: 6). In exilic and post-exilic oracles, he is portrayed as the good shepherd and the lowly king (Ezekiel 34: 23; Zechariah 9: 9). According to the anonymous prophet of the exile, the salvation within history would be achieved through the Servant of the Lord. Despised and rejected by men, led like a lamb to the slaughter, raised from the dead and highly exalted, through his vicarious sufferings he would win salvation for the nations (Isaiah 52: 13 to 53: 12). In the fullness of time these various visions of the prophets were fulfilled in Jesus the Messiah and Servant of the Lord, who through suffering entered into the glory of his kingdom. It was his Spirit who inspired the prophets 'when predicting the sufferings of Christ and the subsequent glory' (I Peter 1: 11). The eternal God was present in history, both in judgment and in salvation, in the person and work of Jesus Christ our Lord.

[1] G. von Rad, *Old Testament Theology*, Vol. II, 185.

II

Amos

Amos of Tekoa has a unique place in the story of Israel. He was the first of the writing prophets. Not the first of the prophets. As we have seen, he was preceded by Moses and Samuel, Nathan and Gad, Elijah and Elisha, Micaiah—and many others. A good deal is known about some of these 'prophets before the prophets'. Nevertheless, their words have not been recorded and transmitted to us. Here and there, a word or two spoken by these earlier prophets has been preserved in the stories about them. We know what Nathan said to David, what Elijah said to the assembly on Carmel, what Micaiah said to Ahab. Yet, apart from such isolated sayings, the words of these earlier prophets have not been preserved and collected. Amos is the first prophet whose utterances have been recorded in a book. It is for this reason that 'the writing prophets' are distinguished from all those great men, also called prophets, who preceded them. The phrase 'writing prophet' does not necessarily imply that Amos himself recorded his own spoken words. There are three kinds of material in the book which bears his name—narrative, visions, and oracles. Since it is in the third person, the one narrative passage was not *written* by Amos (7: 10–17). The prophet himself, however, probably recorded his visions, for they are in the first person singular. Their autobiographical character distinguishes them from the rest of the book. (7: 1–9; 8: 1, 2; 9: 1). It is possible that *some* of the oracles, as well as the visions, were recorded by Amos himself. The greater part of the book consists of these terse, poetic utterances. Beautiful in form, striking in simplicity, vivid in imagery, powerful in impact, they certainly give the impression of having come direct from the prophet.

Many of these oracles, however, transmitted as units, were probably recorded by the followers of Amos after his death. In what way were the words of the Lord Jesus transmitted and recorded? He did not minister alone, but was accompanied and assisted by disciples. They remembered and treasured his words, and for some time transmitted them 'by word of mouth'. Later on, these eyewitnesses or their companions put them into writing. There is no direct evidence that Amos was accompanied and assisted by a band of disciples. Yet some of the seed fell on good ground; there were those upon whom his words made a deep and lasting impression. Believing that he was a man sent from God, they preserved his words in memory and, after his death, committed them to writing. There may have been several collections of these oracles available to the editor of the book. The latter has combined the oracles and the visions with the biographical passage on the call of the prophet and his encounter with the priest Amaziah at Bethel (7: 10–17). In its present form, the book is fragmentary in character; it is a collection of concise, inspired utterances. The reader must remember it is recorded preaching; that prior to the written was the spoken word. This preservation of the words of Amos, whether by the prophet himself, or by those who responded to his message, was an epoch-making event in the history of Israel. It was the outcome of a conviction. The words of the prophet were of value and significance not only for his contemporaries, but also for future generations. The transition from speech to writing meant that the words of the prophet were 'treasured up on purpose to a life beyond life', and his message and influence were 'let loose o'er all the world'.

HISTORICAL BACKGROUND

The words of Amos cannot be fully understood without some knowledge of the situation in which he exercised his ministry. The kingdom established by David was disrupted after the death of Solomon, and divided into the Northern Kingdom of Israel and the Southern Kingdom of Judah. In this prophecy, the Northern Kingdom is not only called Israel, but also 'Jacob' and 'Joseph'—the last because its two main tribes, Ephraim and Manasseh, were sons of Joseph. Established by Jeroboam I, it was the stronger of the two kingdoms, and achieved great power under Omri. This able ruler built the city of Samaria and made it the capital of his realm. He also made an alliance with Phoenicia, and brought about the marriage of his son Ahab to Jezebel, daughter of the king of Tyre. This pagan queen actively promoted in Israel the worship of Baal-Melkart. This menace was challenged by Elijah in the dramatic contest on Mount Carmel. Elijah and his successor Elisha were the champions of the pure faith of Israel against the corrupt worship of the baalim. They instigated the revolution by which the dynasty of Omri was overthrown. This revolt was led by Jehu, a commander in the army, who with great zeal and brutality exterminated both the house of Ahab and the worshippers of Baal. But this 'purge' weakened the Northern Kingdom which, having lost the support of its two former allies Phoenicia and Judah, was now exposed to invasion by its powerful north-eastern neighbour, Syria. From his capital city, Damascus, the Syrian King Hazael oppressed Israel and annexed some of her territory. This yoke was broken in the year 805 B.C. when the Assyrian monarch Adad-nirari III defeated and crippled Syria. Israel, under her kings Jehoash and Jeroboam II, recovered her freedom and lost territories. Lo-debar, Karnaim, and other cities in Gilead were recaptured (6: 13). The Assyrians were then preoccupied for some time with troubles at home.

The Northern Kingdom, thus set free from all foreign interference or domination, entered upon a period of peace and prosperity. During the long reign of Jeroboam II (783–743 B.C.), she attained the zenith of her power. The trade routes of the ancient Near East passed through her territory, which now extended from Mount Hermon to the Dead Sea (II Kings 14: 25). Great wealth and power came into the hands of the nobles and the merchants. This prosperity was especially evident in the capital city of Samaria, whose 'notable men' were proud and self-indulgent, lazy and luxurious. Lolling on divans inlaid with ivory, feasting on lamb and veal, drinking wine by the bowlful, prattling to the sound of the harp, they could not have cared less about the plight of the common people (6: 4–6). The 'ladies' were no better—'Bring, that we may drink' (4: 1). Making continual demands on their husbands for the satisfaction of appetite, they shared with them responsibility for the oppression of the people.

In former times the peasants, the small-holders, the farmers, had been the strength of the nation. Now, in the changed circumstances following the upheavals and wars, they were at the mercy of the newly-rich. They had been dispossessed by the land-hungry and greedy upper classes. The small-holdings had been swallowed up in the large estates. There was a gulf between the rich and the poor. Nor was there any redress for the oppressed in the law-courts. For the judges accepted bribes from the rich, and those without money were given no chance of a hearing. Not that the powerful and wealthy were irreligious! Piety and devotion went hand in hand with injustice and oppression. The sanctuaries at Bethel and Gilgal were thronged with worshippers, offering many costly gifts and sacrifices. Religion was divorced from justice, piety from kindness, sacrifice from mercy. Such was the state of the nation when Amos was taken from the flock and sent to preach in the Northern Kingdom. He prophesied during the reign of Jeroboam II, about 760 B.C. His ministry is dated two years before a disastrous earthquake, which was remembered long afterwards (1: 1; Zechariah 14: 5).

THE SHEPHERD OF TEKOA

Amos belonged to Tekoa, a village about ten miles south of Jerusalem, and six miles south of Bethlehem. He was a shepherd by occupation. The sheep he pastured on the slopes of the limestone hills around Tekoa were probably his own. He had another job as well, for he was both 'a herdsman, and a dresser of sycamore trees' (7: 14). The fruit of the sycamore was the diet of the poor. While unripe, the fig-like fruit had to be punctured to help it ripen to an edible state. This was the seasonal occupation of Amos. Away to the east of Tekoa was the desolate 'wilderness of Judea', a terrain of barren and rocky hills, falling away steeply to the western shore of the Dead Sea. Some of the figures of speech used in this prophecy are taken from this half-desert region. Perhaps it was to sell his produce that Amos, from time to time, visited the cities of Israel. In whatever way he acquired the information, he was certainly well acquainted with the sinful state of the nation. Back in Tekoa, he brooded over what he had seen, and there in the silence of the wilderness he heard the voice of the Lord. Moses and David, Elijah and Amos, John the Baptist and Jesus Christ were all men of the wilderness. 'Under all speech that is good for anything there lies a silence that is better.'[1] In this silent land, Amos felt an inner compulsion to go forth from country to city, to herald the coming judgment.

In the four autobiographical visions, we have the prophet's own account of his call. They follow the sequence of the seasons—spring, summer, autumn. In the spring he sees in

[1] Thomas Carlyle, *Critical and Miscellaneous Essays*.

vision a brood of locusts devouring the grass upon which the flocks depend (7: 1–3). In the summer the blazing sun suggests to his mind that the coming judgment may take the form of a conflagration, licking up the water of spring, stream, and ocean (7: 4–6). He prays that these judgments may be averted, and his prayers are heard. In the autumn, the sight of a basket of ripe fruit (*qayic*) by a play upon words, conveys the message that the end (*qec*), the day of doom, is approaching (8: 1–3). A builder tests a wall, to see if it is upright, by means of a plumb line. God is testing his people, is finding them wanting, and the judgment cannot long be delayed (7: 7–9). The constraint upon Amos to go forth from quiet Tekoa, and to proclaim in the thronged cities this message of impending doom, was overwhelming. The initiative and the pressure were from God. 'The Lord took me from following the flock, and the Lord said to me, "Go, prophesy to my people Israel"'(7: 15). Amos had no option but to go. He who hears the roar of a lion shudders with fear. The reaction is involuntary. The sequence of cause and effect is inevitable. God has spoken; Amos must prophesy (3: 8). God does nothing without revealing his plans in advance to his servants, the prophets (3: 7). Amos has been told of the impending judgment; now he must tell others. He was a man under authority, speaking and acting under divine constraint.

Tekoa was in Judah. Why did Amos not go to Jerusalem, the capital of the Southern Kingdom, and preach there? Why go to Israel, the Northern Kingdom, and denounce 'those who feel secure on the mountain of Samaria' (6: 1)? Israel was larger, stronger, more influential than Judah. While Amos regarded the inhabitants of both kingdoms as one people, and addressed his message to them all, yet he went to the centre of power to deliver it. Evidence for the duration of his ministry is lacking; it may have been short, a year or two years at most. He probably went to the city of Samaria, the capital, for several of his oracles are directed against it (e.g. 3: 9–11). He may have gone to the sanctuary at Gilgal (4: 4). Perhaps he visited several other places. He certainly went to Bethel, and there it was that his ministry came to an abrupt end. Hallowed by the vision of the patriarch Jacob,[1] Bethel was the principal sanctuary of the Northern Kingdom, and was under royal patronage. To the crowds who thronged there to worship, Amos addressed his fiery words, his unpalatable predictions of

[1] See Genesis 28: 10–22.

impending doom. Here one of the decisive encounters of history
took place. Amaziah the priest of the sanctuary confronted
Amos the prophet of Tekoa. The priest had sent a message to
King Jeroboam, accusing Amos of subversion and rebellion.
Now, perhaps in obedience to the royal command, he orders
the prophet to leave the kingdom. In contemptuous words
which imply that Amos is a deluded visionary, a professional
concerned only for his own maintenance, the priest tells him
to be off to the land of Judah, that he may be paid for his
oracles there. In reply, Amos affirms that he is no professional,
does not belong to one of the old prophetic guilds. He is a
prophet by the direct call of God, who took him from the
flock and sent him forth to preach. Let Amaziah not imagine
therefore that by silencing the prophet, he can thereby avert
the doom pronounced by him. For the priest, his wife, family,
and possessions would all be involved in the coming disaster
(7: 10–17). It seems likely that Amos then returned to Tekoa,
and may there have committed his visions and some of his
utterances to writing. This was done in the faith that the words
of God, rejected in the present, would be vindicated in the
future. This has indeed happened in ways which Amos himself
could never have foreseen.

THE HERALD OF JUDGMENT

The message of Amos is as clear as a trumpet call. It sounds
throughout the book like the recurring theme of a symphony.
'I will punish you for all your iniquities' (3: 2). He is the herald
of judgment, the prophet of doom. The Lord is righteous, the
nation is sinful, ruin is inevitable. After a superscription, the
prophecy opens with a series of oracles against the surrounding
nations. Syria and Philistia, Tyre and Edom, Ammon and
Moab are denounced for crimes against humanity—for ruthless
warfare and the slave trade, for broken agreements and lack
of pity, for brutality to mothers and the desecration of the
dead. Because the sins of these nations cannot be counted
('for three transgressions . . . and for four') God will not
'revoke the punishment' (1: 3–15; 2: 1–3). Delivered either on
successive days or on a single occasion, these six oracles would
be heard with warm approval by the Israelite audience. They
were in full agreement with the punishment and doom
announced for their traditional enemies. It was richly deserved!
Then comes the climax; with dramatic suddenness, Amos turns

upon them. For transgressions without number, God will
punish Israel. For there helpless debtors are sold into slavery,
the poor are ground down, and the worship at the sanctuaries
is accompanied by prostitution and oppression (2: 6–8).
True—unlike those surrounding nations—Israel is the chosen
people of God. But election is for vocation, and the greater the
privilege the greater the responsibility. Therefore God will
bring a heavier punishment upon the people with whom he
has been especially intimate (3: 2).

What are these evils which have provoked the indignation
of the Lord? They are social rather than religious. Idolatry,
the worship of Sakkuth and Kaiwan, Assyrian gods, is once
mentioned (5: 26). But Amos is predominantly concerned with
wrongs done to people and society—bribery in the courts,
heartlessness, brutality, prostitution, self-indulgence, the evils
of luxury, the dispossession of the helpless, the oppression of the
poor. For these sins, judgment will fall upon all classes of the
people—upon the king and his house, the royal chaplain and
his family, the leaders and the nobles, the luxury-loving men
and the pampered women, the rapacious landowners and the
idle rich. And the common people will be involved along with
'the notable men' in the destruction which is coming upon the
whole nation. Escape will be impossible. Let them dig down
into Sheol or climb up into Heaven, hide in the thickets of
Carmel or sink into the depths of the sea, the wicked will not
escape the fierce indignation of the Lord of Hosts (9: 2, 3).
And what is the appointed instrument of judgment? Like a
sleeping lion, mighty Assyria was quiescent during the long
and prosperous reign of Jeroboam II. Not until after the
ministry of Amos did Tiglath-pileser III, emperor of Assyria,
begin to menace the western states. Yet, years in advance,
Amos could see what was coming. 'The prophet's mind is the
seismograph of providence, vibrating to the first faint tremors
that herald the coming earthquake.'[1] He discerned 'the signs
of the times'. Assyria was to be the instrument of judgment
(6: 14). The overthrow of the nation would take place on the
field of battle. The swiftness and strength, the experience and
skill of Israel's warriors, would be of no avail (2: 14–16). In
their pride and complacency, the people had imagined that
'the day of the Lord', his final coming in power and glory,
would be to their advantage. Their enemies would be over-

[1] John Skinner, *Prophecy and Religion*.

thrown; they would be exalted. The prophet corrects this gross misconception. The Lord will indeed come—but for *Israel* it will be a day of thick darkness, of inescapable doom (5: 18–20). Inescapable? Unless they repent of their crimes against humanity and let justice roll down like waters.

'LET JUSTICE ROLL DOWN'

In Palestine the ordinary brook (or *wadi*) is a raging torrent in the rainy season. In the summer heat, it dwindles to a trickle or becomes completely dry. On the other hand, a brook fed by a spring is perennial or 'everflowing'. God requires that justice flow like a swollen torrent and righteousness like an everflowing stream (5: 24). The dealings of men with one another in every sphere of life, personal, economic, social, political, must be just and right. Why? Because the God of Israel, made known in his righteous acts and saving deeds, requires it. In the Exodus from Egypt, he had delivered his people from slavery, and at Sinai had established a covenant with them. This bond between Israel and the Lord was the basis of her existence as a people. It had ethical and moral conditions, which Israel was under obligation to fulfil. Thus, in making this demand for justice and righteousness, Amos was no innovator. He was recalling the people to the ancient Mosaic tradition, to the distinctive faith and way of Israel. 'You only have I known of all the families of the earth.' Called into intimate, covenanted relationship with God, she must express in human relationships all that was involved in that divine relationship. These moral obligations are set forth by the prophet with concrete realism and particularity. There are no vague generalities and pious platitudes. He castigates merchants who use false measures, weights, and balances, and sell food of poor quality at high prices (8: 5, 6). The outer garment of the poor man taken in pledge, his only blanket for the chilly night, must be returned to him at sundown (2: 8). Like a man ploughing the sea with oxen, judges who accept bribes and turn the administration of justice into poison, are acting contrary to the divine order of things (6: 12). Amos is specific and particular. His challenging words, unmistakable in their application, must have caused deep offence to the court and the army, to the greedy merchants and the ruthless landowners, to the idle rich and the unjust judges, to the professional priests and prophets. Amos was not banished for mouthing pious platitudes! With scandalous particularity he was demanding right relationships in ordinary life. Such is the basic requirement of the God of the covenant, and he will accept no substitute.

Not even religious services! There were many who were in the habit of substituting cult for conduct, costly offerings at the sanctuaries for rightness in the common relationships of life. The prophet addresses them with ironical words. He calls them to worship at the famous sanctuaries at Bethel and Gilgal —in order that they may continue in their personal and social sins! How they love these happy festivals (4: 4, 5)! But the Lord will smash into fragments their sanctuary at Bethel (9: 1). He hates their festal pilgrimages and solemn assemblies, he rejects their costly offerings and burdensome songs. What he requires is abundant justice and unceasing righteousness (5: 21-24). Is Amos rejecting the cult altogether? Are assemblies and offerings, songs and prayers, rites and ceremonies, not required of the covenanted people? Some scholars take the view that the prophet is repudiating 'organized religion' altogether (see 5: 25). What God requires, he is saying, is not worship at the sanctuary, but obedience in life. From what we know of the faith of Israel and the message of the prophets as a whole, it may be questioned whether Amos would make such an antithesis. For obedience in life is the fruit of a right relationship with God—and how is that sustained if not by worship? Amos is not rejecting the cult, the system of worship, as such. He is rejecting the *corrupt* cult, the false security it encouraged, the depravity that went with it. He is denouncing the *substitution* of cultic acts for right living. God hates and rejects all acts of worship which are substitutes for right personal and social relationships. God is righteous. Therefore cult and conduct must be all of a piece. No man can be in right relationship with God, who is not in right relationships with his fellow men. This truth is taken up in the teaching of Jesus Christ (Matthew 5: 23, 24). We are dealing with the Lord himself in our ordinary human relationships. He who does not love the brother he sees, cannot love the God he does not see (Matthew 25: 31-40; I John 4: 7-21).

'TERRIBLE MAJESTY'

'God is clothed with terrible majesty' (Job 37: 22). These words of Elihu aptly describe the whole atmosphere of this prophecy. Amos was 'a God-intoxicated man'. He was vividly aware of the reality of God, the Lord of hosts, in all his power and majesty. In nature and in history, the prophet saw everything in the light of the sovereignty and activity of God. He was aware of the inescapable presence. Not the impersonal presence 'of something far more deeply interfused'.[1] He knew rather the presence of One who had met him by appointment, who had disclosed his mind to his servant and was active in the events of that age. God and Amos were walking together (3: 3). Although he gives no explicit teaching on monotheism, this truth is an axiom of all the thought and activity of Amos. That there is only one God, he takes as a matter of course. The Lord of hosts is supreme in the universe and has direct control of nature. He is the Maker of mountains and winds, of day and night (4: 13). He created the constellations on high, he causes the sun to rise, he makes darkness and it is night, he directs the clouds and waters the earth (5: 8). He is active in solar eclipse and earthquake (8: 9; 6: 11). Creator and Sustainer of the world, he is also the Lord and Ruler of the nations. He has jurisdiction over mighty Assyria. Amos does not mention that nation by name, yet his reference to an exile 'beyond Damascus' indicates that the prophet regarded Assyria as the instrument in God's hand for the punishment of Israel (5: 27). The judgments of the Lord will also overtake Syria and Philistia, Edom and Phoenicia, Moab and Ammon (1: 3 to 2: 3). All nations are under his control and providential care. He brought Israel up out of Egypt; he also brought the Philistines from Crete and the Syrians from Kir (9: 7). He controls the migrations and movements of all peoples. His concern is universal, his sovereignty over all nations.

This prophetic portrait of the Creator and Ruler of the world, the Lord of transcendent majesty and overpowering will, is austere and awe-inspiring. It has led some to contrast the God of Amos with the God of Hosea, the God of judgment with the God of mercy, the God of wrath with the God of love. While there is certainly a great difference of emphasis, such a contrast, if overdrawn, can be entirely misleading. There is light as well as darkness in the portrait of God which Amos paints. To complete the picture attention must be drawn to complementary aspects of the character of God. For his indignation is but the other side of his compassion, and his

---

[1] William Wordsworth, *Lines composed a few miles above Tintern Abbey.*

activity in judgment is the expression of his concern for men. Gaza has sold men into slavery and Ammon has 'ripped up women with child' (1: 6, 13). God will punish both. Why? Because he cares for the slaves and grieves over the slaughtered mothers. If he did not care he would not be indignant. Why should he, through his prophet, denounce those who 'sell . . . the needy for a pair of shoes' and compel the poor to pay exorbitant rents (2: 6; 5: 11)? Why bother? Because he is deeply concerned about the plight of the poor and has compassion on the oppressed. The judgment of God on the wicked is the consequence of his compassion for their victims. Nor is the love of God confined to the oppressed. For why does he announce to sinners the impending judgment? He does nothing without telling his secret plans to his servants the prophets. He tells them, so that they may tell others (3: 7, 8). But why do this—why warn sinners in advance? So that they may heed the warning. It is because God loves sinful men, that he tells them *in advance* of the coming judgment. He provides the opportunity for repentance, so that they may be saved. Amos laments the fact that up to the time of his ministry, the judgments of God which had already fallen, had not moved the people to repentance. He had visited them with a whole series of calamities—famine, drought, blight, epidemics, earthquake. 'Yet you did not return to me.' Not one of these chastisements had brought Israel to repentance (4: 6-11). But that was their purpose—as it was the purpose of the ministry of Amos. Why preach, why court unpopularity, why face persecution? Because, for some at least, repentance was an open possibility. 'Seek me and live' (5: 4).

Jesus, like Amos, was aware that judgment was coming upon a whole generation. When the tower in Siloam fell and killed a number of bystanders, he made this comment, 'Unless you repent you will all likewise perish' (Luke 13:5). That was the message of Amos—and the 'unless' is the decisive word. It has been maintained by some that Amos was so engrossed with the message of judgment entrusted to him, that he had no word of hope for the people. It is conceded that at the end of the book in its present form, the flame of hope burns brightly. The ruined nation is to be rebuilt, the fertile earth blessed by God is to bring forth abundantly, and the scattered exiles are to return for good (9: 11-15). Many scholars, however, regard this epilogue as a later addition to the book. Even so, it is not true to say that hope is absent from the authentic utterances of Amos. Some may repent—a few. There is no developed doctrine of the remnant in this prophecy, but there are hints of it. A few bits and pieces of a sheep mangled by a lion may be salvaged by a shepherd. Likewise a few may survive the destruction of Samaria (3: 12). If they hate evil and love good, the Lord may yet be gracious to *the remnant* of his people (5: 15). Amos had no hope for the nation as a whole. Yet when the flood destroyed the race 'a few, that is, eight persons, were saved through water' (I Peter 3: 20). It was to save a remnant from impending destruction that Amos prophesied. He who is clothed in terrible majesty, Creator of the world, Ruler of the nations, the Lord of righteousness, the Judge of all the earth, is also the King of love and the God of hope.

III

Hosea

The ministry of the prophet Hosea belongs to the closing years of the Northern Kingdom. His father's name was Beeri; otherwise nothing is known about his family or about his birthplace and upbringing. He was a native of Israel, and to that kingdom most of his messages were addressed. In this respect he is both like and unlike his predecessor. For while Amos too preached in Israel, yet his home was in Judah. It is not known whether Hosea ever saw Amos or listened to his preaching. But the disciples of Hosea who transmitted his messages were probably acquainted with the oracles of the earlier prophet. The two prophets were not alike in character and personality. Hosea resembles the tender-hearted Jeremiah rather than the stern and austere shepherd of Tekoa. He was an embodiment of the loving-kindness he proclaimed. Sensitive, warm-hearted, full of compassion and pity, he loved the people he was compelled to condemn. This lover of men was also a poet, with a keen sense of observation and an imaginative approach to the world. He loved the sights and sounds of the countryside and the commonplace activities of daily life. In a single oracle he speaks of the morning mist, the early dew, the swirling chaff, and the ascending smoke—symbols of that which passes quickly away (13: 3). He refers to the restless dove, the stubborn heifer, the weary oxen, the wild ass wandering alone, the lamb grazing in a broad place, the leopard lying in wait, and the bear robbed of her cubs. Like the parables of Jesus, the illustrations of Hosea are drawn from common life—the farmer sowing and reaping, the driver easing the yoke, the fowler spreading his net, the trader with false balances. These references to country life have led some to suppose that before his call to the prophetic ministry, Hosea was a farmer. Others, noting the references to ovens, have inferred that he was a baker (7: 4–7). But, whatever his former occupation, this lover of men and of nature was also a practical man of affairs, well acquainted with the economic, social, and political state of the nation. He knew all about the political intrigues, the plots and counterplots, the revolutions and dynastic changes which preceded the downfall of Israel. He was acquainted with the vacillating foreign policy of the rulers, who sought for security now in Egypt, now in Assyria, 'like a dove, silly and without sense' (7: 11).

Hosea was a preacher, and it must be remembered that his messages were spoken, before they were committed to writing and collected on one scroll. Because these concise, rhythmic utterances were delivered on many different occasions, it is not an easy book to read. They have been put together without any regard to subject matter, logical sequence, or progression of thought. The same themes are repeated in different words, over and over again. Furthermore the Hebrew text has been badly preserved, and as the existence of many variant readings implies, the meaning is not always clear, and is sometimes a matter of conjecture. Some of the references to current or recent events which would have been understood by the hearers of the prophet, are now meaningless to us (e.g. 6: 8). There are many references to harlotry, and the reader may not be sure whether to take these literally or in a figurative sense. Many of these difficulties disappear when the facts outlined in the next three sections are taken into account.

Most of the messages of Hosea are addressed to the Northern Kingdom of Israel, which in this prophecy, no less than thirty-six times, is called Ephraim. Manasseh and Ephraim, sons of Joseph, were the ancestors of the two tribes thus named, which occupied the central hill country of Palestine. Ephraim soon outstripped Manasseh in importance, and it was an Ephraimite, Jeroboam, who revolted against Solomon and set up the Northern Kingdom. As a result, Ephraim became another name for Israel, and is almost always used by Hosea to designate, not one tribe, but the whole of the Northern Kingdom. It may also be a term of endearment. A few of the oracles of Hosea are addressed to Judah, but some of these, especially those which are commendatory, are regarded by many scholars as later additions, made by an editor or editors who lived in the Southern Kingdom (e.g. 1: 7). In the Book of Hosea there is a small amount of biographical (chapter 1) and autobiographical (chapter 3) material. This constitutes the first main part of the book (chapters 1 to 3) and is the account of the prophet's marriage, of the unfaithfulness of his wife Gomer, and of her restoration through the persistence of his love. This story is symbolic of the faithlessness of Israel and of the loyal and abiding love of God for her. The second main part of the book (chapters 4 to 14) is a collection of oracles, rebuking sin, announcing judgment, calling to repentance, and promising renewal.

THE TIMES

Hosea began to prophesy during the concluding years of the reign of Jeroboam II (783–743 B.C.). In his earliest oracle he predicts the downfall of the dynasty of Jehu, to which Jeroboam belonged (1: 4, 5). The long period of prosperity and peace enjoyed by Israel during the reign of Jeroboam II came to an end very soon after his death. Assyria had been quiescent for half a century. But with the accession of Tiglath-pileser III (745–727, referred to as Pul in the book of Kings), the very existence of the relatively small nations in Syria-Palestine was threatened. After the conquest of Babylonia, the Assyrian king turned towards the Mediterranean, subdued the territory of Hamath, and compelled the neighbouring states to pay tribute. The Assyrian threat coincided with a period of political instability in Israel. At Samaria, the capital, there was a succession of kings. After a reign of only six months, Zechariah, the son of Jeroboam II, was murdered by a usurper called Shallum (II Kings 15: 8–11). Shallum himself survived for one month only, and was then liquidated by Menahem, who retained the throne for six years (743–738). When the Assyrians invaded his territory 'Menahem gave Pul a thousand talents of silver, that he might help him to confirm his hold of the royal power' (II Kings 15: 19). By this policy of appeasement, 'the great king' was bought off for a time. Meanwhile, extending his power to the border of Egypt, he made all the rulers of Syria-Palestine pay tribute. Menahem was succeeded by his son Pekahiah (738–737), who after a reign of under two years was murdered by Pekah, the commander of his army. Hosea refers to this period of dynastic instability, intrigue, and murder. The plotters 'devour their rulers', and the people, although 'all their kings have fallen', do not call upon the Lord for help (7: 7).

Pekah attempted to resist the power of Assyria. To this end, he made an alliance with Rezin of Damascus, king of Syria.

These two kings invited Ahaz of Judah to join them. When he refused, they invaded the Southern Kingdom and besieged Jerusalem, in order to depose him. Contrary to the counsel of the prophet Isaiah, Ahaz of Judah appealed to Tiglath-pileser for help and sent him a present. In any case the Assyrian monarch was bound to accept the challenge of the two allied kings. He subdued Israel in 733, and incorporated Galilee and Transjordan, the plain of Jezreel, and the coastal region into his own empire. Only the city and province of Samaria were left to Pekah of Israel. The upper classes of the annexed territories were deported to Mesopotamia, and were replaced by Assyrian officials and people from other parts of the empire. The Assyrians then crushed Damascus and annexed the whole kingdom of Syria. In 732 Pekah was murdered by Hoshea, who continued to pay tribute to Assyria until the death of Tiglath-pileser (727). Before the new King Shalmaneser V could establish himself, Hoshea, relying upon Egypt and in conjunction with other states, refused to pay any further tribute to Assyria. Three years later Shalmaneser V invaded and occupied what remained of Israel, captured King Hoshea, and besieged the city of Samaria. The siege lasted three years, during which Shalmaneser died. His successor, Sargon II, subdued the city. He deported 27,290 Israelites to other parts of the Assyrian empire, and 'brought people from Babylon, Cuthah, Avva, Hamath, and Sepharvaim, and placed them in the cities of Samaria instead of the people of Israel' (II Kings 17: 24). That was the end of the Northern Kingdom (722–721 B.C.). The prophet Hosea did not live to see this disaster. There is evidence that he was active up to the time when Pekah of Israel and Rezin of Syria invaded Judah. One of his oracles may refer to this event, known as the Syro-Ephraimitic war. For Judah retaliated by invading Israel (5: 8–11). Probably the ministry of the prophet lasted for about ten years, from the concluding days of Jeroboam II, through the period of political intrigue and instability, to the confused days of the Syro-Ephraimitic war. The approximate dates would thus be 743–734 B.C.

FALSE RELIGION

To understand the message of Hosea, it is necessary to have some knowledge, not only of the political, but also of the religious background. When the Hebrews left behind the

D

simplicity of the nomadic life and settled in Canaan, they were exposed to the temptations of a corrupt civilization. The change in their manner of life brought with it a challenge to the Mosaic faith, to the traditions of Sinai and the wilderness. For the art of agriculture which they had to learn from the Canaanites was bound up with the worship of pagan gods—the Baals, to whom the fertility of the earth was ascribed. The Hebrews were now dependent for the necessities of life upon the fertility of the earth, and were thus under strong pressure to acknowledge the Baals, the source of fertility. The word *baal* means 'lord' or 'owner'. It was the title for the male deity who was regarded as the owner of the land in a particular locality, and the donor of its fertility. Thus, there were a large number of gods, the Baals, each one associated with a particular town or locality, and each one having his female partner. Yet, although there were many gods, it was possible to regard all these local gods as manifestations of one great god, the Baal, whose female consort was Astarte. Now it was believed that the fertility of the ground depended upon the sexual relations of the Baal and his partner. The worshippers could help to bring about this union by enacting at the high place the drama of the sacred marriage. Furthermore, by imitating the desired action of the god and the goddess, that is, by having sexual intercourse with the 'sacred' prostitutes at the sanctuaries, the worshippers could exert power over the deities and bring them together (4: 13, 14). The people were like the gods they worshipped. The popular religion, with its highly erotic and grossly sensual conceptions and imagery, encouraged widspread sexual immorality.

Now the Israelites were confusing the worship of God with the worship of the Baal. It was not simply, as Elijah had put it, that they kept hopping from one leg to another, sometimes worshipping the God of Israel and sometimes worshipping the Baals. The national apostasy did take that form, and that was bad enough. What was far worse was the identification of the worship of God with the false religion. The God of Israel was called *Baal*, and his worship corrupted by association with the false beliefs and debased practices of the fertility cults. Many of the shrines where the Lord was worshipped had been taken over from the Canaanites—together with much of the pagan cult. Let us look at a typical pagan sanctuary. It is located on a high place, with an open courtyard in front of the shrine. In

this roofless court is the altar for animal sacrifice. Beside the
altar there is an upright stone pillar (the Massebah, representing the god), and an upright wooden pole (the 'Asherah,
representing the goddess). In the shrine itself is an image of
stone, wood, or metal, before which stands an altar for incense
and a table for offerings. To sanctuaries of this kind individuals
and households came with their gifts and prayers. Here also
the local people assembled in great numbers for the communal
festivals associated with the agricultural year and with new
moons and Sabbaths. They were often occasions for drunkenness and sexual debauchery. It was not that Hosea's contemporaries had abandoned the worship of God for the service of
another god called Baal. At least, they did not see it that way.
They were, they supposed, worshipping the God of Israel
under that name and by those rites.

Let us note here the main features of the false religion. In the
first place, it was akin to magic. It was an attempt to exert
pressure upon or to gain control over the deity for man's own
purposes. Secondly, being a deification of the processes of
reproduction, of fertility, of sex, it was inevitably sensual and
licentious. Thirdly, the worshippers were concerned predominantly with the supply of material goods; it was grossly
materialistic. Fourthly, the religious ritual was divorced from
all moral obligation. As may be seen from the second and third
characteristics of the false religion, the people of this present
age are like Hosea's contemporaries. For this age also is
obsessed with sex and 'the standard of living', with the erotic
and the acquisition of material goods. The third and fourth
features were the result of a basic dualism in the thinking of
the people, who had not yet identified the Redeemer with the
Creator. They did not realize that the earth was the Lord's—
the Lord who had brought them forth out of the land of
Egypt. 'She (Israel) did not know that it was I who gave her
the grain, the wine, and the oil, and who lavished upon her
silver and gold which they used for Baal' (2: 8). The Lord of
history and of the covenant with its moral demands, the God
of the Exodus and the wilderness, is also the Creator and
Sustainer of the universe, the Giver of all good things. When
Hosea refers to the great flaw in the character of Israel as 'a
spirit of harlotry', he is therefore speaking both literally and
metaphorically. The worship of the Baals and sexual immorality go together. Yet the prophet is referring to something

more radical. For Israel to have any part at all in the false religion, with its perverted outlook and corrupt practice, was 'to play the harlot', to be unfaithful to her true Husband. It was the purpose of God, through the discipline of suffering and exile, to bring Israel to the time when the false religion would have been completely discarded. 'And in that day, says the Lord, you will call me, "My Husband", and no longer will you call me, "My Baal". For I will remove the names of the Baals from her mouth, and they shall be mentioned by name no more' (2: 16, 17).

HOSEA AND GOMER: GOD AND ISRAEL

Having looked at the political and religious background of the book, we now turn to the story of the marriage of Hosea and Gomer. For this tragic domestic experience colours the whole message of the prophet. The story is recorded in the first and third chapters. Hosea married Gomer the daughter of Diblaim, in obedience to a command of God. 'Go, take to yourself a wife of harlotry and have children of harlotry' (1: 2). At first sight this appears to mean that he was ordered to marry a woman who was already known to be a harlot. Such a command would be incompatible with the righteousness of God, and it is unnecessary to interpret the words in that way. For the story was told and written down after the tragic outcome. Looking back from the other side of this heart-breaking experience, Hosea could see that he was commanded to marry a woman who *subsequently* turned out to be a harlot. The initial action is interpreted in terms of the result, the divine command is seen in the light of the outcome. At the time of the marriage, Hosea knew nothing of the innate unfaithfulness of Gomer, which was to manifest itself later on in outward act and relationship. The first child to be born of the marriage was a son, who, in obedience to a command from the Lord, was named Jezreel. He was to be a living text for the prophet's sermon on judgment. It was at the city of Jezreel that Jehu, founder of the contemporary dynasty 'slew all that remained of the house of Ahab' (II Kings 10: 11). For this brutality and bloodshed, the judgment of God would now fall upon 'the kingdom of the house of Israel'. It may have been after the birth of their first son that Gomer became unfaithful to Hosea (compare the language of 1: 3 with 1: 6 and 8). Gomer's second child was a daughter, and in obedience to God's command was given the name 'Not pitied'. She was a living sign that the pity of God for Israel was now exhausted. Having weaned her daughter, Gomer bore a second son, who was named by Hosea 'Not my people'. God had rejected Israel, they were no longer his people.

Between the biography of the first and the autobiography of the third chapter, there is a gap in our knowledge of Hosea's domestic life. From what is said in the third chapter, it may be inferred that some time after the birth of her third child, Gomer deserted Hosea. After the lapse of an unspecified period, the prophet received from God the command to go on loving his faithless wife (3: 1). In obedience to God, he went and bought her back 'for fifteen shekels of silver and a homer and a lethech of barley' (3: 2). It is not stated to whom this price in cash and in kind was paid. Perhaps it was handed over to her paramour or to the master who owned her as a slave. On the other hand, she may have been employed as a sacred prostitute at one of the sanctuaries. Having been brought back, Gomer was put on probation 'for many days' by her husband (3: 3). We are left to infer that after this period of separation and discipline, it was the intention of Hosea to take back Gomer as his wife. The message of the book is vitally related to this tragic experience. What Hosea was to Gomer, God was to Israel. His oracles as a whole bear the stamp of his personal suffering, but it is in the second chapter that the allegory is worked out most fully.

Israel has been rejected by God for her disloyalty—yet not beyond recall. Loyal Israelites, perhaps the disciples of the prophet, are urged to plead with their mother (the nation) to put away her harlotry (the worship of the Baals). For, like a faithless wife running after her 'lovers', Israel has turned to false gods. In her ignorance she gives thanks to Baal for the gifts (grain, wine, oil, wealth) which have been lavished upon her by the God of Israel (2: 8). Therefore God will strip her naked, take away those gifts, bring her back into the wilderness, lead her into exile. Israel, like Gomer, will have a period of probation. 'The children of Israel shall dwell many days without king or prince, without sacrifice or pillar, without ephod or teraphim' (3: 4). During the exile they would be deprived of their rulers and of the treasured symbols and sacraments of the sanctuaries. But punishment was with a view to renewal. Through this discipline of suffering, Israel would be purified and prepared for a new betrothal. As in the days after the Exodus, when he made a covenant with his people at Sinai, God would speak again to the heart of Israel and betroth her to himself in loyal love for ever (2: 14, 19, 20). Nature would share in the renewal; the animals would live at peace with men and the earth bring forth abundantly (2: 18 and 21–23).

This allegory sheds a clear light upon the way in which God makes himself known to men. Revelation does not consist of doctrinal propositions, ready-made in heaven, and communicated by God to the mind of man. God reveals, not truths, but himself; and this personal disclosure is made through events and personal relationships. Through the human love of Hosea, God reveals his love. Through the suffering of the prophet, he unveils his heart. Human life and experience can be a window through which we look into the heart of God. We can know by analogy. 'If you then, who are evil, know how to give good gifts to your children, *how much more* will your Father who is in heaven give good things to those who ask him?' (Matthew 7: 11). In applying the analogy, we must not overlook those words 'how much more'. God far transcends the best in our human life. This conviction underlies Hosea's allegory. 'If I, an imperfect and sinful human being, love my wife so much, and in spite of her infidelity cannot cease to love her, then how much more must the Lord love his faithless people Israel.'

THE SIN OF ISRAEL

Hosea had learned the meaning of sin in the school of suffering. Gomer had rejected his love, and by her disloyalty had inflicted great suffering upon her husband. In marriage, the most intimate relationship of life, he had encountered sin directly. He had immediate knowledge of the heartbreak and suffering it brings. His own experience enabled him to understand in depth how God suffered on account of the faithlessness of Israel. Here, sin is understood, not primarily in terms of law, but of love; it is an affront to love, a disloyalty to obligation. In memorable words, quoted by Christ, the prophet sets forth what the Lord requires of his people. 'For I desire steadfast love and not sacrifice, the knowledge of God, rather than burnt offerings' (6: 6). But what God desired, Israel had withheld. Instead of steadfast love there had been disloyalty; instead of the knowledge of God, intimate and personal, there had been a false conception of his nature and requirements. This faithlessness of Israel Hosea describes in language coloured by the conduct of Gomer. 'For the spirit of harlotry is within them, and they know not the Lord' (5: 4). This inner flaw, this innate infidelity, was no recent characteristic of Israel; it was long-standing, ingrained, and persistent. It went back to the time of the conquest of Canaan (9: 10). There were, according to Hosea, two main ways in which it was manifested in the national life. Firstly, there was the corrupt cult, the debased worship of the high places. These fertility rites and the accompanying sexual immorality and drunkenness, we have already described. Hosea also condemns the idolatrous objects associated with this worship. Again and again he refers with contempt to the 'calves', the bull images made of wood or metal and overlaid with silver or gold, which were used to represent the deity (e.g. 8: 4–6; 10: 5, 6; 13: 2). After citing the names of three sanctuaries, centres of this debased and idolatrous worship, the prophet affirms that they are to the worshippers what the hunter's snare, net, and pit are to bird and animal (5: 1, 2).

Secondly, the prophet also sees the infidelity of the people embodied in the institution of the monarchy. This is the sin associated with Gibeah (9: 9; 10: 9). The Lord is the true king of Israel. Yet long ago, the wayward people had clamoured for a human king, and had set Saul of Gibeah over them. In the light of the history of the Northern Kingdom, and especially of the reign of the kings contemporaneous with him, Hosea regarded the monarchy as evil in itself. 'During 253 years Israel had eighteen kings from ten different families, and no family came to a close save by violent death. The rapid succession of usurpers in the closing years was only the final plunge of a disastrous career.'[1] Such men were not appointed by God. 'They made kings, but not through me. They set up princes, but without my knowledge' (8: 4). Since 'all their princes are rebels' (9: 15) God will punish Israel for this misplaced trust in human kings, which goes right back to Gilgal, where Saul was acknowledged as first king (I Samuel 11: 15). Closely associated with the contemporary monarchy itself was yet another sin—the misplaced trust of the rulers themselves. They looked for security in the wrong direction—by entering into alliances with foreign powers. Israel lay between Assyria and Egypt. Some of the notable men at Samaria favoured an

[1] R. F. Horton, *Minor Prophets*, *The Century Bible*, 45.

alliance with Egypt as a bulwark against Assyria; others advocated a policy of appeasement, of friendship with Assyria. 'Ephraim is like a dove, silly and without sense, calling to Egypt, going to Assyria' (7: 11). Called to be a distinctive and separated people, Israel was mixing herself with the surrounding nations, and losing her identity. As a result, like a cake burned on one side and uncooked on the other, she was good for nothing (7: 8, 9; 8: 8, 9). Let her trust in God, her true refuge and strength, instead of seeking the help of foreign powers who had no real interest in her welfare.

The sinful state of the nation is portrayed in a terrible indictment. 'There is no faithfulness or kindness, and no knowledge of God in the land.' God's commandments given through Moses are disobeyed, for there is false swearing, lying, killing, stealing, and adultery (4: 1, 2). But do not blame the people, Hosea adds, for the priests are largely responsible for this state of affairs (4: 4). As 'ministers of the Word', it is their duty to instruct the people, and guide them in the way of the Lord. They have failed completely in this primary duty. Indeed, they are feeding on the sin of the people, since they take their share of the sacrifices of the corrupt cult. The people have become like their priests (4: 4–9). The sinfulness of the nation is so radical, that the prophet despairs of any real change of heart. True, the people know how to put on a show of repentance. They say 'Come, let us return to the Lord; for he has torn, that he may heal us; he has stricken, and he will bind us up' (6: 1). Their words are sound and excellent—but they do not really mean what they say. There is no true conviction of sin, no genuine repentance. The shallowness of their resolve to return is seen in the complacent assumption which underlies it. They assume that an indulgent God will restore their fortunes in next to no time, and without much difficulty (6: 2). They have a gift for *saying* the right thing, for their basic need is indeed that true knowledge of God which dawns upon men like the rising sun (6: 3). But the splendid words are not genuine. Israel's love is like the morning mist or the early dew which passes quickly away (6: 4). What can God do with such people? Their persistent and obstinate wrongdoing has resulted in moral impotence, in an atrophy of the will. Israel cannot repent. 'Their deeds do not permit them to return to their God' (5: 4). What is the use of appealing to them any more? 'Ephraim is joined to idols, let him alone' (4: 17). They

must reap what they have sown, and the harvest is now inevitable. The judgment will come suddenly like the attack of a
leopard, and will be ferocious, like a bear robbed of her cubs
(13: 7, 8). The vulture is about to pounce on the prey; the
Assyrians will be the instrument of divine judgment (8: 1). God
will show no mercy. 'Shall I save them from the power of Sheol,
shall I redeem them from death? Death, bring out your plagues!
Sheol, bring out your power to destroy! I have no mind for
compassion' (13: 14).[1] Is that God's last word? Or is there some
greater power that can transform the call 'Come with your
plagues, O death' into 'O death, where is thy victory?' (I
Corinthians 15, 55). There is. To this we now turn.

COVENANT LOVE

The marriage of Hosea to Gomer is a symbol of the relationship of the Lord to Israel. The prophet loved his wife deeply
and continued to love her in spite of her unfaithfulness. At the
cost of great personal suffering, he bought her back again, and
sought to mend the broken marriage. In making use of this
analogy, the prophet was taking a great risk. His contemporaries, familiar with the fertility cults, might take the
allegory literally, and suppose that the Lord was the husband
of Israel in much the same way that the Baal was regarded as
the husband of the land. Yet the daring of the prophet in
making use, not of abstract language, but of personal imagery
and analogy, is fully justified. For 'the footprints of the Divine
are more visible in that rich soil'.[2] We must be careful, however, not to reverse the direction of the analogy. The starting
point is not the love of Hosea for Gomer, from the existence
and persistence of which we may infer the reality and depth
of God's love for Israel. To use the language of art, the love of
God for Israel is the original; the love of Hosea for Gomer the
copy. Using the same analogy, the apostle Paul does not begin
with the love of husband and wife and thus reveal to us the
love of Christ for his bride, the Church. On the contrary, it is
the love of Christ for the Church which is the pattern for
Christian marriage. The love of Hosea for Gomer had its
source and inspiration in that divine love which it imperfectly
reveals. The human relationship is the symbol, the divine
relationship the reality. The Spirit inspired Hosea to choose

[1] Translation by J. B. Phillips in *Four Prophets*, 53.
[2] C. S. Lewis, *Letters to Malcolm*, 74.

this analogy which sheds a clear light upon the relationship between the Lord and his people.

The way in which the symbol of marriage discloses the nature of this relationship, is best seen by taking in turn the key words *knowledge* and *covenant*. Hosea is deeply concerned because there is 'no knowledge of God in the land' (4: 1). In their better moments, even the sinful people realize that such knowledge is priority number one. 'Let us know, let us press on to know the Lord' (6: 3). By knowledge, however, the prophet is not referring to factual information, to impersonal learning, to intellectual understanding. He is not primarily concerned that the people shall learn more *about* God, as an observer may study and know an object from which he remains detached. He is speaking rather of personal knowledge mediated through encounter and experience. Knowledge of another person in depth is possible only through meeting and revelation, through shared experience and commitment, through trust and love. For knowledge of this kind, marriage is the best analogy, for it is or can be the most intimate of all personal relationships. 'Now Adam knew Eve his wife' (Genesis 4: 1). In the Bible the verb 'to know' is used of sexual intercourse between husband and wife. This is one revealing example of the biblical meaning of the word. To know is to meet, to converse, to share experience, to make response, to disclose and commit oneself, and to be deeply involved in the life of another. For this reason the marriage analogy, better than any other, discloses what God requires of his people. 'I will betroth you to me in faithfulness; and you shall know the Lord' (2: 20). With his people God desires, not a distant, but a close relationship; from his people he desires, not a formal acknowledgment, but a total commitment. Hosea's analogy is employed by the Lord Jesus Christ (Mark 2: 19, 20; Matthew 25: 1–13), by the apostle Paul (II Corinthians 11: 2; Ephesians 5: 21–33), and by John of Patmos (Revelation 19: 7; 21: 2). It has influenced the language of our hymns—especially those by Bernard of Clairvaux. It has imparted depth and warmth to the devotion and relationship of believers to the Lord.

Unfortunately, the analogy has long been individualized by preachers and poets, who seem to have forgotten that the Bride is the People of God—Israel, the Church. And so 'Christ loved the Church' has been changed into 'Jesu, Lover of my soul'. Our relationship with the Lord is both personal and corporate, but it is better to use the many other images given to us in Scripture to describe personal relationship with him. For when the nuptial analogy is individualized, it is often sentimentalized. C. H. Spurgeon, who himself in his eucharistic hymn addresses Christ as 'Thou glorious bridegroom of the heart' draws attention to the dangers of misusing this imagery. In his *Lectures on Preaching*, describing some of the sermons of his own time, he says 'the kissing and hugging which some preachers delight in is disgusting'. Such erotic misinterpretations of the analogy are far removed from the thought of Hosea. For he is setting forth the covenant love of God for his people. This conception of the covenant which lies at the heart of the faith of Israel, was almost bound to lead to the use, sooner or later, of the analogy of marriage. Not that Hosea confines himself to nuptial imagery. In describing what happened at the Exodus and in the wilderness, he also uses the figure of father and son. 'When Israel was a child, I loved him, and out of Egypt I called my son.' Like a father training his child to walk, carrying him in his arms, leading him with a harness, so the loving heavenly Father had set Israel on her feet as a nation, borne her along, and led her with bonds of love (11: 1–4). Yet it is of the marriage analogy that Hosea makes a sustained use. By this imagery he describes how God will do again what he did at the beginning in the wilderness. 'Therefore, behold, I will allure her, and bring her into the wilderness, and speak tenderly to her' (2: 14). It is his purpose to woo and win his bride all over again, as he did when he brought her up out of the land of Egypt. There at Sinai, long ago, he made a covenant with his people (Exodus 24: 3–8). Now, he will betroth Israel to himself again, in a bond never to be broken. 'And I will betroth you to me for ever; I will betroth you to me in righteousness and in justice, in steadfast love, and in mercy' (2: 19).

At the heart of this covenant is *chesed*. In the Authorised Version this Hebrew word is often translated 'loving-kindness', and in the Revised Standard Version it is almost always translated 'steadfast love'. *Chesed* presupposes the existence of a bond or covenant between two or more parties. It is the love which operates within the covenant, and maintains it by discharging all the accepted obligations. The word is often used in conjunction with or as a parallel to the word 'faithfulness' (e.g. Psalm 36: 5). *Chesed* is loyal love, steadfast love, bonded love, covenant love. Because the Lord has betrothed Israel to himself in loyal love, in spite of her infidelity he cannot and will not let her go. 'How can I give you up, O Ephraim! How can I hand you over, O Israel! How can I make you like Admah! How can I treat you like Zeboiim!' (These two cities perished like Sodom and Gomorrah.) 'My heart recoils within me, my compassion grows warm and tender. I will not execute my fierce anger, I will not again destroy Ephraim; for I am God and not man, the Holy One in your midst, and I will not come to destroy' (11: 8, 9). His love is strong and mighty, patient and persistent, warm and compassionate. Here we see into the heart of God; and here in the heart of God there is tension, passion, a tumult of feelings, a conflict of emotions. Punish Israel he will, for he is holy; cease to love her he will not, for he is God and not man. His nature is love, inexhaustible and invincible. In response to this loyal love, the prophet calls upon Israel to return to the Lord her God. And, returning, let her offer in worship, not rams or bullocks, but words; sincere words of penitence for her sin. And let her abandon once for all her trust in foreign alliances and the corrupt worship of the Baals. Then God will heal her disease—faithlessness—and bestow upon her his free, unmerited, boundless love. This is the way to new life and strength, to renewal and salvation (14, 1–6). 'By no other of the Old Testament witnesses is the tender intimacy and triumphant power of the love of God so deeply comprehended and so fully expressed as by Hosea.'[1] The love of God is stronger than the sin of his people, and through suffering will, in the end, be triumphant. This good news Hosea proclaimed with his lips and embodied in his life. In thus bearing witness to the divine love in its tender intimacy and triumphant power, Hosea was foreteller and forerunner. He points forward to Jesus Christ, the Mediator of the New Covenant, whose loyal love, through the sufferings of the cross, was triumphant.

[1] Artur Weiser, *Das Buch der Zwölf kleinen Propheten,* quoted in *The Interpreter's Bible,* Vol. VI, 690.

IV

Micah

Between the plain of Philistia and the mountains of Judea lies a region known in the Old Testament as the Shephelah. The word means 'lowland', for although the hills reach a height of 1,500 feet in the south, the country is low in comparison with the Judean highlands to the east. This territory, traversed by deep valleys, was fertile and populous. The rich red soil of the valleys produced an abundance of grain. The sides of the hills were covered with trees. Indeed this well-wooded region gave to Israel a proverbial saying, 'as plentiful as the sycamore of the Shephelah' (I Kings 10: 27). It was a pleasant land of olive groves and vineyards, of flocks and herds, of shepherds and farmers. Being a buffer region between the maritime plain and the central highlands, it was also of strategic importance. Enemies approaching from the west had to take possession of this region, before attacking the central highlands. Conversely, it was Judah's first line of defence. That is why some of the strongest fortresses in the land were to be found in this territory. Several narrow valleys traverse the Shephelah from east to west, and are the natural highways from the coastal plain to Jerusalem and other places in central Judea. These fortified valleys were the scene of many a battle. The inhabitants of the Shephelah lived in an intermediate zone. On the one hand, they were not very far from Jerusalem the capital; on the other hand they looked out over the plain along which passed the highway from Egypt to Mesopotamia. 'The Shephelah is sufficiently detached from the capital and body of the land to beget in her sons an independence of mind and feeling, but so much upon the edge of the open world as to endue them at the same time with that sense of the responsibilities of warfare, which the national statesman, aloof and at ease in Zion, could not possibly have shared.'[1]

This combination of sturdy independence and international

[1] George Adam Smith, *The Historical Geography of the Holy Land.*

concern was characteristic of Micah, whose home was at Moresheth in the Shephelah. His village, close to the ancient stronghold of Lachish and not far from the modern Beit Jibrin, was about twenty-five miles south-west of Jerusalem. Here Micah grew up among the country folk, his companions peasants and farmers, shepherds and artisans. Nothing is known about his family or his upbringing. He tells us not of the occasion, but of the result of his call to the prophetic ministry. Moved by the Spirit of God, he is conscious of the possession of adequate resources of power. Endowed with wisdom and courage, he is able to judge rightly and to expose and condemn the sin of his people (3: 8). It is possible that the ministry of Amos was used by the Lord to call Micah to his work, or to influence him when he had entered upon it. Tekoa was a little over seventeen miles east of Moresheth, and the impact of the words of Amos on Micah is evident in this prophecy.[1] Both alike cried out for justice; both were spokesmen and champions of the oppressed. Some of the oracles were spoken, not in Moresheth, but in Jerusalem. In one of them we see Micah walking about stripped and naked, howling like a jackal, screeching like an ostrich (1: 8). This lament over the impending destruction of Jerusalem was probably heard as Micah walked through the streets and squares of the capital. Isaiah, his older contemporary, was also in Jerusalem. We simply do not know whether Isaiah, the man of the city, and Micah, the countryman, ever met. There is evidence that the preaching of Micah made a profound impression on both king and people. A century later, the prophet Jeremiah was threatened with death. Attempting to save his life, some of the princes appealed to the precedent of Micah of Moresheth. He too, they pointed out, had predicted the downfall of Jerusalem and the destruction of the Temple. Instead of putting Micah to death, King Hezekiah had responded to his message. He had turned to the Lord, and had carried through certain religious reforms (Jeremiah 26: 16-19).

The date of Micah's ministry is difficult to determine. The editor dates the ministry of the prophet during the reigns of Jotham, Ahaz, and Hezekiah—that is, some time within the period 750 to 687 B.C. (1: 1). But the passage from the Book of Jeremiah just cited is much earlier than the chronological note of the editor, and is evidence for a ministry during the

[1] Compare Amos 2: 12 with Micah 2: 6.

reign of Hezekiah. Did Micah also prophesy earlier, during the reigns of Jotham (750–736) and Ahaz (736–716)? He predicted the destruction of Samaria (1: 6, 7). If this oracle refers to the fall of that city in 721 B.C., then Micah must have been preaching in the reign of Ahaz. We cannot be sure that it does, for Samaria was not literally destroyed when it fell to the Assyrians; it was intact and inhabited long after the fall of the Northern Kingdom. Some scholars believe that Micah began to preach before the fall of Samaria in 721 B.C.; others believe that the whole of the ministry fell within the reign of Hezekiah.

As with the dating of his ministry, so also with the authorship of the oracles, there is a wide diversity of opinion among biblical scholars. It is generally agreed that almost all[1] the oracles in the first part of the book (chapters 1 to 3) are genuine prophecies of Micah. These threats of doom are followed by oracles of promise in the second part (chapters 4 and 5), and by oracles of both doom and promise in the third part of the book (chapters 6 and 7). Parts two and three are collections of oracles from various periods, some of them much later than the time of the prophet. Yet these two anthologies also include some genuine oracles of Micah himself.

THE CITY BUILT WITH WRONG

The Book of Micah begins with 'a tale of two cities'. God comes forth from the temple of heaven, using the mountain tops as his stepping stones. He comes in judgment against the two Hebrew kingdoms, Israel and Judah, as represented by the two capitals, Samaria and Jerusalem. For from these cities which should have been centres of law, order, and justice, moral corruption had spread like a contagious disease all over the land. Like Amos, Micah the countryman is appalled at the wickedness and the degradation, the selfishness and the violence, the enervating luxury and the crass materialism of the inhabitants of the great cities. 'What is the transgression of Jacob? Is it not Samaria? And what is the sin of the house of Judah? Is it not Jerusalem?' (1: 2–5). All the leading citizens are implicated. Hating the good and loving the evil, the men of rank and influence have turned the moral order upside down. The rulers, the guardians of justice, have betrayed their trust. For they oppress the people they govern, and build the prosperity of Jerusalem on violence and injustice (3: 9, 10). The

[1] 2: 12, 13 is one such exception.

prophets are blind guides leading the people astray. Motivated by the love of money, they bless the man who satisfies their material wants, and 'declare war against him who puts nothing into their mouths'. God will forsake them in the days that are coming; he will have no revelation to impart to such men (3: 5–7). The judges cannot be trusted. For instead of administering justice impartially, according to ascertained facts and legal principles, their decisions are influenced by monetary bribes (3: 11). The priests also have their price. They manipulate the sacred oracle, and give instruction in accordance with the size of the fee (3: 11). This mania for money is all the more odious because covered by a veneer of false piety (3: 11). While professing to 'lean upon the Lord' the notable men are in fact worshippers of mammon.

Upon them all—rulers, prophets, judges, priests—Micah pronounces judgment. 'Therefore because of you Zion shall be ploughed as a field; Jerusalem shall become a heap of ruins, and the mountain of the house a wooded height' (3: 12). 'Because of you . . .' Because of the corruption of the leaders, calamity will overtake Jerusalem, the Temple site will be deserted, the once populous city will become a heap of ruins. Such a prediction must have come as a profound shock to both leaders and people. They would regard such words as blasphemous. Because Jerusalem was 'the city of the great king' they believed it was invincible. The presence of God in the Temple was the guarantee of the inviolability of Zion (3: 11). Micah did not share this popular view, this complacent, comforting illusion. With magnificent courage he announced the impending destruction of the city built 'with blood and . . . with wrong'.

The instrument of God's judgment was Assyria. Some of the oracles of Micah were delivered during the two military campaigns undertaken by the Assyrians in 711 and 701 B.C. A description has already been given in the previous chapter of the end of the Northern Kingdom, which Micah may have predicted. 'Therefore I will make Samaria a heap in the open country, a place for planting vineyards; and I will pour down her stones into the valley, and uncover her foundations' (1: 6). It is more likely that these words were spoken against Samaria many years after her occupation by the Assyrians. In any case, the end of the Northern Kingdom was not the end of Assyria's troubles in Syria-Palestine. In 714 B.C. a revolt against the hated enemy, instigated by Egypt, broke out in the Philistine city of Ashdod. When the Assyrian army arrived to put down the revolt, the Egyptians deserted their allies. Ashdod and two other cities were destroyed, and their territory was annexed by the Assyrians. If, in the initial stages, Hezekiah king of Judah was implicated in this revolt, he withdrew in good time, and Judah was not invaded on this occasion. Next time, however, the anti-Assyrian policy of the king brought Judah to the very brink of disaster. For when Sargon died in 705 B.C., Hezekiah took the lead in a widespread movement to throw off the heavy Assyrian yoke. For a time the new king, Sennacherib, was engaged in suppressing risings elsewhere. Eventually he appeared in the west, and, after defeating the Egyptian forces near the city of Ekron and crushing the cities of Philistia, turned in his wrath upon Judah. As the dreaded soldiers of Assyria approached, Micah visited several towns in the south-west to warn them of the impending judgment. The alarm took the form of a pun, a play upon words, in which the name of each city was utilized. Even his own beloved Moresheth would not escape the tidal wave of destruction (1: 10–16). Sennacherib occupied forty-six of the walled cities and towns of Judah, and shut up Hezekiah in Jerusalem 'like a caged bird'. As will be described in the next chapter, when all seemed lost the city of Jerusalem was miraculously delivered, and the Assyrians returned speedily to their own land. This unexpected turn of events may have discredited the ministry of Micah in the eyes of his contemporaries. He had predicted the destruction of the city 'built with wrong'—and Jerusalem had survived intact. 'The mills of God grind slowly.' If to his contemporaries of short sight he appeared mistaken, nevertheless the words of Micah were treasured by his disciples, and in the long run were vindicated by history, when Jerusalem was destroyed by the Babylonians in 587 B.C.

THE CHAMPION OF THE OPPRESSED

Micah stands forth as the champion of the oppressed. He enters the lists on behalf of the peasants against the wealthy landowners. He may himself have been a farmer; in any case he has identified himself with the poor and the middle classes of Judah. The typical peasant farmer owned the small plot of land he had inherited from his fathers. He depended for his livelihood upon the rain and the fertility of the soil, upon his crops and domestic animals, upon his own labour and that of his family. His situation was ofttimes precarious, for he had many enemies—drought, blight, disease, famine. The growth of trade between nations and the resulting increase of wealth in the eighth century, had widened the gap between the small-holders and the upper classes. Those who already had enough and to spare were taking more and more. The wealthy did not always live near the lands they appropriated. There were many absentee landlords living in luxury and idleness in the metropolis, and their greed was insatiable. The mania to possess drove away sleep; they would lie awake at night working out clever schemes to dispossess those who had no defence against their ruthlessness (2: 1). 'They covet fields, and seize them; and houses, and take them away; they oppress a man and his house, a man and his inheritance' (2: 2). These lands and houses were not necessarily acquired by theft, fraud, or violence. More than likely the exploitation would take place well within the limits of the law. A smallholder who had bor-rowed money in a time of distress would find himself unable to repay it. His land would be sold to pay off the debt, and he and his family, having no other means of livelihood, would be reduced to the status of serfs. The exploiters had no mercy even upon defenceless widows, who with their children were ousted from their well-loved homes. The helpless children, the true glory of the nation, were the victims of their rapacity (2: 9). Like a butcher killing and skinning an animal, chopping up the carcass and boiling the joints in a cauldron, the leaders of Judah had oppressed and exploited the common people with utter ruthlessness (3: 1–3). The prophet now declares that the Lord plans to deal with the oppressors as they have dealt with others. Have they dispossessed others of their lands? The Lord has a scheme to take away their own. For a foreign foe will invade the land, measure it out, divide it up and take possession of it (2: 3–5).

The sin which Micah denounces with such fierce indignation is known in the Greek New Testament as *pleonexia*—'the accursed love of possessing'. This is the sin of the selfish egoist who is determined to have more than his fair share of the good things of life. The word denotes a greedy, grasping attitude to others, accompanied by a ruthless disregard for their rights and needs. This sin is portrayed by Christ in the parable of the rich farmer, who has divorced getting from giving, and evaluates life in terms of possessions (Luke 12: 13–21). The apostle Paul says it is as bad as idolatry—to the Jews the worst of all sins (Colossians 3: 5). We are familiar with one aspect of it in contemporary society. 'The profit motive, when it is the sole basis of an economic system, encourages a cutthroat competition and selfish ambition that inspires men to be more concerned about making a living than making a life. It can make men so I-centered that they no longer are Thou-centered.'[1] The strength of Micah's protest against this sin is the measure of his concern for the common people. With his predecessor Amos, and his older contemporary Isaiah, he stands at the head of that great procession of men who through the ages have championed the cause of the oppressed. In this company of the concerned are John the Baptist and James the Lord's brother, Francis of Assisi, and Vincent de Paul, Elizabeth Fry and Anthony Shaftesbury, Charles Kingsley and Thomas Barnardo—and many others. Not all the others are saints, for we may see the spirit of Micah at work in more turbulent figures—for example, in John Ball who took a prominent part in the peasants' revolt of 1381, and in Karl Marx, the fountain-head of a more recent and greater revolution. 'With all of its false assumptions and evil methods, Communism arose as a protest against the injustices and indignities inflicted upon the underprivileged. *The Communist Manifesto* was written by men aflame with a passion for social justice.'[2] They differ greatly; yet Micah and Marx have something in common. The influence of the prophet has not been confined to his contemporaries; like leaven, it has been at work in society down the ages.

BASIC RELIGION

The Book of Micah contains one of the best summaries of true religion to be found in the Bible. It is preceded by a scene in a court of law. The culprit in the witness-box is Israel, the prosecutor is God. 'O my people, what have I done to you?' In view of all his saving deeds, some of which are mentioned, why has Israel behaved so badly? Does the Lord deserve such ingratitude and disobedience (6: 1–5)? Then comes the great oracle, the Mount Everest of the Old Testament, for which alone the Book of Micah deserves immortality (6: 6–8). It begins with a series of four questions. The enquirer stands as

[1] Martin Luther King, *Strength to Love*, 98.   [2] Ibid., 96.

the representative of everyman, for the questions and the answer are of universal importance and timeless validity. 'With what shall I come before the Lord, and bow myself before God on high?' What kind of worship does God require, what is the service he desires of man? The second line of the question implies that God is highly exalted in the heavens, and that the worshipper will bow down before him in reverence and humility. When a man does thus come to worship, what is he required to bring? Ancient peoples erected altars and offered sacrifices; the custom is primitive and universal. In one type of sacrifice—the burnt offering—the whole body of the victim was consumed with fire. A yearling was a specially valuable offering. Did the Lord require offerings such as these? Perhaps he did if they were offered in sufficiently large numbers: Solomon, at the dedication of the temple, had offered to the Lord 'twenty-two thousand oxen and a hundred and twenty thousand sheep' (I Kings 8: 63). Did God require animal sacrifices by the thousand, or vegetable offerings in abundance? Perhaps a yet more costly sacrifice and offering was required— that which Abraham was willing to make when he bound his son Isaac and laid him on the altar on Mount Moriah? Human sacrifice, especially of a first-born son, was widespread in the ancient world. During the lifetime of Micah, King Ahaz 'burned his son as an offering' (II Kings 16: 3). Could a man by offering the fruit of his body atone for the sin of his soul? All four rhetorical questions are, it is implied, to be answered in the negative. Mounting to a climax they serve, by contrast, to introduce the positive answer.

God has made known what is good; he has already revealed to man his will. Three things he desires and requires of every man. Amos, in God's name, had demanded the first of the three essentials. 'Let justice roll down like waters, and righteousness like an everflowing stream' (Amos 5: 24). The relationships and dealings of a person with other persons in every sphere of life—personal, domestic, economic, social—must be just and right. All men are required 'to do *justice*'. Hosea had taught and exhibited the second essential. 'I desire steadfast love (*chesed*) and not sacrifice' (Hosea 6: 6). Loyalty and love, faithfulness and helpfulness, mercy and kindness, are demanded of us in the personal relationships of daily life. All men are required 'to love *kindness*'. The third essential may be regarded as a summary of the message of Isaiah. He appealed for quiet

confidence and faith in God, for reverence and humility before
'the Holy One of Israel' (Isaiah 30: 15). Enoch, who lived in
intimate companionship with his Maker, is said to have 'walked
with God' (Genesis 5: 22). When two friends go for a walk, they
are together all the time and they enter into fellowship through
conversation. God's delight is to be with men in the dialogue of
Word and Answer. Furthermore, the ordering of a man's
conduct, his walk, should be characterized by piety and
reverence, by faith and humility. All men are required '*to walk
humbly with . . . God*'. The teaching of the eighth-century
prophets on cult and conduct is often misrepresented. The
prophet is not asking men to substitute ethics for religion,
justice and kindness for piety and worship. The question he
asks is 'When I come before the Lord *to worship*, what shall
I bring?' The *climax* of the answer to this question is—'to walk
humbly with your God'. Acts of worship are presupposed, and a
life of faith and piety is the supreme demand. Yet it is certainly
significant that two of the three essentials have to do with
people. A humble walk with God, and justice and kindness in
our human relationships—like the two Great Commandments
of Christ—must not be separated (Mark 12: 28–34). 'The one
thing that matters is how men stand with God and the one
test of that is how they stand with men.'[1] The oracle of Micah,
which has been called 'the Magna Charta of the prophetic
religion', provides everyman with a simple but searching
three-fold test. Am I just in all my dealings? Am I kind to all
people? Am I living in humble fellowship with God?

The prophecies which follow in this third main section of the
book, may well be the last extant utterances of Micah. They
probably belong to the period of the Assyrian invasion in
701 B.C., when there was great distress and insecurity (6:
13–16). The prophet makes a final survey of those evils of contemporary society upon which we have already commented.
Like Diogenes with his lantern, looking for an honest man in
Athens, Micah cannot find a single upright man (7: 1, 2).

A psalm from a later period has been appended to the book
(7: 7–20). Israel,[2] already in exile, is hoping for the day of

[1] H. Wheeler Robinson, *The Christian Experience of the Holy Spirit*, 121.

[2] In the earlier chapters of this book, the word *Israel* usually denotes
the Northern Kingdom as distinct from *Judah* the Southern Kingdom.
After the destruction of the two kingdoms, i.e. in exilic and post-exilic
passages, the word *Israel* is often used, as here, as the designation of the
whole People of God.

deliverance. God in his great mercy will pardon her sins (18, 19), give her victory over heathen enemies (10, 16, 17), rebuild the devastated city of Jerusalem (11), bring back the scattered exiles (12), and stand as Shepherd over his gathered flock (14).

VISIONS OF THE FUTURE

The material in the second, but latest, part of the book (chapters 4 and 5) comes from the post-exilic period. Fragments continued to be added to the authentic utterances of Micah until the prophecy was included in the canon of scripture about 200 B.C. On reading through this anthology, it is evident that two contrasting views of Israel's future are intertwined. There are the military fragments, in which the restoration and triumph of Israel is described in terms of warfare and the violent subjugation of her enemies. 'Like a young lion among the flocks of sheep' (5: 8) Israel, restored, uses her political and military power against the heathen nations, being bent on revenge (4: 9–13; 5: 8, 9, 15). Interwoven with this strand are fragments expressing love and goodwill to all nations. 'Like showers upon the grass' (5: 7) Israel, restored, brings blessing and refreshment, and is the centre of a world at peace (4: 1–4, 6–8; 5: 7, 10–14).

In this middle section of the prophecy there are two oracles of outstanding importance, both to the Church and to mankind. There is the announcement of the coming of the Messiah (5: 2–4). It is an exclamatory address to Bethlehem. The author, looking back after the exile over the whole history of the Hebrew monarchy to its origin in David, predicts the advent of a second and greater David. He too will spring from the town of Bethlehem in the district of Ephrathah. O Bethlehem, how marvellous that one so great should come from such a little undistinguished place! His origin is 'from of old'—his ancestry goes right back to the ancient days of the original David. He is said to come forth 'for me'—he comes, in accordance with the divine plan and purpose, to be the agent through whom God himself will rule over his people. But until God does raise up this Anointed One, his scattered exiled people will continue to be oppressed by their enemies. This oppression will end when the prediction made by the prophet Isaiah is fulfilled. 'Behold, a young woman shall conceive and bear a son, and shall call his name Immanuel' (Isaiah 7: 14). For at his coming, the scattered exiles will return and be reunited with their brethren left behind in the land. Like David, the Messiah will be a Shepherd-King. He will use his power to care for the flock, a power which comes not from the people he shepherds, but from God himself. For he will be clothed with divine power and majesty. His reign will bring security and peace, and win universal acknowledgment. This prophecy was fulfilled when Jesus was born of the Virgin Mary at Bethlehem (Matthew 2: 5, 6). His origin is from everlasting, and he comes forth to be the agent of God's rule on earth. He is the Shepherd-King, who feeds, guides, and protects the flock over which he rules. He delivers his people from the captivity of sin and death and unites them in one fellowship. He is the Prince of Peace whose reign will in the end be acknowledged by all creatures.

This universal reign of God in peace is also the theme of the other momentous oracle in this middle section of the prophecy (4: 1-4). It is to be found in a slightly different form in the Book of Isaiah (2: 2-4), and also belongs to the period following the exile. When the age of the Messiah dawns, Mount Zion on which the Temple stands, will be elevated above the hills, so as to be visible to all the inhabitants of the earth. Then the nations of the world will go on pilgrimage to Jerusalem to be taught by the God of Israel, that they may order their lives in accordance with his word. They will go because they will then recognize that Jerusalem is the true source of divine revelation. The result of this recognition of God's sovereignty, the fruit of this obedience to his word, will be universal peace. For the powerful nations of the world will then accept the arbitration of God, will submit their differences to him and abide by his decisions. In those days there will be no further need for the instruments of war. So the weapons of destruction will be transformed into instruments of fruitfulness, into agricultural tools and implements, and the art of war will no longer be taught to the rising generation. Every individual will then enjoy peace and security. This vision of a world at peace under the kingly rule of God has exerted a powerful influence over the minds of men in all subsequent ages. It makes articulate the longings of the common people in all lands for permanent security and peace. The persistent attempts to secure the universal peace apart from the universal recognition of the sovereignty of God have led to frustration, disillusionment, and cynicism. Yet, in spite of these repeated failures, the bright vision continues to haunt the minds of men, not only within, but also far outside the bounds of the Christian Church. The two great oracles—the coming and reign of the Messiah, and the vision of universal peace and security—belong together. 'Sword shall be sickle when Jesus is King.'[1]

[1] C. Silvester Horne, in the hymn 'Sing we the King who is coming to reign'.

V

Isaiah

The Book of Isaiah is a collection of oracles from a number of prophets. In this respect the first scroll of the Latter Prophets is like the fourth. As the name implies, the Book of the Twelve contains the oracles of a number of prophets on one scroll. Likewise the Book of Isaiah is one scroll on which are written the oracles of a number of prophets—but in this case, with the exception of Isaiah of Jerusalem, all the prophets are anonymous. Therefore within the Book of Isaiah it is necessary to distinguish the words (and the biography and autobiography) of the prophet of that name, from the words of his disciples and of other, anonymous, prophets. It is not implied that material of the latter kind is of no value or is necessarily of less value than the authentic utterances of Isaiah. As we treasure the inspired words of Peter and Paul alongside those of Christ himself, so we may value the words of the disciples of Isaiah who interpreted and continued the work of their master. In this present chapter we are not concerned with the material in chapters 40 to 66 of the Book of Isaiah. The oracles in chapters 40 to 55 are two centuries later than the time of Isaiah, and belong to the period at the end of the exile when Cyrus of Persia was about to overthrow Babylon. We shall study them in chapter XI of this book. The oracles collected in chapters 56 to 66 are later still, and presuppose the situation in Palestine after the return from exile. We shall study them in chapter XIV of this book.

The material in chapters 1 to 39, with which we are now concerned, falls into six main sections. (i) Chapters 1 to 12. This is a collection of oracles mostly from the earlier period of Isaiah's ministry, together with an account of his call and other autobiographical material. (ii) Chapters 13 to 23. A series of oracles against foreign nations. Some of this material is Isaiah's, some comes from a later age. (iii) Chapters 24 to 27. An apocalypse—prophecies, psalms, and prayers relating to world judgment and the future blessedness of Israel. The collection is several centuries later than the time of Isaiah. (iv) Chapters 28 to 33. Most of these oracles are from the later period of Isaiah's ministry. (v) Chapters 34 and 35. Two exilic poems on the end-time intervention of God in judgment and salvation. (vi) Chapters 36 to 39. A historical narrative, concerning Sennacherib, Hezekiah, and Isaiah, reproduced with some alterations from II Kings.

From this classification, it will be seen that the oracles of Isaiah are concentrated in sections one (chapters 1 to 12) and four (chapters 28 to 33). We can learn from the book itself how these two main collections were originally made. Right up to the time of the Syro-Ephraimitic war in 734 B.C., the people and the court disregarded the message and the counsel of the prophet. Since therefore his words were rejected in the present, Isaiah was commanded to preserve them for the future. All his prophecies and testimony to date (i.e. most of the material in chapters 1 to 11) were committed to writing and sealed, until events should verify the truth proclaimed. 'Bind up the testimony, seal the teaching among my disciples. I will wait for the Lord, who is hiding his face from the house of Jacob, and I will hope in him' (8: 16, 17). Later on, for the second time in his ministry the words of Isaiah were rejected by the king and his advisers. Prior to Sennacherib's campaign, they disregarded the counsel of the prophet and made an alliance with Egypt. Again Isaiah was commanded to commit his messages to writing. 'And now, go, write it before them on a tablet, and inscribe it in a book, that it may be for the time to come as a witness for ever' (30: 8). The oracles written down on that occasion are to be found in chapters 28 to 33. To these two original collections of the prophet's oracles, other collections were added. The Book of Isaiah is essentially a collection of collections of oracles.

CALL AND COMMISSION

Isaiah, son of Amos, was a citizen of Jerusalem. He was married and had two sons. A man of culture and learning, he had a thorough knowledge of national and international affairs. Since he had access to the court, it may be inferred that he was of noble birth. He may have been a priest, since his inaugural vision took place *in* the Temple, which only priests were allowed to enter. Alternatively, it may have been as a

cultic prophet that he participated in the Temple services. His
call to the prophetic ministry of the word of God is dated 'in
the year that King Uzziah died' (740 B.C.). That was a critical
year for both Israel and Judah. It marked the end of the long
period of peace and prosperity that had characterized the
reigns of Jeroboam II of Israel and Uzziah of Judah, and the
beginning of the period of tension and peril occasioned by
the westward expansion of Assyria.

Chapter 6 is autobiography; the moving story of his call and
commission is told by Isaiah himself. As he stood in the
sanctuary, or perhaps at the open doors looking into it, he had
a vision. He was caught up by the Spirit into the temple of
heaven. The worship of the sanctuary on earth, its objects and
activities, its symbols and ceremonies—the red-hot stones of
the altar, the clouds of incense, the antiphonal singing of the
Temple choir, the winged cherubim, the ark throne in the
holy of holies—all these earthly things were taken up into
the heavenly vision. 'I saw the Lord sitting upon a throne, high
and lifted up.' With a reserve born of reverence the prophet
makes no attempt to describe the appearance of the majestic
King, the skirts of whose royal robe filled the Temple. The
Lord of hosts was attended by fiery creatures, the six-winged
seraphim. The three pairs of wings may be taken as symbols of
adoration, humility, and service—they veiled their faces before
his overwhelming glory, they screened their naked bodies from
his awful purity, they stood poised to go on his service. This
seraphic choir was praising God without ceasing. 'Holy, holy,
holy is the Lord of hosts; the whole earth is full of his glory.'
The Hebrews expressed the superlative by repeating a word
three times. In antiphonal song, the seraphim were extolling
the perfect holiness of the Lord, who reigns over the hosts of
heaven, and whose glory fills the whole earth. As if by an
earthquake, the foundations shook at the cry of the seraphim,
and the Temple was filled with smoke, both of which, as at
Sinai, were signs of the divine presence (Exodus 19: 18). In
response to this vision of God in his perfect holiness, Isaiah
was constrained to confess his utter unworthiness—'Woe is
me! for I am lost.' He acknowledged that both he, and the
nation to which he belonged, were sinful and unclean. In
response to this confession of sin, God sent a seraph to touch
the mouth of Isaiah with a red-hot stone taken from the altar.
This action, symbol of the divine forgiveness and cleansing,

the seraph accompanied by a declaration of pardon. 'Your guilt is taken away, and your sin forgiven.' Cleansed by contact with the divine holiness, Isaiah had now both the capacity to hear and the desire to obey the word of God. He was present at the heavenly council, listening to the dialogue between God and the heavenly beings. The decision had already been made to send a messenger to Judah, and the Lord was enquiring of the council 'Whom shall I send, and who will go for us?' Isaiah volunteered for service: 'Here I am! Send me.' God accepted the offer and commissioned Isaiah to be his messenger. He was warned that his mission to a people spiritually blind and deaf would meet with failure. This insensitivity and obstinacy of the people was not the purpose, but the result, of his preaching, here announced by God in advance. In response to his question, 'How long, O Lord?', he was told to continue his work until the whole nation had been destroyed—all except a tiny remnant which would survive.

In this story we see represented and foreshadowed many of the insights and convictions the prophet was destined to proclaim throughout the whole course of his long ministry. Here are disclosed the perfect holiness of God and his sovereignty over all creation; and, in contrast with that holiness and sovereignty, the radical sinfulness of man and his need of divine forgiveness and cleansing. In this story the nature of the prophetic ministry is unveiled: a prophet is a man who has stood in the heavenly council and is commissioned to declare what he has heard. Here at the outset is the doctrine of the remnant—the faithful community which survives the judgments of God in history, and through which he continues to work out his purpose of salvation. In addition to these insights about God, Man, and the Church, which are taken up in the teaching of Isaiah, we can also see essential elements in our Christian worship and experience foreshadowed in this story of the prophet's call. Every time the Sanctus is said or sung at the Eucharist, we are reminded of the influence of this vision on the liturgy of the Church. Here is vision and awe, adoration and song, penitence and confession, absolution and cleansing, the hearing and obeying of the word of God, revelation and response. Here above all is disclosed the pattern of Christian experience, for the sequence—vision of God, confession of sin, commissioning for service—has been reproduced in countless lives down the ages. When we see God, then we become aware of our sinfulness; when we are cleansed by God, then we are ready for service.

The story of his call and commission was written down by Isaiah after the delivery of most of the messages now recorded in the chapters which precede it. To his original oracles, he added the account of his call, because it is the warrant for his authority and preaching. But in the time sequence, the call of the prophet *preceded* the delivery of the messages which are set in the book before it. We are now to study the oracles in chapters 1 to 5, most of which come from the early years of his ministry. Here Isaiah exposes and condemns the corruption and rebellion of the people in the light of his vision of the holiness and sovereignty of God. 'Sons have I reared and brought up, but they have rebelled against me.' The father is deeply grieved; he has lavished care upon his children only to be rewarded with open rebellion. Even dumb animals know their owners, but Israel does not know the Lord (1: 2, 3). The behaviour of the people is contrary to nature, a monstrous perversion of the true order of things.

The rebellion manifests itself in character and conduct as self-sufficiency and arrogance. Man has confidence in his own unaided reason (5: 21), and takes pride in his own creations and achievements (2: 7). This primal sin of pride is like a serpent with many heads. There is scepticism: disbelief in the reality or in the activity of God (5: 19). There is moral darkness and confusion: the depravity of those who can no longer distinguish between good and evil (5: 20). There is superstition and idolatry: looking to the diviner and the fortune teller for guidance, and bowing down in worship before sticks and stones (2: 6, 8). There is the gross indulgence of bodily appetite: men are to be seen drinking the whole day long, unaware of what the Lord is doing in the world (5: 11, 12). There is vanity and wantonness: the women of Jerusalem, obsessed with dress, decked with costly ornaments, flirting with their eyes, are lovers of luxury, ostentation, and pleasure (3: 16 to 4: 1). This vaunting pride in all its forms is destined for destruction. The judgment which is coming upon the nation will expose the hollow pretensions of self-sufficient man. 'For the Lord of hosts has a day against all that is proud and lofty, against all that is lifted up and high . . . and the haughtiness of man shall be humbled, and the pride of men shall be brought low; and the Lord alone will be exalted in that day' (2: 12, 17).

This denunciation of human pride in the earlier prophecies of Isaiah is accompanied by the condemnation of social injustice. This is the message of the finest parable in the Old Testament (5: 1–7). Nathan had once concealed the truth in a parable, and by that stratagem had compelled the unwary David to pronounce judgment on himself (II Samuel 12: 1–15). Isaiah also uses a parable as the sword of the Spirit. It has the form of a popular love song, and may have been spoken or sung at the festivities of the grape harvest. A dear friend of the singer had made a vineyard. He had prepared the soil thoroughly, planted choice vines, and secured the protection of the plants from animals and thieves. When vintage time came, he found nothing but wild grapes. Since nothing more could have been done for the vineyard, what could the owner now do but give it up? The useless vineyard would be utterly destroyed, and the land become a thorn-choked waste. Thus far the crowds, captivated by the story, have enjoyed the song. Now comes the thrust of the sword. *You*, the men of Israel, the house of Judah, are the vineyard on which the Lord has lavished such care. Yet when he came expecting fruit, what did he find? He looked for justice (*mishpat*) and found bloodshed (*mispah*), he expected to see righteousness (*cedhāquāh*) but instead he heard a cry from the oppressed (*ceāqāh*). To the loving care of God the nation has responded with violence and oppression.

The city of Jerusalem, once renowned for faithfulness, has become as wicked as a harlot. For, like silver mixed with dross, or wine mingled with water, her rulers have spoiled justice by admixture with injustice. They are far too obsessed with money to pay any attention to the needs of the oppressed (1: 21–26). The Lord will call them to account for robbing and crushing the poor (3: 13–15). In the coming judgment, he will take away the guilty rulers and officials, and the leaderless society will lapse into anarchy (3: 1–8). The rapacious landowners who have built up large estates at the expense of their defenceless neighbours, will be left in solitude. The punishment will fit the crime; those who have turned out their neighbours will in the end have no neighbours (5: 8).

It was probably in the courts of the Temple that Isaiah

delivered these oracles against social unrighteousness. For the exploitation and oppression of the poor and helpless did not mean that the worship of the Temple was being neglected! Injustice and piety, oppression and worship, immoral conduct and sacrificial cult went hand in hand together. The prophet tells the people that their worship is hateful to God. He will not accept their holocausts of rams and calves, bulls and goats. He cannot stand their festivals and assemblies; he is weary of them, they are a burden to him. Nor will he listen to their prayers, for their outstretched hands are stained with innocent blood. If they really desire to offer acceptable worship, they must cleanse themselves, put away all evil, learn to do good, search for justice and champion the cause of the oppressed. Isaiah is not rejecting the cult as such. He himself had received his call and commission in the Temple, and may have been a priest, or a cultic prophet. Like Amos, Hosea, and Micah, he is condemning, in God's name, the substitution of cult for conduct, of rite and ceremony for justice and kindness, of sacrifice and offering for personal holiness and social righteousness. Not only sacrifices, but also prayers, not only ceremonies, but also words are included in this indictment. Worship, however costly and splendid, can never be an acceptable substitute for obedience to the moral demands of God. True worship should inspire such obedience. After this indictment, as in a court of law, the people are invited to 'reason together' with God as judge. Their sins are grave and heinous; they are like scarlet, red like crimson. Can they become like wool, white like snow? It all depends. The magnanimous offer of forgiveness is conditional. The alternatives are set forth—'if you are willing and obedient . . . if you refuse and rebel'. Israel must choose between the way of life and peace and the way of destruction and death (1: 10–20).

About six years after his call to the ministry, Isaiah was brought into public prominence by a political crisis which confronted Judah. About 734 B.C., the Southern Kingdom was threatened with invasion by the combined armies of Israel and Syria. Stricken with panic, Ahaz king of Judah appealed to the Assyrian monarch Tiglath-pileser III for help. From that time, throughout the whole course of his long ministry, directly or indirectly, the prophet was concerned with Assyria. We shall therefore look first at what Isaiah has to say about Assyria, before studying the other early prophecies and those of his middle years and later ministry.

For almost 300 years, Assyria was the greatest power in the ancient Near East. From her capital Nineveh, the dread of her spread to every country from Persia in the east to Egypt in the south-west. With the accession of Tiglath-pileser in 745 B.C., the small states of Syria-Palestine began to feel the full impact of this aggressive military power. The many campaigns of the Assyrian monarchs and their commanders inflicted untold sufferings upon the common people. 'Upon whom has not come your unceasing evil?' (Nahum 3: 19). Aggressive, ruthless, irresistible, the invasion of her armies was as destructive as a mighty river in flood (8: 7, 8). The Assyrian cavalry advanced with incredible speed. Each soldier was vigorous and alert, smart and well-equipped, armed with bow and arrows, poised and ready for battle. The hoofs of their steeds struck sparks like flint, and the rumble of the chariot wheels was like a tornado (5: 26–30). There is a second imaginative description of the swift advance of the Assyrian soldiery. 'He has gone up from Rimmon, he has come to Aiath . . . they have crossed over the pass, at Geba they lodge for the night.' Here the enemy is depicted as marching down from the north, through the territory of Benjamin, to a hill within sight of Jerusalem. The inhabitants of the towns and villages flee in panic before the advancing Assyrian army (10: 28–32).

Why did God permit such aggression and cruelty? Why was this tyrant and taskmaster allowed to overrun and oppress the nations? Was there some hidden meaning in her military campaigns, was some purpose being served by her conquests? Isaiah answers these questions in a lament over the downfall of Assyria (10: 5–19; 14: 24–27). The Lord of history addresses the aggressive empire. 'Ah, Assyria, the rod of my anger.' A master chastises his slave with a rod; Assyria is the instrument in the hand of God for the punishment of his disobedient people (5, 6). The rod is an unconscious instrument; the Assyrian monarch is not aware of the purpose for which he is being used. The arrogant king is concerned only with conquest and glory (7). He boasts of the cities already captured by the Assyrians, whose gods were unable to save them. Soon he will treat Jerusalem as these cities have already been treated (9–11). All his conquests he has achieved unaided, by his own wisdom and power, annexing the territories of other peoples and plundering their treasures, none daring to protest (13, 14). The prophet then breaks in upon the soliloquy of the proud conqueror. How ridiculous for an axe to vaunt itself over him who wields it, for an instrument to get the idea that it controls the person who uses it (15)! Bombastic and self-sufficient, the conqueror is destined to be struck down with disease. Like a forest ravaged by fire, whose few remaining trees a child can count, Assyria and her armies will be destroyed. For 'the light of Israel will become a fire, and his Holy One a flame' (16–19).

This poem enshrines the prophetic interpretation of history. In spite of all appearances to the contrary, ultimate power in the world belongs to God, and he is absolutely supreme in human affairs. He works out his purposes not only through the agency of those who in trust and obedience co-operate with him, but also through the instrumentality of those who are unaware of those purposes and pursue their own ends. He can turn the wrath of men to praise him (Psalm 76: 10). Even the acts which violate his will, he can use to carry out his will. In the world today there are great powers which do not acknowledge the existence, still less the sovereignty, of God. Trusting in no power other or greater than themselves, they are guilty of the self-idolatry which characterized imperial Assyria. Yet they are being used by the God whose existence they deny; unaware of his purpose, they are instruments in his hand. Through their plans, both good and evil, he is working out his purposes of judgment and mercy. The Assyrian monarch was known as the King of Kings (cf. 10: 8). The knowledge that the Lord God is the true King of Kings, is the secret of that quiet trust and firm faith which Isaiah required and commended.

IMMANUEL AND THE REMNANT

The political crisis of 734–733 B.C. was caused by the attempt of the Northern Kingdom and Syria to resist Assyrian expansion under Tiglath-pileser. The kings, Pekah of Israel and Rezin of Damascus, attempted to persuade Ahaz of Judah to join the anti-Assyrian coalition. When he refused, they made preparations to invade the Southern Kingdom, in order to depose Ahaz and place on the throne of Judah a puppet of their own. Ahaz was seized with panic, and it was probably on this occasion that he offered up his own son in sacrifice (II Kings 16: 3). 'His heart and the heart of his people shook as the trees of the forest shake before the wind' (7: 2). The cowardly king was minded to send a substantial gift to Tiglath-pileser, and to appeal for Assyrian aid against Pekah and Rezin. To this policy Isaiah was resolutely opposed.

At God's command he went forth to meet the king, to warn him against taking such a course. He was accompanied by his son Shear-jashub who, like the children of Hosea, had received at birth a symbolic name. The presence of the boy whose name meant 'Only a remnant will return', was itself an embodied warning against seeking the help of the Assyrian monster. A besieged city would need a supply of water, and that was why, at the time, Ahaz was inspecting the aqueduct which brought water from the spring Gihon to a reservoir in the city. Isaiah, addressing the king, urged him to be calm and fearless, for the outcome of events would be determined, not by the schemes of little men, but by the sovereign will of God. Pekah and Rezin were but 'two smouldering stumps of firebrands' already almost extinguished. Each was head of his own country and capital only, and would not be permitted to replace the Davidic dynasty at Jerusalem. Let the king conquer his fears and have faith in God. The message was reinforced by a play upon words. If your faith is not firm and sure (*tha'aminn*), then you will not be established and secure (*the'amenn*) (7: 1–9).

Since Ahaz was not willing to commit himself unreservedly to God, Isaiah went to him again after a short time, with a proposal designed to strengthen his faith. This interview took place in the council chamber. As proof of the truth of his word, the Lord invited Ahaz to ask for a sign, and gave him the option of naming it. With a hypocritical show of piety, Ahaz declined the offer, on the ground that it was not right to put the Lord to the test. Provoked to indignation by the faithless king, the prophet affirmed that the Lord himself would give the sign for which Ahaz had refused to ask. A maiden was with child and would soon bear a son, and would call him Immanuel (God-with-us). Before the child reached the age of discrimination the lands of the two kings who now threatened Jerusalem would be desolate. This sign of deliverance would also be to Ahaz, who had refused it, a sign of disaster. For the land, saved from the two little kings he so greatly feared, would be overwhelmed by Assyria. They would be shaved by the razor they had hired (7: 10–20).

What had Isaiah in mind when he predicted the birth of a son who was to be called Immanuel? The prophet expected the birth of the child to take place in the immediate future, for he was to be a sign to Ahaz of the destruction of Israel and Syria. Some interpreters believe that the maiden was the queen, and her expected child the future King Hezekiah. Taking the sign of Immanuel in conjunction with the messianic poem (9: 2–7), it is evident that Isaiah was referring to the birth of a son of the royal line. His coming would be a decisive intervention, and in his person and reign God would be present with his people. With this true king they would pass through a period of severe privation and suffering, when the food would be a wilderness diet of curds and honey. Yet through this wilderness they would be led to the 'milk and honey' of the Promised Land. The words of Isaiah addressed to the contemporary situation, had reference to a more distant situation. 'A prophecy may have a proximate fulfilment which nevertheless does not exhaust its meaning.'[1] The Christian evangelist, quoting the Septuagint, in which the Hebrew word 'maiden' ('almah) is rendered by the Greek word 'virgin' (parthenos), sees the prediction of Isaiah coming to ultimate fulfilment in the birth of Jesus Christ of the Virgin Mary. He is the sign that God is with us (Matthew 1: 23).

Some time after these encounters with Ahaz, a second son was born to Isaiah. Before his conception, the name given to him at birth had already been placarded before the eyes of the people. His symbolic name, Maher-shalal-hash-baz, means 'speed the spoil, hasten the prey'. He was an embodied warning—especially to the Northern Kingdom. For before the child could say 'father' or 'mother', the wealth of Damascus and the spoil of Samaria would have been carried away by the king of Assyria (8: 1–4). Yet all these signs and messages were in vain. Ahaz refused to turn away from the policy dictated by his fears. He appealed to Tiglath-pileser for help, sending to him the treasures of the Temple and of his own palace (II Kings 16: 7, 8). Isaiah denounced this misplaced trust by contrasting the waters of Shiloah with the river Euphrates. Shiloah was the canal or aqueduct which conveyed water from the spring

[1] C. R. North, article Immanuel, The Interpreter's Dictionary of the Bible, Vol. II, 688.

Gihon. Isaiah takes these waters 'that flow gently' as a symbol of quiet faith in God. Because the people had rejected that faith, the Assyrians, like the mighty river Euphrates in flood, would overwhelm the land (Isaiah 8: 5–8). The messages of Isaiah had fallen on deaf ears and his counsels had been persistently rejected. So he now withdrew from public affairs and concentrated on his disciples. The words his contemporaries had refused to hear were committed to writing (i.e. the prophecies, biographical and autobiographical material in chapters 1 to 8). The papyrus scroll on which they were written, the first collection of Isaiah's oracles, was sealed, and committed to his disciples for preservation; for his inspired words, rejected in the present, would be vindicated in the future. Meanwhile, he would wait quietly for the Lord to act. 'For the Lord spoke thus to me with his strong hand upon me, and warned me not to walk in the way of this people' (8: 11). He felt a divine compulsion to withdraw from the society in which policy was based on the rejection of God.

This withdrawal of Isaiah and his disciples was an epoch-making event. Here there emerges within a nation a distinctive group, dissociating itself from the outlook and aims of contemporary society, yet bearing witness within that society to a higher allegiance. It is the birth of the Church. The idea of the remnant must have taken shape in the mind of Isaiah in the early days of his ministry, since the conception is embodied in the name he gave to his first son—Shear-jashub. The name contained the twin-ideas of judgment and salvation. '*Only* a remnant will return'. A few only would survive the impending judgment. 'For though your people Israel be as the sand of the sea, only a remnant of them will return. Destruction is decreed, overflowing with righteousness' (10: 22). When, however, the emphasis is placed on the verb the name is a promise. 'A remnant *will return*, the remnant of Jacob, to the mighty God' (10: 21). Noah and his family survived the judgment, the destruction of civilization by the waters of the flood, and became the progenitors of the new human race. God would visit his disobedient people in judgment—the flood waters of Assyria—but in his mercy he would continue his work of salvation through the righteous remnant which would survive that judgment. Isaiah and his disciples are the type of the new Israel which was to be gathered out of the world by Jesus Christ.

THE MESSIAH

In the sign of Immanuel, we have already seen that Isaiah was anticipating the birth of a royal son. This expectation comes to sublime expression in the two passages of his prophecy best known to Christians (9: 1–7; 11: 1–9). Centuries earlier, God had assured David through Nathan the prophet of the permanence of his dynasty. 'And your house and your kingdom shall be made sure for ever before me; your throne shall be established for ever' (II Samuel 7: 8–16). This promise was a source of confidence and hope, especially in times of upheaval and danger. It was because Ahaz did not believe this divine promise concerning the permanence of the Davidic dynasty, that he was terrified by the threat of Pekah and Rezin to depose him. So, while Isaiah affirmed his faith in the king that was to be born of David's line, Ahaz looked to another king for deliverance. In response to his appeal, Tiglath-pileser invaded Israel, and made Galilee and other parts of her territory into Assyrian provinces. It was after this Galilean deportation in 733–732 B.C., and before the fall of Samaria in 722–721 B.C. that Isaiah delivered the first of his two great messianic oracles (9: 1–7).

Galilee, the territory of Zebulun and Naphtali, traversed by the ancient caravan route from Damascus to the western sea, overrun by the Assyrians and annexed by Tiglath-pileser, had been brought into contempt and plunged in heathen darkness. But now, into the land of deep darkness, a great light has shone. The people rejoice as when the harvesters bring home the sheaves, or the victors divide the spoils of battle. For as Gideon once defeated the Midianites and liberated his country, so God has now broken the rod of the Assyrian oppressor. The boots and blood-stained garments of the enemy soldiers have been consumed by fire. 'For to us a child is born, to us a son is given; and the government will be upon his shoulder, and his name will be called "Wonderful Counsellor, Mighty God, Everlasting Father, Prince of Peace".' Two of these titles have reference to the character and two to the reign of the king. He will be endowed with both the wisdom and the power of God. Like a father, he will care for the people without ceasing, and under his beneficent and harmonious rule, they will enjoy life to the full. From David's throne, he will rule over a wide dominion in justice and righteousness. This poetic oracle may have been composed by the prophet to celebrate the accession of a monarch. Each successive king of the dynasty of David was 'the Lord's *anointed*'. (That is the meaning of the Hebrew word *Messiah*.) Consecrated with holy oil, the new king was thereby brought into a special relationship with God, and was regarded as his adopted son. His life as God's son began when he was anointed king, and it is possible that the words 'is born . . . is given' should be understood in this sense. 'You are my son, today I have begotten you' (Psalm 2: 7). The original covenant with David was reaffirmed at the accession of each king, and the hope was reborn that this particular king would be the ideal ruler, the true son of God. None of the successors of David fulfilled this expectation. Yet with the destruction of the Davidic monarchy in 587 B.C. the vision did not fade. The deferred hope was projected into the future, and at length found fulfilment in Jesus the Messiah. When this poem is read as the Old Testament lesson for Christmas Day, or its words are sung to the music of Handel's *Messiah*, its full meaning is seen in the light of its fulfilment in Christ (Matthew 4: 12–16).

There is a second portrait of the ideal king (11: 1–9). He is to be of Davidic stock: a shoot will spring from the stump of Jesse, father of David. Permanently endowed with the Spirit, he will rule as God's representative. The Spirit will confer upon him six outstanding gifts. He is to be endowed with *wisdom*, the practical ability to order affairs successfully; and with *understanding*, the keenness of perception which can penetrate beneath outward appearances to underlying truth. He will be endowed with *counsel*, the ability to make right decisions; and with *might*, the strength of purpose to carry them into effect. He will be endowed with *knowledge*, the intimate personal knowledge of God; and with *the fear of the Lord*, the reverence which 'the Holy One of Israel' inspires. These gifts of the Spirit of God will enable the king to rule with wisdom, justice, and might. As a judge, he will not rely on outward appearance. In dealing with the poor and needy he will decide according to the right, and will use his authority to strike down the tyrant and the oppressor. Righteousness and integrity will be the clothing he wears. When he reigns, nature herself will be transformed, and paradise restored. Wild beasts and reptiles will live in harmony with domestic animals and children. Brutality and violence will cease, for all creatures acknowledging the sovereignty of God will live at peace. As with the previous poem, no ancient Hebrew king fulfilled this hope. It is a portrait of the Christ, whose kingdom has come but is not yet complete. For justice is not yet enthroned with might, nor is creation yet at peace. It is also a portrait of the Holy Spirit, manifested in the person and work of the Messiah, and given to those who trust in him. To the six gifts of the Spirit mentioned in the Hebrew text, the Septuagint added a seventh, piety (in the first part of verse 3). The Vulgate, the Latin version, followed the Septuagint, the Greek version. Here, for the first time, we have the list of the seven gifts of the Spirit, frequently mentioned in our Christian hymns. Furthermore, the Hebrew prophet's vision of nature transformed, of a renewal which would include the animal creation as well as mankind, was taken up by the Christian apostle. The whole creation now groans and travails in pain, but it is not without hope. At the advent of Christ, with the arrival of the messianic kingdom, all creation, animate and inanimate, will share in the freedom and glory of the sons of God (Romans 8: 18–25).

PROPHECIES FROM THE MIDDLE YEARS OF ISAIAH'S MINISTRY

When his messages were rejected at the time of the Syro-Israelite war, Isaiah withdrew from public activity. From this retreat he emerged to announce the impending destruction of the two kingdoms, which had earlier joined forces against Judah. Damascus, capital of Syria, would become a deserted ruin, and on the sites of the once populous Syrian cities, flocks would graze. Like 'two or three berries in the top of the highest bough' left behind by the harvesters of the olive crop, only a remnant of Israel would survive the coming disaster (17: 1–6). The prophet describes the condition of the Northern Kingdom in those last years before her destruction by Assyria. Like the blows of a hammer, disaster follows disaster; yet the self-confidence of Ephraim is not shattered. Invaded by Syrians and Philistines, misled by elders and lying prophets, bereft of her young men by war, torn to pieces by civil strife, evil, like a forest fire, was destroying the nation (9: 8–21). The city of Samaria, built on a hill encircled by walls, was like a faded garland on a reveller's head. There the magnates, drunken and dissolute, lolled in false security. But Assyria, like a hurricane, would destroy the faded garland, and 'like a first-ripe fig' Israel would be devoured (28: 1–4). This destruction took place in two stages. Tiglath-pileser invaded and overran the Northern Kingdom in 733 B.C., and incorporated Galilee, Gilead, and the coastal plain in his Assyrian empire. This first disaster had already befallen the nation when Isaiah delivered his first oracle concerning the messianic King (9: 2–7). The little of the 'ripe fig' that remained, the city and province of Samaria, was also devoured by the Assyrians a decade later, when the capital was besieged by Shalmaneser and fell to Sargon in 724–721 B.C.

Soon after the fall of Samaria, the new Assyrian monarch Sargon II was confronted with a rising organized by the king of Hamath, and supported by the Philistines. The latter, mistaking a temporary reprieve for a permanent deliverance from Assyria, were rebuked by the realistic prophet for wishful thinking and premature rejoicing. 'Rejoice not, O Philistia, all of you, that the rod which smote you is broken' (14: 28–32). Hezekiah, the new king of Judah, who had succeeded Ahaz (about 716 B.C.) was making the same mistake. He was inclined to believe that the time had come to cast off the Assyrian yoke, and was disposed to lend an ear to the intrigues against Assyria which the Egyptian Pharaoh was instigating. Egypt had been passing through a period of disorder and civil strife, leading up to the establishment in 714 B.C. of an alien Ethiopian dynasty. Isaiah's announcement of God's judgment on Egypt, to be manifested in civil war, natural and social calamity, and the rule of 'a hard master . . . a fierce king', probably belongs to this period (19: 1–15). The new Pharaoh Shabaka was concerned to check the power of Assyria. One year after his accession an anti-Assyrian revolt broke out in the Philistine kingdom of Ashdod. The Pharaoh attempted to involve Judah, along with Edom and Moab, in the uprising. This policy was strenuously opposed by Isaiah. When the ambassadors of the Ethiopian Pharaoh arrived in Jerusalem to persuade Hezekiah to join the anti-Assyrian revolt, Isaiah had a message for them to convey to their tall fellow-countrymen in the land of buzzing insects! The Lord was in control of the nations of the world, and he would give the signal for the final overthrow of Assyria. He was waiting for the harvest, and before Assyria was ripe, he would intervene and cut down her armies. That time had not yet come, and so to resist Assyria, who for the time being was God's agent, was to resist his purpose (18: 1–7).

It was during this period that Isaiah was commanded by God to walk 'naked and barefoot for three years as a sign and a portent against Egypt and Ethiopia'. That was how a prisoner of war was marched off into captivity. The purpose of this symbolic act, which reinforced the spoken word of the prophet, was to warn Hezekiah and the nation of the folly of trusting in the new Ethiopian dynasty of Egypt. His dramatic action symbolized the conquest of Egypt by Assyria (20: 1–6). Shebna, the governor of the palace of Hezekiah, was probably an advocate of the policy of alliance with Egypt against Assyria. He was an opponent of Isaiah and his message. The prophet predicted his downfall. Like a ball, the Lord would toss him away, and the key of the palace would pass to Eliakim (22: 15–25). In the New Testament, this key of the house of David, the symbol of authority, has passed into the possession of Jesus Christ. He has power to open and shut, to admit others to or exclude them from the presence of the King in the new Jerusalem (Revelation 3: 7). Shebna did in fact fall from power, although he was allowed to continue in a subordinate position. It was probably the influence of Isaiah that prevented the king, in spite of the earlier negotiations with Eypt, from becoming deeply implicated in the anti-Assyrian revolt. Although this had broken out in 713 B.C., Sargon, who was preoccupied elsewhere in his far-flung empire, did not attempt to suppress it until the third year. In 711 B.C., he sent the Tartan, the commander-in-chief, with an army to Ashdod. The Egyptians deserted their allies, who were left to their cruel fate. The revolt was ruthlessly suppressed and the king-dom of Ashdod became an Assyrian province. Because Hezekiah withdrew from the conspiracy just in time, Judah escaped invasion. Yet the king did not learn his lesson. Next time, he took a lead in the anti-Assyrian movement, and brought his country to the very verge of disaster. To this series of events we now turn.

PROPHECIES FROM THE LATER YEARS OF ISAIAH'S MINISTRY

The death of Sargon in 705 B.C. was soon followed by disturbances in many parts of the empire, and his successor Sennacherib was preoccupied for several years dealing with these. The ring-leader against Assyria was Merodach-baladan, who had seized the throne of Babylon and was endeavouring to

stir up trouble for Sennacherib among the subject peoples. He
sent an embassy to Jerusalem, which was welcomed by
Hezekiah, who showed them all his treasures (39: 1–4). The
reform of worship which Hezekiah carried out at this time, and
which probably included the removal of the Assyrian altar
placed by Ahaz in the Temple, was one manifestation of the
king's determination to regain political independence. Together with other neighbouring states, Judah joined the anti-
Assyrian uprising. The Pharaoh of Egypt (the Ethiopian,
Shabaka), hoping to hasten the collapse of Assyria, fanned the
flames of revolt. Envoys of Hezekiah were sent to Egypt to
negotiate an alliance and arrange for effective military aid.
Many of the oracles in chapters 28 to 31 belong to this period,
and were directed against the political and military alliance
with Egypt—the 'covenant with death'. The counsel of Isaiah
was clear and consistent—stay out of the revolution. This
reiterated message was persistently rejected by Hezekiah and
his political advisers.

Here is a summary of what the prophet said at this period.
Untaught by the disaster which had overtaken the Northern
Kingdom, the rulers of Jerusalem, like the former magnates
of Samaria, are fuddled by drink and stupefied by self-
indulgence (28: 1–4, 7, 8). They mock God's messenger. Is he a
schoolmaster and are they children, that he must needs say the
same words to them over and over again? The prophet replies
with indignation: if they will not listen to the lesson in familiar
Hebrew words, God will spell it out to them bit by bit—in
Assyrian (28: 9–13)! Let these scoffers not suppose that their
alliance with Egypt will serve as a shelter from the storm. The
Lord himself would provide the true shelter, erected in justice
and righteousness on the cornerstone of faith. That stone bears
the inscription—'he who trusts will not be alarmed'. The stone
is God's chosen people, the remnant, the renewed community.
(In the fullness of time that ideal remnant was represented in
the Messiah. Jesus Christ is the precious cornerstone, 'and he
who believes in him will not be put to shame' [I Peter 2: 4–8].)
But as for the shelter in which Hezekiah and his advisers were
trusting, it would be swept away by the Assyrian flood (28:
14–19).

The misguided policy of the rulers has blinded the people;
they are in a condition of spiritual stupor, and can neither see
what the Lord is doing nor hear what he is saying (29: 9–11).

These deceitful leaders, negotiating an alliance with Egypt, fondly imagine that the Lord cannot see what they are doing; they insult the intelligence of their Creator (29: 15, 16). Woe to the rebels who carry out this plan which is not of God, who set out for Egypt without seeking his guidance. The delegates who are leading asses and camels laden with gifts across the Negeb, the home of the lion and the serpent, are labouring in vain. 'For Egypt's help is worthless and empty' (30: 1–7). Once again, Isaiah is commanded to put into writing the messages which the rulers have rejected 'that it may be for the time to come'. For at present the people listen only to the prophets who say what they want to hear (30: 8–11). But God's prophet sets forth the true way of deliverance. 'In returning and rest you shall be saved; in quietness and in trust shall be your strength.' Their salvation and strength lie in conversion and surrender to God. But they will have none of it, preferring to trust in armaments for deliverance. 'No! We will speed upon horses.' So be it! If it's speed they want, they shall have it—as they flee in panic and in vain before their foes (30: 15–17)! Have these scheming politicians overlooked the fact that the Lord too is wise, and that he also has a plan? If they were really wise, they would not be putting their trust in the weak and transitory, but in the omnipotent and eternal. For 'the Egyptians are men, and not God; and their horses are flesh, and not spirit' (31: 1–3).

These various oracles against the Egyptian alliance belong to the period between 705 and 701 B.C. The rebellious states had this period of respite, because Sennacherib was fully engaged in putting down risings in other parts of his empire. But in 701 B.C., having defeated Merodach-baladan and pacified the east, Sennacherib appeared in the west. We have his own account of this campaign in Syria-Palestine, as well as the biblical account in II Kings (chapters 18 and 19) from which the account in Isaiah (chapters 36 and 37) is taken. Passing through Phoenicia, he crushed Sidon and other coastal cities, and, reaching Philistia, he defeated the Egyptian forces on the plain of Eltakeh near Ekron. The small rebellious states were now completely at his mercy, and after crushing the Philistines, he turned on Judah. At Jerusalem, Hezekiah's workmen had cut a tunnel through 1,777 feet of rock, to bring the water from the spring Gihon to a pool inside the city wall. The fortifications were also feverishly repaired and strengthened

(22: 8–11). Sennacherib records how he overran the whole of Judah. 'As for Hezekiah the Judean, he did not submit to my yoke. I laid siege to forty-six of his strong cities and conquered . . . I drove out 200,150 people . . . himself I made a prisoner in Jerusalem, his royal residence, like a bird in a cage.' Like a slave severely flogged, bruised, and wounded from head to foot, the whole land was afflicted, and Jerusalem was isolated 'like a booth in a vineyard, like a lodge in a cucumber field' (1: 5–9). Many of the soldiers of Hezekiah deserted to the enemy, and the Assyrians besieged Jerusalem. In response to a demand from Sennacherib who was encamped at Lachish, Hezekiah surrendered, and a heavy tribute was imposed upon him (II Kings 18: 13–16). Unexpectedly the city had been saved from destruction and there was much feasting and wild rejoicing. Isaiah was shocked by the behaviour of the populace. 'What do you mean that you have gone up, all of you, to the housetops, you who are full of shoutings, tumultuous city, exultant town?' Some of their soldiers had fled before the enemy, some of their fellow-citizens had been executed or sold into slavery, and they themselves had vainly trusted in their own defence preparations and had not looked to the Lord. It was a day for weeping and mourning, not for joy and gladness (22: 1–14).

The summary of Sennacherib's invasion in II Kings 18: 13–16, is followed by two separate accounts. The first of these is found in II Kings 18: 17 to 19: 8, and in Isaiah 36: 2 to 37: 8; and the second account is found in II Kings 19: 9–37 and in Isaiah 37: 9–38. Some scholars believe that the events recorded in both these accounts took place ten or more years later than the events just described. They are believed to be records of a second invasion of Judah by Sennacherib about the year 688 B.C., when he was involved in putting down a rebellion backed by Tirhakah of Egypt (37: 9). According to the first of these accounts, the Assyrian king sent his deputy, the Rabshakeh, to demand the unconditional surrender of Jerusalem. Accompanied by a detachment of the Assyrian army, the Rabshakeh made a clever propaganda speech to the officials and soldiers standing on the city walls. He underlined the futility of resistance and the advantages of surrendering to the invincible army of Sennacherib (36: 1–22). In this crisis, Hezekiah consulted Isaiah, and was counselled by him not to submit to the arrogant Assyrian. For God would cause

Sennacherib to hear a rumour (perhaps of unrest or revolution in some part of his empire) and he would return to his own land (37: 1–7).

According to the second account, the Assyrian monarch sent an impertinent letter to Hezekiah, insulting the Holy One of Israel. Did the gods of all the other nations subdued by the Assyrian kings save them, that Hezekiah should be so stupid and misguided as to trust for deliverance in his God? The Lord responded to Hezekiah who took the letter to him in prayer, by sending Isaiah with a promise of speedy deliverance. 'He shall not come into this city, or shoot an arrow there, or come before it with a shield, or cast up a siege-mound against it . . . for I will defend this city to save it, for my own sake and for the sake of my servant David' (37: 33, 35). Large numbers of soldiers in the Assyrian camp were destroyed, probably by a plague, here interpreted as the sword of 'the angel of the Lord' (37: 36). Jerusalem was miraculously delivered. The anti-Assyrian and pro-Egyptian policy of Hezekiah and his advisers had inflicted untold suffering upon Judah, and had brought the state to the very edge of the precipice. Yet it was not the purpose of God that Jerusalem, at that time, should fall to the enemy. Working through the events of history and the words of his prophet, the Lord had delivered Zion.

PROPHECIES LATER THAN ISAIAH'S TIME

After the deliverance of Jerusalem from Sennacherib, Isaiah disappears from the scene. Hezekiah died in 687 B.C., and was succeeded by Manasseh. According to Jewish tradition, Isaiah was sawn asunder during the reign of that apostate king (II Kings 21: 16; Hebrews 11: 37). The influence of the prophet did not cease with his martyrdom, and his disciples continued to cherish and transmit his teaching. Furthermore, the tradition associated with Isaiah became the medium through which the Spirit of God inspired others to interpret and amplify the message of the prophet, and apply it to the changed circumstances of their own time. It is not always possible to distinguish the oracles of the prophet himself from the words of his spiritual descendants. In the long discourses in the Gospel of John it is impossible to determine with precision where the words of Jesus end and the meditation of the evangelist begins. So in this prophecy, there may be material which comes from the prophet, but which has been expanded and applied to later situations by those who belonged to 'the school of Isaiah'.

The sixth and last part of the First Book of Isaiah (chapters 36 to 39) does not now concern us, since it is taken with some modifications from II Kings. Taking the other five sections in order, we now look at the material later than Isaiah contained in the First Book.

(i) Almost all the oracles in chapters 1 to 12 come from Isaiah, but there are a few exceptions. The oracle, found also in Micah, on world peace (2: 2–5), the vision of Zion purified by judgment (4: 2–6), the prophecies concerning the restoration of the scattered exiles (11: 10–16), are probably all post-exilic.

(ii) In chapters 13 to 23 we have a collection of oracles most of which are directed against foreign nations. Those which may be attributed to Isaiah with assurance are: God's plan to destroy Assyria (14: 24–27), the rebuke to Philistia (14: 28–32), the doom of Syria and Ephraim (17: 1–11), the destruction of the Assyrian army (17: 12–14), the message to the ambassadors (18: 1–7), concerning chaos in Egypt (19: 1–15), an acted and spoken prophecy against Egypt (20: 1–6), the rebuke of exultant Jerusalem (22: 1–14), the downfall of Shebna the king's minister (22: 15–25). Alongside these utterances of Isaiah are other oracles, three of them of great length, which probably come from a later period. The oracle concerning Babylon which stands at the head of the collection and is ascribed by the editor to Isaiah, probably belongs to the period just prior to the destruction of that city by Cyrus of Persia (between 550 and 538 B.C.). In the remarkable dirge on the fall of the king of Babylon, we have a vivid description of Sheol, the dark and dusty realm of the shades, the underworld of the ghostly dead (13: 1 to 14: 23). There is a lament over the destruction of Moab, the nation to the east of the Dead Sea, which had been overwhelmed by disaster. It could be by Isaiah, following the Assyrian devastation of Moab, but it is also possible that it was composed much later, after the Arab incursions into that land about 650 B.C. (15: 1 to 16: 14). Some of the oracles concerning Egypt belong to the Persian or Hellenistic periods. They affirm that the God of Israel will be worshipped in that foreign land and the Hebrew tongue be spoken in five of its cities. One of these is remarkable for its universalism. The author foresees the day when the Egyptians, like the Israelites, will be the people of God, and when Egypt, Assyria, and

Israel, reconciled and united, will be a blessing to all mankind
(19: 16–25). The city of Babylon fell to Sargon in 710 B.C.,
to Sennacherib in 689 B.C., and to Cyrus of Persia in 539 B.C.
It is not known with certainty to which of these periods the
oracle on the fall of Babylon, and the two brief oracles which
follow it on Edom and the Arabs, belong (21: 1–17). The
judgment of God on the sea-faring Phoenicians was announced
by Isaiah himself. To his oracle against Sidon (23: 1–4, 12–14)
later writers added the material about Tyre (23: 5–11, 15–18).

(iii) All the prophecies, psalms, and prayers in chapters 24
to 27 refer to the last days and the age to come. The main
ideas embodied in them are much later than Isaiah's time,
and have been assigned to various periods between the fourth
and second centuries B.C. A great catastrophe is about to overwhelm the earth, and, except for a small remnant, to destroy
the whole human race (24: 1–20). The triumphant Lord,
having punished his enemies in heaven and on earth, will reign
in Zion. There he will prepare a great banquet for all nations,
and will take away sorrow and abolish death (24: 21 to 25: 9).
A hymn of thanksgiving for God's victory is followed by a
prayer of entreaty. Let God deliver his people, not only from
their human enemies, but also from 'the last enemy', death.
The prayer is answered. 'Thy dead shall live, their bodies shall
rise. O dwellers in the dust, awake and sing for joy!' While
there are intimations of immortality in the Psalter and in Job,
this is the earliest mention in the Bible of the resurrection of
the (righteous) dead (26: 1–19).[1] Meanwhile, the people are
invited to hide and to wait until the judgment is past (26: 20,
21). For the Lord will then make Israel like a fruitful vineyard
(compare 5: 1–7) and his people, gathered from exile and
reunited, will worship him at Jerusalem (27: 1–13).

(iv) The oracles in chapters 28 to 31 come mostly from
Isaiah, and belong to the period 705–701 B.C. There are a few
passages which come from a later time: the promise of blessing
to the remnant (28: 5, 6), the description of the transformation
of nature and the redemption of society (29: 17–24), and the
prediction that the Lord will teach and guide his people in an
age of material prosperity (30: 18–26). In chapters 32 and 33
we have the words of Isaiah and of his spiritual descendants—
the passages 32: 1–5, 9–14 and 33: 1–6 are usually attributed
to the former, and 32: 6–8, 15–20 and 33: 7–24 to the latter.

[1] Compare I Corinthians 15: 26, 54.

We are familiar with the beautiful words of the prophet about the king who reigns by integrity and the princes who rule by justice, and are like a shelter from the wind, a refuge from the storm, like streams in the desert and the shade of a great rock in a thirsty land. While these words are true in part of many a great and noble character, they are fulfilled completely only in Jesus Christ. To us, he is the promised messianic king who in royal splendour reigns over a wide dominion, a spacious land (32: 1, 2; 33: 17).

(v) The two poems in chapters 34 and 35, the one on judgment and the other on salvation, are complementary. They come from the period of the exile in Babylon. In the first, all nations are summoned to hear God's sentence of destruction, which falls especially upon Edom, and is described in terms of a sacrificial feast. The Edomites, hated by the Jews for their active participation in the destruction of Jerusalem in 587 B.C., are taken as a type of all the enemies of God. Indignation against, and judgment upon evil is always one aspect of his intervention in the world (chapter 34). In the second poem, the redemption of his people is depicted as a new Exodus. The despondent exiles are summoned to have courage, for the Lord is coming to deliver them. At his advent, men will be made whole and nature will be transformed. Led by the Lord himself along a Sacred Way, across deserts flowing with streams, the ransomed exiles will march to Zion with everlasting joy in their hearts (chapter 35).

THE MESSAGE OF ISAIAH

The prophet Isaiah, whose ministry extended for over half a century, was undoubtedly the greatest man of his time. As statesman and reformer, poet and prophet, his whole personality and outstanding gifts were dedicated to the service of God. His extensive knowledge of men and affairs was included in the self-offering. Although he was probably a person of high rank, for he had easy access to kings, he did not refrain from rebuking the privileged classes. With rare courage he exposed and denounced social injustice and oppression. External as well as internal affairs were the concern of this great statesman, who sought to change the foreign policy of kings, to save his country from disaster. This practical man of affairs was also a creative artist, whose literary output is unsurpassed elsewhere in the Bible. 'He has all the qualities which are generally supposed to

be characteristic of a great poet—nobility of thought, wealth
of imagination, the observant eye, the power of graphic description, deep feeling and sincerity.'[1] His style is clear and
direct, his language concise and often majestic, his images
drawn from city and rural life, vivid and unforgettable. Above
all, Isaiah was a prophet of God, the king's friend who, having
stood in the heavenly council, was commissioned to declare
what he had seen and heard. He had seen the King, the Lord
of hosts, seated upon a throne, high and lifted up, upon whose
sovereignty the destiny of Israel and of all nations depended.
'As I have planned, so shall it be, and as I have purposed, so
shall it stand.' Even mighty Assyria God can use—and break
(14: 24–26). The phenomena of nature are likewise under his
control. When in storm and earthquake he comes in judgment,
the inhabitants of the earth flee 'before the terror of the Lord,
and from the glory of his majesty' (2: 12–22). Isaiah had also
overheard the seraphim extolling the perfect holiness of the
Divine Majesty. From that day the prophet was a man who
stood in awe of 'the Holy One of Israel' (he uses this title twelve
times), who is God and not man, separate from and over
against all that he has made. Holiness is the distinctive characteristic, the essential nature of the divine. The Holy One is
the mysterious, incomprehensible God, in his majestic exaltation. The holy is that which evokes reverence and awe in all
rational and sensitive creatures, and stirs within them the
impulse to worship. Holiness is also perfect goodness, absolute
purity, moral perfection. In the Holy One of Israel these ethical
and moral qualities are combined with the numinous; he is
exalted and pure, transcendent and good.

When Isaiah thus saw the King and heard the Sanctus, he
confessed his radical sinfulness. It was because the prophet was
aware of the sovereignty and holiness of God, that he was, by
contrast, aware also of the sinfulness of Israel and of mankind.
Sin is rebellion against the King and uncleanness in the
presence of the Holy One. God's sovereign-holiness must
express itself in judgment against that sin. Man's pride and self-
sufficiency, his sensuality and injustice would be consumed as
with fire on 'the day of the Lord'. This retribution, mediated
through the events of history, could be averted by repentance
and faith. 'Come now, let us talk this over . . . if you are willing
to obey, you shall eat the good things of the earth. But if you

[1] T. Henshaw, *The Latter Prophets*, 136.

G

persist in rebellion, the sword shall eat you instead' (1 : 18–20).[1]
This spirit of rebellion and disobedience, in the case of the
rulers of the nation, was manifested in their foreign policy.
Instead of looking to God for security and deliverance, they
sought it in alliances with foreign powers. Ahaz appealed to
Assyria; had he trusted in the Lord he would have been established in security (7: 9). Hezekiah made a covenant with
Egypt; had he but turned to the Lord with a quiet mind and a
trustful heart, he would have found deliverance and strength
(30: 15). We may not infer from this teaching that alliances
between nations are always contrary to God's will, or that
passive acquiescence is better than active diplomacy. Isaiah
calls for faith in the living God, who is the principal actor on
the stage of the earth in the drama of history. The contemporaries of Isaiah were unaware of the dynamic activity of
God in the world. It was wrong for Ahaz to appeal to Assyria,
because God would maintain the Davidic dynasty; later on, it
was wrong to resist Assyria, for God was then using her as his
rod. It was needless for Israel, Egypt, and their allies to hasten
the downfall of Assyria, for God would take care of that; later
on it was right for Hezekiah to resist the Assyrians, for it was
the purpose of God to deliver Zion. What was required at all
times was trust in the plan and in the activity of God.

That was why the prophet affirmed the inviolability of
Zion. It was not because he had made a careful assessment of
the political and military forces involved, that he was con-
fident Zion would not be overthrown. (Such an assessment, at
the time of Sennacherib's invasion, led his contemporaries to
the opposite view.) Isaiah encouraged Hezekiah to resist what
up to then (as the Rabshakeh pointed out) had been an
irresistible force, because he believed that it was God's purpose
at that time to preserve the royal line and 'the mountain of the
temple of the Lord'—the house and the city of David. His
faith was vindicated by a mighty act of God which, in the
memory of Israel, was cherished along with the Exodus from
Egypt and the Return from Babylon. Later on, Jeremiah had
to contend with those who had transformed the conviction of
Isaiah, that God would *at that time* deliver Jerusalem, into the
inflexible dogma that he would always in all circumstances
save Zion and her Temple from destruction (Jeremiah 7:
1–15). That was to substitute a static for a dynamic conception

[1] *The Jerusalem Bible.*

of the purpose of God, who has not promised to deliver his people irrespective of the circumstances or apart from their moral obedience.

Furthermore, the ultimate concern of Isaiah was not for stones, but for living stones; not for Zion as a city, but for Zion as a community. And God was in fact at that time establishing a community which survived the eventual destruction of the city (28: 16). Throughout the whole course of his long ministry, at the very beginning of which he was commissioned to announce the destruction of the nation as a whole (6: 11–13), Isaiah never ceased to cherish the hope that a purified remnant would survive that judgment. The righteous remnant is the true Zion, secure and inviolate. That faithful community is built on a foundation stone which binds all the stones into one. Like the city, the Davidic dynasty did not survive the disaster of 587 B.C. Yet as the city survived in the community, so the Davidic line was destined to survive in the Messiah. Isaiah was convinced that God would honour his promise to David. 'Your throne shall be established for ever' (II Samuel 7: 16). Deeply dissatisfied with the contemporary kings, the prophet announced the advent of the ideal king, who would share the attributes of God, and would establish justice and peace in a kingdom having no end. It was a long-deferred but an unfading hope. Seven centuries later, the Archangel Gabriel announced to the Virgin Mary—'Behold, you will conceive in your womb and bear a son, and you shall call his name Jesus . . . and the Lord God will give to him the throne of his father David . . . and of his kingdom there will be no end' (Luke 1: 31–33).

VI

Zephaniah

After Isaiah came Zephaniah—but not immediately. For a period of almost three-quarters of a century separated the ministries of these two men of God. Other prophets may have been active during that period; but if so, we have no knowledge of them. It was the dark age of reaction and apostasy, during which Judah was completely subservient to Assyria. Sennacherib had been murdered in 681 B.C. His able successor, Esarhaddon, after dealing with the civil war which followed his father's death, greatly extended the boundaries and influence of Assyria in the west. He planned to subdue Egypt, for that nation was constantly inciting rebellion against Assyria in Palestine. He invaded her territory, defeated and captured Pharaoh Taharqa, subdued lower Egypt, and established his dominion as far south as the city of Memphis. His son, Ashurbanipal, extended the conquests of his father, by pushing on beyond Memphis into upper Egypt. In 661 B.C. he captured and destroyed Thebes, the stronghold and capital of the realm. With the conquest of Egypt, Assyria had reached the zenith of her power.

The reign of Manasseh, king of Judah (687–642 B.C.), coincided with this period of Assyrian conquest and ascendancy in the west. Son and successor of Hezekiah, his reign of forty-five years surpassed, both in length and in wickedness, that of any other king of Judah. Quite apart from the choice or the desire of Manasseh, little Judah was a vassal of mighty Assyria. Only by the regular payment of tribute could the king retain his throne and live at peace. The sin of Manasseh was not political capitulation but religious apostasy. The small vassal state would have found it difficult in any case to resist the inroads of Assyrian culture and religion; but far from attempting to resist these influences, Manasseh actively encouraged them. Rejecting the teaching of the great eighth-century prophets and reversing the reforms of his father Hezekiah, he led the people into a dark age of idolatry and immorality. The tale of woe is told in II Kings 21: 1–18. 'He rebuilt the high places which Hezekiah his father had destroyed.' The old local sanctuaries, with their corrupt worship, were reinstated. 'He erected altars for Baal, and made an Asherah.' He revived the old Canaanite nature worship with its fertility gods and goddesses. He 'worshipped all the host of heaven, and served them' (II Kings 21: 3). The sun, moon, and stars, regarded as heavenly beings, were worshipped by the Assyrians. Either to curry favour with his masters, or perhaps under compulsion from them, Manasseh introduced astral worship, and erected altars for that purpose in the Temple itself. 'He burned his son as an offering, and practised soothsaying and augury, and dealt with mediums and with wizards' (II Kings 21: 6). Various ancient abominations, such as child sacrifice, magic, divination, the cult of the dead, were also revived by this arch-villain. 'Moreover Manasseh shed very much innocent blood, till he had filled Jerusalem from one end to another' (II Kings 21: 16). According to Josephus and Jewish tradition, this blood-bath included the contemporary prophets, and Isaiah was sawn asunder at this time. Whether or not these later inferences from this verse are true, it is clearly affirmed that many innocent people were murdered. Even in those dark days there were some who opposed the wicked king, and raised their voices at the cost of their lives.

Amon (642–640 B.C.), who succeeded Manasseh at the age of twenty-two, 'walked in all the way in which his father walked, and served the idols that his father served' (II Kings 21: 21). After a reign of only two years, he was assassinated by his courtiers, and his son, Josiah, was then set on the throne 'by the people of the land'. At his accession, Josiah was only eight years old, and it was not until he came of age that he began the Reformation that we now associate with his name. Meanwhile, for ten years the affairs of state were in the hands of regents, and no concerted attempt was made to rid the national life of the evils introduced or revived by Manasseh. Now it was during this period of the minority of Josiah, that the Scythians invaded the western provinces of the Assyrian empire. These nomadic hordes, from the steppes of Southern Russia, had crossed the Caucasus Mountains into the Near East. Mounted on horseback, they swept through Phoenicia, and passed down the maritime plain to raid Egypt. The Pharaoh

Psammeticus, who at that time was besieging Ashdod, was driven back across his own border. According to Herodotus, he eventually turned them back, not by force of arms, but by giving to them a large sum of money (1: 18 may be a reference to this bribe). The raids of these wild men terrorized the people of the eastern Mediterranean, and the memory of their savagery persisted for centuries. (For example, the apostle Paul uses the word 'Scythian' for rude barbarian [Colossians 3: 11].)

The Scythian invasion of Palestine was probably the occasion of the call of Zephaniah to the prophetic ministry. The invaders were seen by the prophet as forerunners of the judgment of God which was 'hastening fast' against sinful Judah and all nations. The prophecy has four main divisions. (i) The Day of the Lord (1: 1–18; 2: 1–3). (ii) Judgment on the pagan nations (2: 4–15). (iii) Against Jerusalem (3: 1–8). (iv) Promises (3: 9–20). As in the books of Amos, Hosea, Micah, and Isaiah, some oracles of a later period are placed alongside the authentic utterances of the prophet. The following passages are all later than the time of Zephaniah—2: 8–11; 2: 15; 3: 9–20. The idolatry, scepticism, and immorality denounced in the authentic oracles of the prophet, are the legacy of the reigns of Manasseh and Amon. They are characteristic of the period *before*, but not after the great Reformation under Josiah (621 B.C.), when the Book of Deuteronomy was published and its enactments enforced. The ministry of Zephaniah may be dated about the year 625 B.C.

THE MAN WITH THE LAMP

About Zephaniah himself nothing is known, except the little that may be inferred from the prophecy that bears his name. It is the only book in which the ancestry of a prophet is carried back four generations. The purpose of the editor in doing this was to show that Zephaniah was the grandson of Hezekiah, the former king of Judah (1: 1). The prophet was therefore related to the contemporary King Josiah and, like Isaiah, belonged to the upper classes. He was probably a citizen of Jerusalem, for he was well acquainted with the topography of the city, and calls it 'this place' (1: 4). He also refers to the Fish Gate, probably in the middle of the northern wall, and to a new suburb near to it called the Second Quarter. He speaks of hills within the city itself, and of a district called the

Mortar, probably some part of the Tyropoean Valley, a centre
of trade (1: 10, 11).

God is represented as searching the streets of this city, like
a night-watchman with a lamp. No sinner will be hidden from
his eyes or escape his judgment (1: 12). It is this figure which
led medieval artists to represent Zephaniah himself as the man
with the lamp of the Lord. It is a fitting image of the tempera-
ment and character, the message and ministry of the prophet.
Like Amos of Tekoa, he was stern and austere, a prophet of the
justice and judgment of God. A man of intense earnestness
and dauntless courage, he exposed and denounced sin wherever
it was to be found. The city which the Lord is about to search,
as with a lamp, is described by the prophet in several oracles.
Jerusalem is rebellious and polluted, and the strong oppress the
weak. To the voice of God, who has spoken through his
prophets, the people have turned a deaf ear. The citizens do
not trust the Lord and are neglecting their religious duties
(3: 1, 2). The coming judgment is represented by means of a
grim figure. Let all be silent before the Lord, for he is about to
offer a sacrifice. He has consecrated his guests for the feast—
the Scythians; he has selected his victim for the altar—Judah!

The prophet is then more specific and describes those who
are to be punished. The young king, Josiah, cannot be
held responsible for the prevalent evils. The indictment is
directed against the princes, the members of the royal family
and of the court, together with all who are aping foreign
fashions and pagan customs. The foreign attire is the outward
sign of inner disloyalty to the traditional faith of Israel. Some
are guilty of the pagan superstition of leaping over the threshold
of the house, regarded as demon haunted. Others are enriching
the royal treasury through fraud and oppression (1: 7–9). Five
leading classes are condemned. The princes and judges,
appointed to be shepherds of the flock, are behaving like
greedy wolves. The prophets are reckless, faithless men, and
the priests are failing in their duty of safeguarding the holy
and upholding the law (3: 3, 4). The merchants have enriched
themselves with treachery and injustice and will be cut off
(1: 10, 11). In addition to these leading classes, various kinds
of idolatry are condemned by the prophet. The Lord is about
to punish the men of divided allegiance. Some are worshipping
God *and* Baal; they will be destroyed to the last remnant. Some
acknowledge the Lord *and* burn incense on the housetops to the

sun, moon, and stars. Others bow down to the God of Israel *and* to Milcom the god of the Ammonites. They will all be cut off. From the men of divided allegiance the prophet goes on to castigate the men of no allegiance—the backsliders and apostates who have rejected God altogether (1: 4–6).

The prophet also announces the doom of some of the surrounding nations. Naming four of her five cities, he foretells the destruction of Philistia; her depopulated towns will become pasture ground for flocks (2: 4–7). Like Philistia on the west, Moab and Ammon on the east are to be made desolate. (This passage is probably later than the time of Zephaniah.) When Jerusalem was destroyed in 587 B.C. these enemies of Judah, who had encouraged the Babylonians, taunted the Jews and helped themselves to their territory. For this heartlessness they are to be destroyed as completely as Sodom and Gomorrah (2: 8–11). The Ethiopians in the far south and the Assyrians in the far north, are also to be punished by the Lord. Nineveh, capital of Assyria, will be a deserted ruin, and her beautiful palaces will be the haunts of owls and ravens (2: 12–15). The sins of these foreign nations are the wrongs they have done to Israel; moreover—as elsewhere in the prophets—their arrogance is regarded as a direct affront to God.

Attention may now be drawn to two evils which underlie this charge of Zephaniah against his fellow-countrymen. Foremost is the sin of divided allegiance. With the exception of a small minority, the people as a whole had not abandoned the worship and service of the Lord. Rather, under the continuing evil influence of her apostate kings, and the constraint of pagan Assyria, many were attempting to combine that allegiance with the observance of foreign cults and superstitions. The message of Zephaniah was a mighty affirmation of the first commandment—'You shall have no other gods besides me' (Exodus 20: 3 margin). The prophet himself, with his moral earnestness and single-hearted devotion to the Lord, was a living embodiment of the message he preached. That message is timeless. For those who acknowledge the true and only God are constantly tempted to acknowledge someone or something else alongside him. Nowadays it is not Baal or Milcom—the idol may be another person or the family, ambition or success, pleasure or power, money or security, the party or the state. The oriental proverb reminds us that there are some activities which cannot be reconciled—'No one can carry two melons in one hand.' We have also the warning of Christ—'No one can serve two masters' (Matthew 6: 24). The invitation and plea to worship and serve the Lord with singleness of heart, is the obverse side of Zephaniah's denunciations.

The other underlying evil is the practical atheism of the indifferent. Perhaps it was because the great hopes kindled by Isaiah had been deferred, that many of the people of Judah had become sceptical and cynical. The yoke of Assyria had not been broken, and the ideal king, the Son of David, was not reigning over them in justice and peace. God had neither hindered nor helped them; he had done nothing either favourable or un-favourable. He just did not count in human affairs, and could be ignored by all practical, level-headed men. These sceptics are described by the prophet as 'the men who are thickening upon their lees' (1: 12, 13). If, in the process of maturing, wine is left to stand too long on its sediment, the quality is impaired. It needs to be poured off from vessel to vessel (see Jeremiah 48: 11, 12). The men of Jerusalem have been too long at ease, they have become complaisant and stagnant, self-satisfied and indolent. They are no longer on the move but have settled down; they are not open to new truth and experience but are content to stay as they are. Scepticism and self-indulgence can lead to a loss of interest in the things of God, and to a lack of concern for the true priorities of life. As we see in our own time, indifference is more difficult to combat than active hostility. It was the sin of the Laodicean Christians, who were neither hot nor cold. In Dante's *Inferno*[1] we meet the 'souls of those who lived without infamy or praise', commingled with those angels 'who have not rebellious been, nor faithful were to God'. Such is the fate of the indifferent.

THE DAY OF THE LORD

Zephaniah is the prophet of the Day of the Lord. He was not the originator of this conception, which probably derives from the Hebrew practice of describing the decisive events of history as 'days'. For example, the victory of Gideon over the Midianites was designated by Isaiah 'the day of Midian' (Isaiah 9: 4). It was believed in Israel that at some time in the future, God would intervene decisively in the affairs of the world and overthrow all his enemies. This intervention and victory was known as the Day of the Lord. The earliest reference

[1] Canto 3.

to it in the Bible is in the prophecy of Amos. As we have seen, his contemporaries believed that the intervention of the Lord would be to their advantage. The enemies of Israel would be destroyed and she herself would be exalted. The prophet also believed that the enemies of God would be punished on that Day—but the sinful Israelites would be among them! It would not, as they expected, be a day of light and salvation, but of darkness and doom.[1]

This teaching of Amos is developed by Zephaniah. The advent of the Lord will be a day of doom for the whole world. At the time of Noah, God destroyed man and beast by the flood. On the impending day of his intervention, he will destroy man and beast, the birds of the air and the fish of the sea; he will sweep away everything from the face of the earth (1: 2, 3). The proximity, the imminence of the day is empha-sized; it 'is at hand . . . near and hastening fast' (1: 7, 14). It is so bitter and painful, that even the tough warrior cries out with fear (1: 14). 'A day of wrath is that day, a day of distress and anguish, a day of ruin and devastation, a day of darkness and gloom, a day of clouds and thick darkness.' At the inter-vention of the Lord, chaos triumphs over order, darkness over light, and the horrors of war are unleashed against fortified cities (1: 15, 16). Groping like the blind, sinners will vainly attempt to escape. For the blood of the people will be poured out like dust, and no bribe will avail to save them—as when the Pharaoh saved Egypt from the Scythians (1: 17–18).

Although Zephaniah does not explicitly mention the Scythians, it is likely that he regarded them as the dreadful forerunners of the Day of the Lord. Assyria and Egypt are not regarded as instruments of divine retribution, for they are both included in the punishment. It is significant that the horrific description of the Day of the Lord includes not only natural calamity, but also 'trumpet blast and battle cry'. The divine indignation is to be manifested through human enemies and armies. Not that Zephaniah has the Scythians only in mind; they are the harbingers of other forces, which God will unleash to chastise Judah and the nations. It is unlikely that the message of Zephaniah was simply and solely the proclamation of impending judgment and doom. True, the Lord would search Jerusalem with a lamp, and not a single wicked family would escape. On the other hand, the people of the 'shameless nation'

[1] See pages 40, 41.

are invited to 'come together and hold assembly' in order to escape the coming judgment. They need not be like chaff scattered by the wind. 'Seek the Lord, all you humble of the land, who do his commands; seek righteousness, seek humility; perhaps you may be hidden on the day of the wrath of the Lord' (2: 1–3). A ray of hope shines here in the darkness; for the humble there is a way of escape.

Some scholars believe that these words of hope are from Zephaniah, but there is no doubt that the visions and promises in the last part of the book (3: 9–20) are post-exilic. The speech of the peoples is to be purified, all nations are to be converted and offer worship to the true God (3: 9, 10). The proud are to be removed from Judah, leaving behind 'a people humble and lowly'. Trustful and blameless, this remnant will enjoy peace and security (3: 11–13). Here we have a lovely description of that spirit of poverty, of trustful simplicity, of humble submission, which Jesus pronounced blessed (Matthew 5: 3). The prophecy ends with a picture of the golden age (3: 14–20). Whether from Zephaniah himself, or from a later age, these oracles of hope and promise are the necessary complement of his dire and dreadful description of the Day of the Lord. For the Lord comes in compassion as well as in anger, he brings salvation as well as judgment.

Yet the main, if not the exclusive, emphasis of Zephaniah, is on the Day of Judgment. Herein lies his message to us and all mankind. The Scythian invasion was not the prelude to the end of the world. The prophet was viewing in timeless sequence events which are historically separate. The Lord draws near again and again in the events of this present age. He comes in retribution in the great crises of history. He came at the time of the fall of Jerusalem to Nebuchadrezzar the Babylonian in 587 B.C. and to Titus the Roman in A.D. 70. These were 'days' of visitation and judgment. In this twentieth century, we have seen fearful chastisement fall upon men and nations. These manifestations of divine retribution in history should be seen as so many phases of one whole. For these days of judgment, like the Scythian invasion, are stages within a process. They are leading up to *the* Day of Judgment at the consummation of the age. The heralds of the climax, which must not be mistaken for the climax itself, are warnings that the Day of the Lord is coming with all speed. John of Patmos describes *the* event in picture language. 'Then I saw a great white throne and him who sat upon it; from his presence earth and sky fled away, and no place was found for them. And I saw the dead, great and small, standing before the throne, and books were opened. Also another book was opened, which is the book of life. And the dead were judged by what was written in the books, by what they had done' (Revelation 20: 11, 12). It was Zephaniah's description of the Day of the Lord which inspired Thomas de Celano (A.D. 1190–1260) to write the hymn 'Dies Irae', now used as the sequence in the Roman Mass for the Commemoration of the Faithful Departed.

> 'Oh, what trembling there shall be
> When the world its Judge shall see,
> Coming in dread majesty!
> Judge of justice, hear my prayer;
> Spare me, Lord, in mercy spare;
> Ere the reckoning-day appear'.[1]

The stern message of Zephaniah, with its complement in the gospel, can rouse us from complacency, confirm us in penitence, lead us to faith and lift us to hope.

[1] For another and complete translation, see *The English Hymnal*, 351.

VII

Nahum

THE FALL OF NINEVEH

In Iraq, on the east bank of the Tigris, on the opposite side of the river from the city of Mosul, are two large mounds. Surrounded by the remains of walls nearly eight miles in circumference, they mark the ruins of the ancient city of Nineveh, which from the time of Sennacherib was the capital of the Assyrian empire. The library of a later Assyrian monarch, Ashurbanipal, was discovered on this site and has been partly excavated. The cuneiform tablets are the records of a civilization distant from us in time by over twenty-five centuries. This library was assembled at Nineveh by the same king who in 661 B.C. captured Thebes, the chief city of Egypt. During Ashurbanipal's reign, Assyria reached the zenith of her power, and her capital, Nineveh, was without rival anywhere in the world. Yet only a few decades later the Assyrian empire collapsed and, as the prophet Zephaniah had predicted, Nineveh became a deserted ruin. The empire which had for so long been irresistible disintegrated with surprising speed. In their lust for power and glory, the great Assyrian rulers and commanders had overreached themselves, leaving a widespread empire exposed to new and vigorous enemies. Established and maintained by brute force, Assyria had evoked the hatred of all the subject peoples, who were ready to seize the first favourable opportunity to revolt against the oppressor.

Egypt, at the south-western end of the Fertile Crescent, soon regained her independence; but the most dangerous threat to the dominion of Assyria came from Babylonia in the south-east. The brother of Ashurbanipal, Shamashumukin, was the subject king of Babylon. In 652 B.C. he revolted, and it took six years of civil war to subdue him and his many allies. Assyria was seriously weakened by this long struggle, and the son and successor of Ashurbanipal, Sinsharishkun, was unable to arrest the process of disintegration. Nabopolassar, a general in his army, revolted and made himself king of an independent Babylon.

This able general began to advance northwards along the Euphrates, capturing the large cities. Meanwhile, another enemy of Assyria advanced from the east; in 614 B.C. the Medes from Iran captured the old capital, Asshur. Cyaxares, king of the Medes, then established an alliance with Nabopolassar of Babylon, and the two armies advanced against Nineveh itself. Aided by the Scythians, the allied forces assaulted and captured the city in 612 B.C. The remnants of the Assyrian army fled to Harran, the great palaces and temples were destroyed and the proud city became a deserted ruin.

The prophecy of Nahum is concerned with this epoch-making event. Since the prophet refers to the fall of Thebes, his ministry must be later than 661 B.C. (3: 8). It is not certain, however, whether the poem should be dated before or after the fall of Nineveh. Nahum's graphic and detailed description of the conquest of the city has led some scholars to the conclusion that the prophet wrote after the event (see also 3: 18, 19). On the other hand, there are passages which suggest that the fall of the city is imminent (e.g. 3: 12, 13). The poem as a whole glows with expectation and hope, and it is likely that the vivid details of the assault were *foreseen* in the imagination of this superb poet. The prophecy should probably be dated just before the fall of Nineveh in 612 B.C. Except that he was a native of Elkosh, nothing is known of Nahum himself (1: 1). According to tradition, that town was in Southern Judea, near the modern village of Beit Jibrin, about twenty miles southwest of Jerusalem.

The prophet is exclusively concerned with the fall of Nineveh, and his prophecy is a paeon of triumph, occasioned by the impending destruction of that wicked city. The introduction is an acrostic poem, each line of which begins with a letter of the Hebrew alphabet from *aleph* to *kaph*. Its theme is the indignation of God against his enemies, manifested in storm and drought, in earthquake and volcanic fire (1: 2–8). This is followed by prophecies addressed alternatively to Judah and Nineveh. Once, Sennacherib planned the destruction of Judah; now God has decreed the destruction of Nineveh and all her idols (1: 11, 14). Judah is promised liberation from the yoke of Assyria and is invited to observe her festivals once more in joy and peace (1: 9, 10, 12, 13, 15). The prophet then describes the capture of Nineveh by the army of the Medes and Babylonians. The soldiers are clad in scarlet, the horses are impatient for action, the chariots gleam like fire. The rampart is assaulted, the water-gates are forced, the palace is in panic. The queen is carried off into exile, the fugitives escape, the dwellings are looted (2: 1–9). The lion (the Assyrian army) used to carry the prey (the treasures of the nations) to the cubs in his den (Nineveh). The Lord is about to destroy them all, together with their place of refuge (2: 10–13).

Then follows a second description of the downfall of 'the bloody city, all full of lies and booty'. After the cavalry charge there are 'hosts of slain, heaps of corpses' over which the victors stumble (3: 1–3). Nineveh is a harlot who has seduced the nations and is about to receive the customary punishment (3: 4–7). The strong city of Thebes (No-Amon), defended by the flood waters of the Nile and by the Egyptians and their allies, fell to Ashurbanipal, who slaughtered the children and carried away the nobles into captivity. Nineveh will fare no better; her fortresses will fall as ripe figs fall when the tree is shaken (3: 8–13). With irony, the prophet orders the men of Nineveh to prepare for the siege and to strengthen the defences —for the city is to be destroyed by fire and sword, and her vast population will vanish like a swarm of locusts 'when the sun rises' (3: 14–17). The prophecy ends with a lament, probably written after the fall of the city. The leaders of Nineveh sleep in death, her citizens are scattered, her wound is fatal; and all who hear the news rejoice over the fall of the cruel and hated tyrant (3: 18, 19).

HOLY ANGER

Nahum was angry with Assyria. On many occasions the land of his birth had been invaded and devastated, and the race to which he belonged had been humiliated and oppressed by her soldiers and rulers. As an enthusiastic patriot, Nahum bitterly resented these wrongs. As the collapse of Assyria drew near, his pent up anger burst forth like the eruption of lava from a volcano. His heart burned with indignation against Judah's ancient enemy. The prophecy, a masterpiece of Hebrew poetry, was the creation not of a detached thinker, but of a patriot moved to a white heat. His own passion and depth of feeling were embodied in the written words. As a poet, Nahum was endowed with unrivalled powers of imagination and description. The warlike scenes he portrays with such detail are brought vividly before our eyes. Take, for example,

his description of the cavalry and chariotry charge. 'The crack
of the whip! The rumble of wheels! Galloping horse, jostling
chariot, charging cavalry, flash of swords, gleam of spears . . . a
mass of wounded, hosts of dead, countless corpses; they
stumble over the dead' (3: 2, 3).[1] Luther maintained that he
himself wrote better when he was angry. Yet this same power
of indignation which inspired Nahum to write superb poetry,
also impelled him to hate Assyria and to rejoice at the prospect
of her collapse. 'The whole prophecy is a paeon of triumph
over a prostrate foe and breathes out the spirit of exultant
revenge.'[2]

Christ taught us to love our enemies. In the light of his
teaching, what are we to make of the prophecy of Nahum?
Can we condone this fierce hatred of Assyria, this rejoicing over
doomed Nineveh? What a contrast to the Book of Jonah!
There God is moved with compassion for the people, the
infants, and even the cattle of Nineveh (Jonah 4: 11). The
contrast cannot be denied, and it must be admitted that the
Book of Nahum does not contain *the whole* truth about God.
There are aspects of the divine character which are not revealed
in this brief prophecy. Nevertheless one facet of the jewel of
truth is to be seen here. For there is a hatred and an anger
which is legitimate; indeed, not only legitimate, but necessary
and excellent. God himself hates that which is evil and reveals
his anger against it. 'The Lord is a jealous God and avenging,
the Lord is avenging and wrathful; the Lord takes vengeance
on his adversaries and keeps wrath for his enemies' (1: 2). This
does not mean that God is vindictive. He is the vindicator whose
holy indignation is but the reverse side of his holy love. God
executes judgment and maintains justice; he is active in righting
wrong and in making whole. Because he upholds the right and
vindicates the oppressed, he could not and would not ignore
the wrongs done by Assyria. 'For who has not felt your un-
relenting cruelty?' (3: 19).[3] Against the people to whom that
query was addressed, the anger of God was revealed from
heaven, through the words of Nahum, and the events of
history. 'Behold I am against you, says the Lord of hosts'
(2: 13). In retributive justice and holy indignation, God was
actively opposed to the brutality and ruthlessness, the

[1] *The Jerusalem Bible.*
[2] J. M. P. Smith, *A Critical and Exegetical Commentary on Nahum*, I.C.C., 281.
[3] *The Jerusalem Bible.*

imperialism and militarism, the misuse of and reliance upon brute force, which was characteristic of ancient Assyria. This indignation of the Lord was conveyed through a man. 'I am full of the wrath of the Lord; I am weary of holding it in' (Jeremiah 6: 11). Nahum did not hold it in; he allowed the hot indignation of God against wrong to flow through the narrow channel of his own heart.

Hatred is not necessarily a bad thing. There are some things we ought to hate, because God himself hates them. 'The Lord loves those who hate evil' (Psalm 97: 10). The ministry of Nahum was before Christ, and we must make distinctions which may not have been clear to him. Hating people is always wrong; hating sin is always right. Hatred of the latter kind needs constantly to be evoked and reinforced. No man is truly good who does not actively hate evil. The rebirth of indignation at wrong is one of the great needs of our time. Abraham Lincoln was very angry when he said of slavery—'if I ever get a chance to hit that thing, I'll hit it hard'. Supine acquiescence in or indolent indifference to entrenched evil is itself a monstrous evil. There are times when we do well to be angry. 'There is an anger without which the world would be a poorer place. The world would have lost much without the blazing anger of Wilberforce against the slave trade, and of Shaftesbury against the conditions in which men, women, and children worked in the nineteenth century.'[1] Temper, resentment, vindictiveness, are perversions of anger and manifestations of self-centredness; indignation is consecrated anger, evoked by wrong done to *others*, and is a manifestation of concern for their welfare. The prophecy of Nahum prefigures one aspect of the character and work of Christ. For in the gospels we see not only the kindness and compassion, but also the anger and indignation of Jesus (e.g. Mark 3: 5; 10: 14; Matthew 23: 13–36; John 2: 15). He is the full and final revelation both of the righteousness and of the wrath of God (Romans 1: 17, 18).

[1] W. Barclay, *The Epistle to the Ephesians*, 101.

H

VIII

Habakkuk

The prophet Habakkuk lived to see the collapse and extinction of one great empire and the rise and triumph of another. Nineveh, capital of Assyria, fell before the combined onslaught of the Babylonians, Medes, and Scythians in 612 B.C. Some of the Ninevites escaped to the city of Harran in western Mesopotamia and, under a new king, Assur-uballit, attempted to carry on the struggle. The Babylonians captured Harran in 611 B.C. and Assur-uballit was driven into Syria. At that stage the Pharaoh, Necho, completely reversed the traditional Egyptian policy of hostility to Assyria. For he could see that the threat to his dominion no longer came from Assyria, but from the formidable Nabopolassar of Babylon. His policy, therefore, was to preserve the reduced and weakened Assyria as a protection and buffer against the new Babylonian empire. Necho also hoped to re-establish the former Egyptian sovereignty over the states of Syria-Palestine. This policy led him into conflict with the king of Judah. For Josiah hoped to restore the United Kingdom of Israel and Judah, and had no intention of allowing former Israelite territory, recently occupied by Assyria, to pass under Egyptian control. So when the Pharaoh marched northwards to the aid of prostrate Assyria, Josiah intercepted him at the pass of Megiddo. In the ensuing battle, Josiah was defeated and killed, and the victorious Necho went on his way to the Euphrates (II Kings 23: 29, 30). The son of the dead king, Jehoahaz, after a reign of only three months, was deposed by Necho. The Pharaoh placed another son of Josiah, Jehoiakim, on the throne of Judah as his vassal.

The sovereignty of Assyria had been replaced by that of Egypt—but not for long. For the new Babylonian government was determined to gain possession of the territory formerly occupied by Assyria in the western part of the Fertile Crescent. The great battle between the Egyptians and their allies, led by Necho, and the Babylonians under the command of Nabopolassar's able son, Nebuchadrezzar, took place at Carchemish on the Euphrates in 605 B.C. (Jeremiah 46: 2). The Egyptians were decisively defeated. 'And the king of Egypt did not come again out of his land, for the king of Babylon had taken all that belonged to the king of Egypt from the Brook of Egypt to the river Euphrates' (II Kings 24: 7). The power of Egypt was broken, and the whole of Syria-Palestine became part of the neo-Babylonian empire. Judah yielded without resistance, and Jehoiakim became a vassal of Nebuchadrezzar, who had succeeded his father Nabopolassar as king of Babylon.

For a time Jehoiakim remained loyal to his new Babylonian master. Unlike his father, good King Josiah, Jehoiakim was an irreligious man, who scorned and rejected the messages of the prophet Jeremiah. A selfish and worldly man, a lover of luxury, he was more concerned about the enlargement of his royal palace at Jerusalem than with the welfare of the nation. He was a cruel tyrant who oppressed the people and shed much innocent blood (Jeremiah 22: 13–17; II Kings 24: 4). Three years after his submission to Babylon he rebelled against Nebuchadrezzar. Chaldean soldiers and bands of Edomites, Moabites, and Ammonites were sent to harass him (II Kings 24: 1, 2). Later on, the armies of Nebuchadrezzar himself invested Jerusalem. During the siege Jehoiakim died, or may perhaps have been killed. His son, Jehoiachin, after a reign of only three months, was compelled to surrender the city. He and his court were taken as captives to Babylon, together with 'all the mighty men of valour, ten thousand captives, and all the craftsmen and the smiths' (II Kings 24: 14). The Temple was plundered, and another son of Josiah, Zedekiah, was placed on the throne as a vassal of Nebuchadrezzar. This first deportation in 598 B.C. was the beginning of the Babylonian exile. The ministry of Habakkuk was exercised in the setting of these tumultuous events. His messages were delivered after the battle of Carchemish in 605 B.C., and during the tyrannical reign of King Jehoiakim. It is likely that some of them should be dated after the capture of Jerusalem in 598 B.C., when many of the people were deported to Babylonia. Habakkuk was a contemporary of Nahum and Jeremiah, and a citizen of Judah. Beyond what may be inferred from the book which bears his name, nothing is otherwise known about him.

DIALOGUE, TAUNT SONG, AND PSALM

The book begins with a dialogue between the prophet and

the Lord. The sequence is—complaint, reply, second complaint, second reply. This structure may be due to the fact that the book was used originally as a prayer liturgy. More probably it is a literary device. The dialogue is initiated by the prophet, who complains bitterly about the miseries the Judeans are suffering. To repeated cries for deliverance, the Lord makes no response, and to the prevalent oppression and injustice, tyranny and violence, he appears to be indifferent. The law is made impotent, justice is perverted, the wicked oppress the righteous. Some scholars believe that the sins mentioned in this lament are those of a foreign power, variously identified, according to the date, as Assyria, Egypt. or Babylonia. It is more likely, however, that the prophet is complaining about the sins of Judeans under Jehoiakim. The wicked king, together with the rich and powerful in Judah, was responsible for the internal disorder and oppression (1: 2–4).

In reply to his complaint, the prophet is told that the Lord is about to do a new and surprising thing. He is raising up the Chaldeans to be the instrument of his justice on the wicked Judeans. Nabopolassar, who established the neo-Babylonian empire, came from Chaldea, a province of southern Babylonia. That is why the Babylonians are called Chaldeans. They are described as hard and cruel. Their horsemen are swifter than leopards, fiercer than wolves; they swoop on the prey like a vulture. Intent on plunder and captives, they scorn kings and fortified cities. Their own strength is their god. Yet these Chaldeans are the instrument of God's judgment and chastisement (1: 5–11).

This reply creates a new and greater difficulty for Habakkuk, and leads to his second complaint. For how can God possibly use such a wicked people as the instrument of his purpose? The eyes of the Holy One, the ever-living God, are too pure to behold evil and to look on wrong. Why then does he look on with apparent indifference while the ruthless Chaldeans swallow up a people more righteous than themselves? For like fish caught in a fisherman's net, the Judeans are trapped by the conqueror, who is dealing mercilessly with them as with other nations (1: 12–17). Unable to see the answer to this perplexing problem, Habakkuk retires to brood over it. 'I will take my stand to watch, and station myself on the tower' (2: 1). Maybe the prophet is speaking literally, and 'the tower' is a quiet and secluded place of retreat. More probably the language is figurative. For us also it may be necessary to withdraw from activity for a time, in order to see life and its problems in perspective. As from the top of a high tower one can see the landscape as a whole, so a clearer and larger vision may be given to the man who ascends the hill of the Lord. He reveals himself to those who wait upon him with eager expectancy. For the Christian, 'the tower' has various names—private prayer and public worship, Bible reading and meditation, the Quiet Time and the occasional Retreat.

While in this attitude of quiet and hopeful receptivity, Habakkuk receives in a vision the message for which he waits. He is commanded to write it on tablets in large characters, so that even a runner may read it. There are two reasons why it is to be put into writing. Intended for all, it must be available for all to see. Furthermore, the written word is the pledge of a reality not yet manifested. The prophet is told to wait patiently for the fulfilment of the divine word, which has its own inherent power and energy. The revelation is couched in the following words: 'Behold, he whose soul is not upright in him shall fail, but the righteous shall live by his faithfulness' (2: 2–4).

This message (which we shall interpret in the next section) is followed by a taunt-song against the Chaldean oppressor, which consists of a series of five woes. A prelude introduces the restless conqueror, who is as greedy as Sheol, as insatiable as death (2: 5). (i) The Chaldean oppressor is a relentless creditor, who has amassed the wealth of the peoples; he will himself be plundered by the nations he has oppressed (2: 6–8). (ii) Having sought security through wealth, the Chaldeans are destined to lose their ill-gotten gains (2: 9–11). (iii) The cruel oppressor is making use of slave-labour to build his cities; but it is not the purpose of God that the peoples should work for that which is to be destroyed (2: 12–14). (iv) The conqueror is like a rogue who tempts others to get drunk, so that he may enjoy their degradation. He himself will be made to drink of the Lord's cup of indignation (2: 12–17). (v) He trusts in Bel and Marduk, lifeless and speechless gods of wood and stone. The living God who speaks is in his heavenly temple; let all men stand in awed silence before him (2: 18–20). The taunt-song has a theme: evil is self-destructive. It is like a boomerang which, thrown from the hand of the tyrant, comes back to strike him who threw it. The harsh treatment he has measured out to others will be given back to him again.

This taunt-song is followed by a Psalm, which may have
been added to the prophecy at a later date. This third chapter
of the book is not found in the scroll from 'Ain Feskha, discovered in 1947–8 in a cave near the Dead Sea, which is the
oldest witness to the text of Habakkuk. In a magnificent poem,
the Psalmist pictures the Holy One coming from the direction
of Edom, enthroned upon a storm cloud. His glory fills the
world, and all nature is convulsed before him (3: 3–11). He
comes to save his anointed people from the enemy, the
oppressor. Overawed by his vision, the poet is resolved to
'quietly wait for the day of trouble to come upon people who
invade us' (3: 13–16). The book concludes with one of the
greatest passages in the Old Testament. The poet foresees
that, through drought or war, crops and flocks may fail
altogether. But his devotion does not depend upon the steady
receipt of material benefits. He does not revere God for what
he gets out of it. Unlike Jacob at Bethel, his prepositions are
not 'if . . . then' (Genesis 28: 20, 21); they are 'though . . .
yet'. He strikes no bargain; his allegiance is independent of the
payment of dividends. His trust is unconditional, his love disinterested. Since God is his chiefest joy, communion with him
is its own reward.

THE PROBLEM AND THE ANSWER

Like the author of the Book of Job, Habakkuk was a courageous man who dared to question God's government of the
world. He was not prepared to assent to traditional dogmas if
they were in conflict with observation and experience. The
basic problem raised by the prophet has troubled and baffled
thoughtful men in all ages. God is righteous and omnipotent;
he is absolutely good and able to do all things which are in
harmony with his purpose. Given this axiom, it was believed
that in his government of the world he would always uphold
and vindicate the righteous and resist and overthrow the
wicked. This clear and simple dogma, however, does not fit the
observed facts of life and history. The wicked prosper and
injustice goes unpunished; the righteous are oppressed and
virtue goes unrewarded. Why does God allow evil to go un-
checked and unpunished. Why does the Holy One allow the
wicked to oppress the righteous? Why had good King Josiah,
the pious reformer, been killed in battle? Why was bad King
Jehoiakim, the selfish tyrant, on the throne? Why were the

cruel and arrogant Chaldeans allowed to conquer the Judeans,
who, for all their faults, were more righteous than the oppressor (1: 13)? How could God himself possibly make use of such
a wicked nation? A three-fold answer is given by the Lord to
the prophet's complaint. We must not, of course, regard this
as a complete answer to the problem of evil. Rather, we have
three related insights into a problem, which in this life will
always lie beyond our understanding. Other complementary
insights are to be found in other parts of scripture.

First, the prophet is told to 'wait for it' (2: 3). The word of
the Lord which he has received, being power-laden, will, like a
runner, hasten on and triumph. If the athlete serves to illustrate the inherent and dynamic energy of the word, the
complementary truth may be illustrated by the *slow* growth of
a tree. In due time the acorn becomes the oak; the vision given
to the prophet will, in due time, flower, ripen, come to fulfilment. Impatient men demand immediate answers to perplexing
problems, but usually the full meaning of events can only be
seen after a long period of time. *We* can see *now* why, for a time,
Judah was made subject to Babylon. We may have to wait a
long time to see the meaning of some of the events within our
own life-span, and only in the clear light of eternity will the
complete answer be given. The true Church is a waiting
community.

The message itself has a negative and a positive aspect. A
statement is made about the destiny of the Chaldean oppressor,
the temporary instrument of God's purpose. 'Behold, he whose
soul is not upright in him shall fail' (2: 4). In place of 'shall
fail' the margin reads 'is puffed up'. The outstanding characteristic of the conqueror is his arrogance and self-sufficiency. He
scorns kings and fortified cities and worships his own physical
strength and military might (1: 10, 11, 16). In his presumption
he makes himself god, aspiring 'to set his nest on high, to be
safe from the reach of harm' (2: 9). (Compare Isaiah 14: 13—
'You said in you heart "I will ascend to heaven; above the
stars of God I will set my throne on high."') But nemesis
awaits 'aspiring pride and insolence'. It is a basic law of the
moral order created by God that he who exalts himself will be
humbled. 'Pride goes before destruction, and a haughty spirit
before a fall' (Proverbs 16: 18). Tyranny is self-destructive:
the oppressor evokes the resistance which eventually brings
about his downfall. In less than a century the new Babylonian

empire disappeared. He whose soul was puffed up and not straight within him came to his inevitable end.

While the self-sufficient Chaldeans are destined to perish, the positive aspect of the message has reference to the faithful Judeans destined to live. 'The righteous shall live by his faithfulness' (2: 4 margin). The Holy One, the Rock, is absolutely sure, completely trustworthy. He, the living God, is faithful. These qualities of his nature are reproduced in those who put their confidence in him. They become—and remain—reliable and trustworthy, loyal and faithful. Such men cannot always read the meaning of events or understand intellectually the problems by which they are confronted. Like the prophet, they too may ask 'why?' and cry out 'how long?' In a given situation they may be quite unable to 'justify the ways of God to men'.[1] In such circumstances, as at all times, they live by fidelity, steadfastness, faithfulness. Although for the time being they are unable to see the working out of the divine purpose, yet they hold on and go on; they continue with dogged perseverance to trust in the word and promises of God. While such faithfulness includes intellectual assent, it involves more, goes far deeper. 'It is a profound and abiding disposition, an ingrained attitude of mind and heart towards God which affects and gives character to all the activities.'[2] Encountering opposition and adversity, faithfulness becomes endurance, which has been defined as 'masculine constancy in holding out under trials'.[3] 'For you have need of endurance, so that you may do the will of God and receive what is promised . . . my righteous one shall live by faith' (Hebrews 10: 36, 38). Paul also quotes the message revealed to Habakkuk, in support of the doctrine of justification by faith (Romans 1: 17; Galatians 3: 11). In doing so he reinterprets the meaning of the key word. Whereas for the Hebrew prophet 'faith' means loyalty, faithfulness, for the Christian apostle it means trust in and commitment to God in Christ. The former meaning depends on the latter. He who has faith in the faithful God, becomes faithful; he who trusts in the trustworthy Christ, becomes trustworthy. In both the active and the passive senses of the word 'the righteous shall live by his faith'.

[1] John Milton, *Paradise Lost*, Book I.
[2] B. B. Warfield, article on *Faith* in *Dictionary of the Bible*, edited J. Hastings, Vol. I, 827.
[3] Waite on II Corinthians 6: 4.

IX

Jeremiah

THE BOOK

The Book of Jeremiah is the second of the four scrolls known as the Latter Prophets. It is the record of the ministry and preaching of the greatest of the Hebrew prophets, extending over a period of about forty-six years (626–580 B.C.). Jeremiah began to preach during the reign of Josiah, and his ministry continued throughout the reigns of Jehoiakim, Jehoiachin, and Zedekiah, until a few years after the fall of Jerusalem. Of that ministry, exceptional both in length and quality, this book is the written legacy. Yet in spite of the great wealth it contains, it is not easy to read. For one thing, the events are not set out in chronological order. Furthermore, except in a few places, the messages of the prophet are not arranged according to subject or sequence. The prophecy appears to be a confused jumble. In fact this book, like Isaiah, is a collection of collections. To an original nucleus, other compilations have been added, without any attempt to order or rearrange the material as a whole. It is best regarded as *an anthology* of the sayings and sermons of Jeremiah, and of stories written about him by Baruch the scribe, to which later material has been added.

The whole book may be divided into four parts. (i) Chapters 1 to 25. Poetry and preaching. Although this first section contains a few narratives, it is largely a collection of oracles written in the first person. These prophecies against Judah and Jerusalem are mostly from Jeremiah himself. (ii) Chapters 26 to 45. Prose and biography. With the exception of a few sermons, this section consists of stories about the prophet written by his secretary, Baruch. (iii) Chapters 46 to 51. Prophecies against foreign nations. In the Septuagint, this section follows chapter 25. As in the books of Isaiah and Ezekiel, there is a collection of oracles directed against the surrounding heathen nations. Some of these are Jeremiah's, some are from later periods. (iv) Chapter 52. Historical appendix. This story of the fall of Jerusalem is taken from II Kings 24: 18 to 25: 30.

Much of the book of Jeremiah was written by Baruch. A member of a prominent Judean family, he was the devoted disciple of the prophet. During the reign of Jehoiakim, in 605 B.C., Jeremiah dictated to Baruch the oracles he had spoken during the twenty-one years which had elapsed since the beginning of his ministry. When Jehoiakim destroyed the original scroll, Baruch rewrote it 'and many similar words were added' (36: 4–32). This second scroll is the original nucleus of the Book of Jeremiah, and the chief source of the material in chapters 1 to 25. Additional material was subsequently added by Jeremiah or Baruch and by later editors. The biographical passages, most of which are in the second main section (chapters 26 to 45) were almost certainly composed by Baruch himself, probably in the last years of the prophet's ministry. This account by the disciple of the sufferings of his master, is the passion story of the Old Testament. Baruch's scroll and Baruch's biography—these are the two main sources of the book of Jeremiah.

So great was the impact of the prophet on the life of the people, that many oracles later than his time were ascribed to him, and his spiritual descendants made their anonymous contributions to the prophecy which bears his name. Indeed, whole books were attributed to him. 'Jeremiah also uttered a lament for Josiah; and all the singing men and singing women have spoken of Josiah in their laments to this day. They made these an ordinance in Israel; behold, they are written in the Laments' (II Chronicles 35: 25). It was probably this statement of the Chronicler which gave rise to the tradition that the prophet was the author of the Book of Lamentations. Our English versions, following the Septuagint and the Vulgate, put Lamentations immediately after Jeremiah. These five poems, occasioned by the fall of Jerusalem in 587 B.C., belong to the period of the exile, and were not written by Jeremiah. Lamentations should be grouped not with the Prophets, but—as in the Hebrew Bible—with the Hagiographa or Writings. The Apocrypha contains a book entitled 'The Letter of Jeremiah', which purports to be 'a copy of a letter which Jeremiah sent to those who were to be taken to Babylon as captives'. It also has a book named after his disciple, which according to its Introduction was written by Baruch in Babylon after the deportation into exile. Both these writings are much later than the time of Jeremiah and Baruch; they belong to the Greek

period, and may be as late as the middle of the second century
B.C. This ascription of later writings to the prophet and to his
disciple is eloquent testimony to their continuing influence in
the life of Israel.

<h2 style="text-align:center">THE CALL</h2>

Jeremiah was born towards the close of the long reign of the
apostate King Manasseh. His home was at Anathoth, a village
about three miles north-east of Jerusalem in the territory of
Benjamin. Centuries earlier, Solomon had banished Abiathar
the priest, a survivor of the house of Eli, to Anathoth. It is just
possible that the father of Jeremiah, the priest Hilkiah, was a
descendant of Abiathar, and therefore of Eli of Shiloh. It is
reasonable to assume that Jeremiah was brought up in a pious
home; otherwise, nothing is known about his early life. His
call to the prophetic ministry took place in 626 B.C., in the
thirteenth year of the reign of Josiah (1: 2). At that time
Jeremiah was 'only a youth'; he may have been under twenty
years of age (1: 6).

The narrative of his call takes the form of a dialogue; God
speaks, Jeremiah answers, God speaks again. First, it is revealed
to him that God's selection and purpose go back to his pre-natal
life and conception. The choice was from the beginning, the
plan was predetermined. Before birth, he was chosen, set aside,
and appointed to the prophetic office. He was predestined to
the task to which he was now being called (1: 5). As with the
prophet, so with the Christian. There is a divine plan which is
prior, not only to our response, but also to our existence. God
chose us in Christ before the foundation of the world (Ephesians 1: 4). 'Our being Christians is no doing of ours, any more
than our being civilized; it is something done to us and for us,
not by us, though we have to make appropriate response in the
form of obedience prompted by love.'[1] The response of
obedience may be costly. Jeremiah is not willing at first to
accept the task assigned to him. He excuses himself on the
grounds of his inexperience and lack of eloquence (1: 6). Like
Moses and Gideon, he attempts to escape from an uncongenial
task and a dangerous mission (Exodus 4: 10; Judges 6: 15). In
his reply, the Lord rebukes Jeremiah and sets aside his
excuses. At the same time the young prophet is encouraged and
fortified with the assurance that he is to speak and act not in his

[1] William Temple, *Readings in St. John's Gospel*, 269.

own strength or in his own name, but in the power and by the authority of God (1: 7, 8). This assurance is followed by a symbolic act. The Lord puts forth his hand and touches the mouth of his spokesman (1: 9). Henceforth he is to speak the words given to him by God, power-laden words which will accomplish the divine purpose in history. That purpose, which includes the nations surrounding Israel, has two aspects, negative and positive, destructive and constructive. The old building is to be pulled down before the new can be erected, the old tree uprooted before the new can be planted (1: 10). First exile, then restoration.

The audition is followed by two visions, in the first of which there is a play upon words. Jeremiah is gazing at the branch of an almond tree in blossom. The first tree to wake after winter, it was named 'wake-tree'. In the mind of the prophet the branch (*shākēdh*) becomes a symbol of the activity of God who was awake and watchful (*shōkēdh*) over his word, to bring it to fulfilment (1: 11, 12). In the second vision the prophet sees, perhaps at the hearth of his own home in Anathoth, a boiling saucepan or cooking pot, with its mouth facing away from the north. It is a symbol of the destructive forces which 'out of the north' are about to 'break forth upon all the inhabitants of the land' (1: 13–16). Jeremiah is then encouraged by the Lord with the promise of divine power for his task. Young and inexperienced, he would be resisted and persecuted by kings and officials, priests and people. Yet upheld and empowered by the Lord, he would be like 'a fortified city, an iron pillar, and bronze walls' (1: 17–19).

THE FOE FROM THE NORTH AND THE CORRUPT RELIGION

Jeremiah prophesied during the reigns of Josiah, Jehoiakim Jehoiachin, and Zedekiah. As far as possible we shall study his life and words in chronological order. We begin with the period of five years between the call of the prophet in 626 and Josiah's Reformation in 621 B.C. Most, although not all, of the oracles in chapters 1 to 6 belong to this period, during which the prophet was preoccupied with a mysterious foreign foe in the north, and with the corrupt religion and apostasy of his own people. The northern peril was revealed to Jeremiah in his inaugural vision of the boiling cauldron. The last great Assyrian ruler, Ashurbanipal, died shortly before Jeremiah was

called to the ministry. Under his successors, the empire swiftly
disintegrated. The Scythians, from the steppes north of the
Black Sea and the Caucasus Mountains, swept down into the
Assyrian territories. According to the historian Herodotus,
these predatory nomads invaded Syria and reached the border
of Egypt.[1] Jeremiah, like his older contemporary Zephaniah,
does not refer to the Scythians by name. There is little doubt,
however, that he had these dreaded raiders in mind, in his
descriptions of the mysterious foe from the north (4: 5–8,
13–22, 27–31; 5: 15–17; 6: 1–8, 22–26).

That does not mean that the descriptions apply only to the
Scythians. 'The north was a perpetual symbol of the threat to
Israel's integrity and well-being, and the use of it enables
Jeremiah to employ a greater variety of language than could
be applied to any one invader.'[2] When these poems were first
committed to writing by Baruch, the Scythian invasion of
Palestine was a thing of the past. They were then interpreted
in the light of the contemporary Babylonian threat from the
north. Whatever the identity of the foe, the invasion of Judah
is described in vivid and horrific language—the warning blast
of the trumpet, the flight of the panic-stricken people to the
walled cities, the onrush of the foe, the horses swifter than
eagles, the death shriek of Zion. These savage hordes, of un-
couth speech, are like a lion from the forest or a wolf from the
desert. 'They lay hold on bow and spear, they are cruel and
have no mercy, the sound of them is like the roaring sea; they
ride upon horses, set in array as a man for battle, against you,
O daughter of Zion' (6: 23). As he identifies himself with his
people, upon whom these sufferings are to be inflicted by the
cruel foe, the emotions of the prophet are in turmoil. 'My
anguish, my anguish! I writhe in pain! Oh, the walls of my
heart! My heart is beating wildly; I cannot keep silent; for
I hear the sound of the trumpet, the alarm of war' (4: 19). In
a poem of extraordinary power, the prophet describes the
return of the primeval chaos—the earth waste and void, the
heavens devoid of light, the mountains and hills moving and
quaking, the birds of the air all gone, the cities deserted and
ruined (4: 23–26). The wild men from the north, whether
Scythians or Babylonians, are the agents of God's judgment
upon a corrupt and sinful people.

[1] See pages 101–102.
[2] H. Cunliffe-Jones, *The Book of Jeremiah*, 65.

Here we pass to the second theme in these early messages of Jeremiah. The alarm of war is being sounded in order to call unfaithful Israel to repentance. The influence of Hosea upon this second aspect of the early preaching of Jeremiah is evident. He had fully assimilated the message of the prophet he most closely resembles. Hosea had set forth the relationship of the Lord to Israel in terms of marriage; Jeremiah develops and applies the analogy. 'I remember the devotion of your youth, your love as a bride, how you followed me in the wilderness, in a land not sown' (2: 2). As between a young bride and her husband there is tenderness and affection, so during the sojourn in the wilderness there was wondrous fellowship between Israel and her God. From this original faithfulness Israel had declined into faithlessness. After the settlement in Canaan, the wife had forsaken her true husband and had played the harlot, i.e. Israel had succumbed to the corrupting influences of the nature-cults, to the false worship of Baalism.[1] In thus yielding to the idolatrous impulse, she had cast off all restraint. 'You broke your yoke and burst your bonds . . . upon every high hill and under every green tree you bowed down as a harlot' (2: 20). In her abandonment to the false worship of the high places, with its deification of sex and its grossly sensual rites, Israel was like 'a restive young camel interlacing her tracks', or a wild ass sniffing the wind in her heat (2: 23, 24).

To the prophet this declension and degeneration, this faithlessness and apostasy, is utterly monstrous and almost incredible. Go west and go east, cross the sea to Cyprus, send across the desert to Kedar, search and enquire everywhere! Has any other nation ever changed its gods, even although those gods were in fact nonentities? 'But my people have changed *their glory* for that which does not profit.' By thus turning away from the living God, the true glory of men, to idolatry, they have forsaken 'the fountain of living waters' for 'broken cisterns, that can hold no water' (2: 9–13). Through his prophet, the Lord appeals to the people to return to the ancient covenantal relationship of the wilderness period. 'Stand by the roads, and look, and ask for the ancient paths, where the good way is; and walk in it, and find rest for your souls' (6: 16). But the people are obdurate. When shewn the true way they reply 'we will not walk in it'; when invited to listen to God's prophets they reply 'we will not give heed' (6: 16, 17). There

[1] The characteristics of this false religion are described on pages 49–52.

are several such passages in which the prophet appears to entertain no hope of the people's repentance. On the other hand, in a poem of great tenderness he overhears the people 'on the bare heights', the very places of idolatrous worship, weeping in genuine penitence. To the divine invitation, 'Return, O faithless sons, I will heal your faithlessness', the people reply 'Behold, we come to thee; for thou art the Lord our God' (3: 21, 22). Aware of the radical sinfulness of the human heart, Jeremiah fears that the people will remain faithless and perverse to the end. Aware of the power and love of God, he hopes that the people will repent, and the impending judgment be averted.

JOSIAH'S REFORMATION

Josiah came to the throne at the age of eight, and reigned for thirty-one years (640–609 B.C.). 'Before him there was no king like him, who turned to the Lord with all his heart' (II Kings 23: 25). Outstanding for his piety and religious zeal, he was also commended by Jeremiah as one who did 'justice and righteousness' and 'judged the cause of the poor and needy' (22: 15, 16). After the death of Ashurbanipal, taking advantage of the weakness of Assyria he was resolved not only to regain political independence for Judah, but also to re-establish the rule of the house of David over the territory of the former Northern Kingdom. The reform of religion, begun in the twelfth year (II Chronicles 34: 3), received a new and powerful impetus in the eighteenth year of his reign. When the Temple at Jerusalem was being repaired, Hilkiah the priest found 'the book of the law in the house of the Lord' (II Chronicles 34: 15). Shapan the secretary read it to Josiah; the king was alarmed, and after consulting Huldah the prophetess, he assembled the people in the courts of the Temple. The scroll was read to the great assembly, after which king and people covenanted to perform all the words written in it. This lawbook has been identified with the core of our Book of Deuteronomy (chapters 12 to 26, and chapter 28). While incorporating much older material, it may have been written during the reign of Manasseh. Here the ideals of the prophets are expressed in the form of sermonic exhortation and legislation, and put into the mouth of the traditional lawgiver, Moses. There is a demand for exclusive loyalty to the Lord, and for justice and humanity in personal relationships, together with a stern condemnation of all idolatrous worship and immoral conduct. The book also insists upon the centralization of worship at the place chosen by the Lord; there is to be one altar only for offering and sacrifice.

The discovery and acceptance of this law-book was followed by a thoroughgoing reformation of religion. All idolatrous cult-objects were removed from the Temple and burned in the Kidron. The local high places throughout the land were destroyed. The idolatrous priests were deposed, the houses of sacred prostitutes were destroyed, and child sacrifice was suppressed (II Kings 23: 4–20). What was the attitude of Jeremiah to Josiah's reformation? He is not *explicitly* associated with the reform movement, either in the book of Jeremiah or in the history books of Kings and Chronicles. He would certainly be in sympathy with some of its aims—the suppression of idolatrous worship and immoral customs, the insistence on justice and humanity, the renewal of the ancient covenant, the appeal for single-hearted devotion to the Lord. From one passage it may be implied that Jeremiah was commanded by God to itinerate and to preach the principles of the Reformation. 'Proclaim all these words in the cities of Judah, and in the streets of Jerusalem: Hear the words of this covenant and do them.' This divine impulse he obeyed. 'Therefore I brought upon them all the words of this covenant, which I commanded them to do, but they did not' (11: 6–8).

This same chapter records how Jeremiah was persecuted in his own town (11: 18–20). The members of his family, friendly to his face, were criticizing him behind his back (12: 6). The men of Anathoth even plotted to kill him. 'Let us destroy the tree with its fruit, let us cut him off from the land of the living, that his name be remembered no more' (11: 19). Although he likens himself to 'a gentle lamb led to the slaughter' he prays 'let me see thy vengeance upon them'. What had the prophet done to provoke such extreme hostility? The sanctuary at Anathoth, as in other places, would have been destroyed by Josiah's reform and the local priests thrown out of work. By preaching the reform, Jeremiah had lent his support to the suppression of the local high places and had thereby earned the bitter hostility of his fellow-townsmen. As Jesus was rejected at Nazareth, so Jeremiah was rejected at Anathoth. It was in this context that he received the memorable challenge. 'If you have raced with men on foot, and they have wearied you, how

will you compete with horses? And if in a safe land you fall
down, how will you do in the jungle of the Jordan?' (12: 5).
Leaving little Anathoth for metropolitan Jerusalem, he would
have to encounter not less, but greater opposition and persecution. God strengthened his servant, not by granting his prayer
for revenge, but by entrusting to him a wider service, a more
difficult task.

The reformation did not result in spiritual renewal, and as
time went by Jeremiah became increasingly disillusioned with
the movement which had at first won his support. Josiah's
reform could not be sustained by the resurgent nationalism and
the ardent desire for political independence with which, from
the outset, it had been associated. The centralization of worship at Jerusalem was not an unmixed blessing; it increased
the power and pretensions of the priesthood, and engendered
in the people a false sense of security. God dwelt in the Temple
in their midst and all would be well (7: 4)! Like the sanctuary,
the written word could also be the object of a misplaced confidence. 'How can you say, "We are wise, and the law of the
Lord is with us"? But, behold, the false pen of the scribes has
made it into a lie' (9: 9). Jeremiah 'was perhaps objecting to
the very idea that God's will can be crystallized in a book,
especially if that book demands sacrifice and glorifies the
temple, and if those who use it become proud and reject the
living oral word of the Lord through the prophet'.[1] The reforms
were superficial. They were concerned more with externals
than with the springs of conduct in the heart. A sinful people
could not be legislated into sound morality and true religion.
Jeremiah saw that these surface solutions were of no lasting
value. 'Break up your fallow ground' (4: 3). Like a plough
breaking up the soil, there must be deep and thoroughgoing
repentance. 'Circumcise yourselves to the Lord, remove the
foreskin of your hearts' (4: 4). Only by a real change of heart
could they become true members of the covenant community.
While it is true that religion cannot be purely spiritual, for
man is animated body, yet the danger always exists of making
externals ends in themselves. The law written in a book failed
to renew the life of the people. This experience was destined
to lead Jeremiah in due course to foretell the coming of the
time when God would make a new covenant with his people
and write his law upon their hearts.

[1] James P. Hyatt, 'Jeremiah' in *The Interpreter's Bible*, 882.

I

TEMPLE AND SACRIFICE

Josiah hoped to restore the kingdom of David. It may have been to preserve his independence, and to prevent the Egyptians from gaining control of Palestine, that he attempted to prevent Pharaoh Necho from joining forces with the Assyrians. In the attempt at the pass of Megiddo to halt the Egyptian advance to the Euphrates, Josiah was killed (609 B.C.). The people set his son Jehoahaz on the throne of Judah; but after a reign of only three months, he was summoned to the headquarters of Necho at Riblah, deposed, and sent as a prisoner to Egypt. To the people mourning the death of Josiah, Jeremiah said, 'Weep not for him who is dead, nor bemoan him; but weep bitterly for him who goes away, for he shall return no more to see his native land' (22: 10).

The Pharaoh set another son of Josiah, Jehoiakim, on the throne of Judah. He was then twenty-five years old and he reigned for eleven years (609–598 B.C.). Jeremiah contrasts the character of the son with that of the father. Jehoiakim was selfish, extravagant, unjust, and tyrannical. He enlarged his palace, 'panelling it with cedar, and painting it with ver-milion'. The workers on that project received no wages. 'Your father . . . judged the cause of the poor and needy . . . but you have eyes and heart only for your dishonest gain, for shedding innocent blood, and for practising oppression and violence.' In describing the conduct of Jehoiakim's father, Josiah, who—unlike his son—was concerned to see that the poor and needy received fair treatment, the prophet, speaking in God's name, asks 'Is not this to know me?' Knowing God and caring for people are here correlated. God meets us in our personal relationships, and it is in that 'down to earth' context that he is to be known, served, and loved (22: 13–17).

The wickedness of Jehoiakim was manifested in an act which rarely occurred in ancient Israel. Uriah, otherwise unknown, prophesied against Jerusalem and Judah 'in words like those of Jeremiah'. When he fled to Egypt, the king sent a deputa-tion to that land; Uriah was arrested and brought back to Jerusalem. Jehoiakim 'slew him with the sword and cast his dead body into the burial place of the common people' (26: 20–23).

Josiah's reformation was now reversed. The worship of Ishtar the Queen of Heaven was revived (7: 16–20). Idols were reintroduced into the Temple, and child sacrifice was practised in the Valley of Ben-Hinnom (7: 30–31). Soon after the accession of Jehoiakim, Jeremiah preached what is now called his Temple Sermon. The event is recorded in chapter 26, but the sermon delivered on that occasion is outlined in chapter 7: 1–15. Standing at the gate between the inner and outer courts, he summoned the assembled worshippers to repentance. 'Amend your ways and your doings.' He then quoted some 'deceptive words' which the people were accustomed to repeat like a magical formula: 'This is the temple of the Lord, the temple of the Lord, the temple of the Lord.' The misinterpretation of Isaiah's doctrine of the inviolability of Zion,[1] together with the Deuteronomic reform which had led to the centralization of sacrificial worship at Jerusalem, had encouraged a misplaced trust in the Temple. They were looking upon it as a talisman: the presence of the sanctuary of the Lord, irrespective of their conduct, ensured safety and protection. This illusion the prophet shattered. What the Lord required was moral obedience, social justice, and sincere worship. He would certainly not protect and deliver those who were breaking his commandments, and using the Temple as if it were a cave of refuge for robbers (cf. Mark 11: 17). As formerly he had destroyed the sanctuary at Shiloh through the Philistines, so God would destroy the sanctuary at Jerusalem. Like the people of the Northern Kingdom, the Judeans also would go into exile.

Jeremiah risked his life in speaking these courageous words. The priests and the prophets regarded the utterance as blasphemy, and, having seized the preacher, demanded that he be put to death. The royal officials who came out to try the case upheld the right of a prophet to speak in God's name. They were supported by the people and by the elders, some of whom cited the precedent of Micah of Moresheth; he had predicted the destruction of Jerusalem and the Temple, and had not been put to death. The additional support of Ahikam, an official of the king, secured the prophet's release. Although they may not have been spoken on the same occasion, the Temple Sermon is followed by the words of the prophet concerning sacrifice. The people may as well eat their sacrifices, for they are of no value to God! At the beginning, following the Exodus, God did not ask for sacrifice but for obedience. From that original devotion to, and relationship with the Lord, the people

[1] See pages 98, 99.

had fallen away; they had persistently refused to listen to the prophets sent to call them to repentance (7: 21–28—cf. 6: 20).

Jeremiah here states explicitly that the Lord does not now, and never has in the past, required offerings and sacrifices (cf. Amos 5: 25). He makes no attempt to reconcile this affirmation with statements in the Scriptures, some of which (e.g. the nucleus of Deuteronomy) must have been known to him, in which sacrifice is commanded by God and offered by man. Is he then condemning sacrifice as such, or simply rejecting outright the *corrupt* sacrificial worship of his own time? Is it right to interpret the unqualified affirmations of prophecy as if they were carefully weighed logical arguments, or the invective of a man moved with indignation as if it were a disinterested historical statement? 'For I desire steadfast love and not sacrifice' (Hosea 6: 6). Is Jeremiah likewise including a denial within an affirmation, in order to assert that one thing is far more important than another? Scholars disagree in their answers to these questions. Yet two things are beyond doubt. For Jeremiah, obedience to the will of God is of primary importance. 'Obey my voice, and I will be your God, and you shall be my people' (7: 23). Along with this primary affirmation, goes the polemic of the prophet against trusting in any *thing* for security and well-being. The means of grace must not be made ends in themselves. The Deuteronomic code, misinterpreted by the scribal legalist, can become a substitute for God (8: 8). It is useless for Judah to rely upon the outward rite of circumcision, which she shared with other nations, if she lacks the inward circumcision of the heart (9: 25, 26). In God's sight, sacrifices divorced from obedience are just so much flesh (7: 21). Those who trust in the Temple are destined for exile even although they say 'We are delivered' (7: 10, 14). The teaching of the prophet is equally applicable to Christians. Private prayers and church services, scriptures and sacraments, sermons and ceremonies, holy seasons and sacred buildings, are all intended to be 'means of grace'. Made ends in themselves they become talismans and idols. The prophet calls for trust in God, the true end of man.

BARUCH'S SCROLL

The battle of Carchemish in 605 B.C. marked a turning point in the history of the ancient world. After the collapse of Assyria, Egypt had gained control of Syria-Palestine, and for four years

Jehoiakim had accepted the sovereignty of the Pharaoh. For some time it remained in doubt whether Egypt or Babylon was to succeed Assyria as the dominant world power. The decisive battle between the two giants took place at the Euphrates near Carchemish (46: 2). The Egyptians were defeated and routed; according to the chronicle of the victorious general, Nebuchadrezzar, 'not a single man escaped to his own country'. As a result of this victory, Babylon gained control of Syria-Palestine and Jehoiakim became the vassal of Nebuchadrezzar.

Jeremiah was deeply moved by this world-shaking event, and soon after the capitulation of Jehoiakim to Babylon, the prophet was commanded by the Lord to commit all his oracles to writing. 'Take a scroll and write on it all the words that I have spoken to you against Israel and Judah and all the nations, from the day I spoke to you, from the days of Josiah until today' (36: 2). For over twenty years Jeremiah had addressed one message after another to the people without effect. Perhaps if those spoken messages were now put into writing, and *all* of them read to people on a single occasion, they would be moved to repentance. So Jeremiah summoned Baruch. At his dictation the scribe wrote all the oracles 'with ink on the scroll'. Some months later, on the occasion of a national fast, the opportunity came to read the scroll to a large assembly. As the prophet himself was prohibited from entering the Temple (as a result, no doubt, of his Temple Sermon), he sent Baruch to read the words to the people. They were deeply impressed, and listened to it all without interruption.

One of those who heard it, Micaiah, went off to report to the state officials, who at that very time were conferring at the palace. They sent for Baruch, who read the scroll to them. On hearing the prophet's words, they were afraid, and after advising Baruch and his master to go into hiding, they reported the matter to the king. Jehoiakim ordered Jehudi, one of his courtiers, to fetch the scroll and read it to him. 'The king was sitting in the winter house and there was a fire burning in the brazier before him. As Jehudi read three or four columns, the king would cut them off with a penknife and throw them into the fire in the brazier' (36: 22, 23). Disregarding the courageous protest of three of his ministers, the king destroyed the entire scroll, rejecting with contempt all the messages of God spoken through his prophet. He also ordered the arrest of Jeremiah and Baruch, but through the agency of human friends 'the Lord hid them'.

Baruch's scroll, which probably contained much of the material of chapters 1 to 25 of our present book, was read three times over on that memorable day. The same words provoked a dissimilar response. The royal councillors received them with awe; the king and his courtiers rejected them with contempt. Men pass judgment upon themselves by their response to the word of God. In what may have been the foreword, we have a summary of the preaching contained in the scroll (25: 1–14). For twenty-three years the prophet had 'spoken persistently' to the people, calling them to repentance. His words had fallen on deaf ears, and because of their continued disobedience, the Lord was about to punish them. For this purpose he was sending the foe from the north, now identified with the Babylonians. The destruction of the nation would be complete. 'I will banish from them the voice of mirth and the voice of gladness, the voice of the bridegroom and the voice of the bride, the grinding of the millstones and the light of the lamp' (25: 10). For 'seventy years' (i.e. for two or three generations) Judah would be subject to Babylon. This then was the substance of the message rejected by Jehoiakim—the Lord of history was about to use the Baby-lonians to chastise and to overthrow sinful Judah and Jerusalem.

This message of doom the prophet continued to proclaim, not only by word but also by action. He was ordered by God to buy a linen loincloth, and to go and hide it in a hole in the rock beside the river Euphrates. On returning later to fetch it, he found that it was soiled and useless. This is a description not of a literal journey, but of the contents of a symbolic vision. God had chosen Judah to cling to him, as a loincloth clings to a man's waist; but the people had been soiled and polluted through association with heathen religion and culture. They were good for nothing, and destined for destruction (13: 1–11). On yet another occasion, the prophet was commanded to take an earth-enware flask and go out to the Gate of the Potsherds. There, in the presence of many witnesses, he was to smash the flask into pieces and then to say in God's name 'so will I break this people and this city' (19: 1–13). This and other symbolic actions of the prophet were not just dramatic illustrations of the spoken word. Done in obedience to God, they were acts of God, helping to bring about that which they signified.[1]

After breaking the flask at the city gate, Jeremiah went to the Temple, and there repeated his announcement that the Lord

[1] See pages 24, 89, 156–158.

would destroy the state by the Babylonians. Pashhur the priest, who was also responsible for public order, had Jeremiah arrested and flogged, and fastened in the stocks which were by the gate of the Temple. In that painful and shameful condition he was left throughout the rest of the day and the night following. When he was released next morning, he gave to Pashhur a new name—'Terror on every side'—and declared to him that he and his family were destined for captivity and death in Babylon (20: 1–6).

For three years after the battle of Carchemish, Jehoiakim acknowledged the sovereignty of Nebuchadrezzar. 'Then he turned and rebelled against him' (II Kings 24: 1). The Babylonian monarch, who was preoccupied with the affairs of state and the equipment of his forces, did not deal with this revolt for some years. Meanwhile, he despatched some of his own soldiers, together with bands of Syrians, Moabites, and Ammonites, to harass Judah. It was not until 598 B.C. that the Babylonian army laid siege to Jerusalem. Jehoiakim died at this juncture, leaving his son Jehoiachin, only eighteen years of age, to face the consequences of his disastrous policy. After a reign of three months, the young king capitulated, and together with his family was carried into exile. The craftsmen, the warriors, the state officials, the cream of the population, together with the treasures of the Temple and city, were also removed to Babylonia. This first deportation of exiles (numbering 3,023—see 52: 28)[1] was the beginning of the Babylonian captivity.

THE FALL OF JERUSALEM

The faithful disciple who wrote down the oracles of his master also recorded some of the outstanding events of his ministry. Baruch's biography, the second main source of the book of Jeremiah, which is to be found mainly in chapters 26 to 46, becomes more detailed as we approach the siege and fall of Jerusalem. We turn now to these last events and stories. After the first deportation, Nebuchadrezzar set Zedekiah on the throne of a weakened Judah, depleted of its upper classes. Neither a good man like his father Josiah nor a wicked man like his brother Jehoiakim, he was 'a weak, irresolute, characterless individual, extremely anxious to know what was right, but utterly incapable of doing it'.[2] He revered Jeremiah, often

[1] II Kings 24: 14 gives the number as 10,000.
[2] J. Skinner, *Prophecy and Religion*, 255.

sought his advice, and recognized the truth of his words. Yet he lacked force of character, and so was unable to resist the pressure of the pro-Egyptian faction, whose misguided policy led the nation to disaster.

His task was the more difficult because Nebuchadrezzar had deported the old nobility, with the result that he was left with advisers who had little or no knowledge of statecraft. Indeed, according to Jeremiah, all those who were left behind in Judah, including the king and his counsellors, were like a basket of 'very bad figs, so bad that they could not be eaten'. The future of the nation lay with those who had been deported to Babylonia; they were like a basket of 'very good . . . first-ripe figs' (chapter 24). Zedekiah, in his fourth year, was confronted with a crisis. Pharaoh Necho had died in 594 B.C., and had been succeeded by Psammeticus II. About the time of this change of dynasty in Egypt, the smaller nations of the west began to cherish hopes of political independence. Envoys from Tyre, Sidon, Edom, Moab, and Ammon, appeared in Jerusalem, to urge Zedekiah to join in the revolt against Babylon. At this juncture, Jeremiah appeared wearing a yoke on his neck. He declared to the envoys that God had given to his servant Nebuchadrezzar, king of Babylon, sovereignty over the nations. The nation that refused to accept the yoke of Babylon would be punished with sword, famine, and pestilence. The nation that accepted the yoke of Babylon would be left 'on its own land, to till it and dwell there' (27: 1–11). He then proceeded to warn Zedekiah, together with the priests and people of Judah, not to listen to the false prophets who were predicting the over-throw of Babylon and encouraging resistance to her (27: 12–22). These phoney prophets, men of shallow optimism, were represented by Hananiah from Gibeon. In the Temple, in the presence of Jeremiah, the priests and the people he announced that God was about to break the yoke of the king of Babylon, and that within two years the exiles would return, and the sacred vessels of the house of the Lord be brought back from Babylonia. He then took the yoke-bars from the neck of Jeremiah and broke them (chapter 28). At that critical time, no doubt because of the strenuous opposition of Jeremiah, Zedekiah did not attempt to cast off the yoke of Babylon.

Not only in Judah, but also among the exiles in Babylonia, Jeremiah was compelled to resist and contradict the popular prophets. Predicting the speedy downfall of Babylon, they were discouraging the exiles from settling down where they were. To counteract their influence, Jeremiah wrote a letter to the exiles. In this he encouraged them to build houses, to plant gardens, to marry, to let their sons and daughters marry, to have children— in a word to settle down to a normal life. For they were destined to stay where they were for a long time. They were even to work and pray for the welfare of Babylon. The Lord had a future for his people in exile, and since his presence was not limited to Jerusalem, they could seek him and would find him in Babylonia. With these words, remarkable alike for sound common-sense and profound religious insight, he sought to discourage the hopes of a speedy return from exile incited by the false prophets (29: 1–14).

In spite of the ministry of the prophet, however, the anti-Babylonian faction in Judah gained in strength, and with the accession in 588 B.C. of the aggressive Egyptian Pharaoh Hophra, Zedekiah succumbed to the popular pressure and renounced his allegiance to Babylon. Nebuchadrezzar established his headquarters at Riblah in Syria. His forces soon over-ran Judea and laid siege to Jerusalem. Zedekiah then despatched two messengers to Jeremiah, asking for divine guidance and expressing the hope that the Lord would deliver the city. In his reply, the prophet declared that resistance to the Babylonians was futile, for the Lord himself would fight, not for, but against the city. He set out the alternatives. 'Behold, I set before you the way of life and the way of death.' Those who went forth and surrendered to the Chaldeans would save their lives; those who stayed in the city would die by sword, famine, or pestilence (21: 1–10). Hoping to gain the Lord's favour, king and people covenanted to set free all Hebrew slaves. Soon afterwards, owing to the advance of the Egyptian army, the Babylonians raised the siege. At once, those who had been emancipated were taken back into slavery. This breach of faith, a clear sign of the radical faithlessness of the people, was vigorously denounced by the prophet (34: 8–22).

The temporary withdrawal of the Chaldean soldiers gave rise to false hopes. The king sent a message to the prophet, requesting him to pray for the welfare of the nation. In his reply, Jeremiah told him that the Babylonian army would return, and even if it should then consist only of wounded soldiers, it would certainly conquer the city (37: 1–10). During the interruption of the siege, Jeremiah set out to visit Anathoth. At the gate of the city he was arrested, accused of desertion, and brought before the princes. 'Enraged at Jeremiah . . . they beat him and imprisoned him in the house of Jonathan the secretary' (37: 11–15). To this improvised prison, the king sent for him, and then questioned him in secret. 'Is there any word from the Lord?' Jeremiah replied 'There is . . . you shall be delivered into the hand of the king of Babylon.' He then pleaded with the king not to send him back to the prison in the house of Jonathan, and on Zedekiah's order he was committed to the court of the guard and allotted a daily ration (37: 16–21). The princes, however, convinced that he was undermining the morale of the people and weakening the resistance of the soldiers, demanded that he be put to death. Against his better judgment, the feeble king gave way to their persistent pressure, and they took Jeremiah and cast him into a cistern. 'And there was no water in the cistern, but only mire, and Jeremiah sank in the mire.' Learning of his sorry plight Ebed-melech, an Ethiopian eunuch went to the king and pleaded for the life of the prophet. When his request was granted, his courage was matched by his considerateness. For he padded 'with old rags and worn-out clothes' the ropes with which he and three helpers drew up the prophet, lest they should chafe his armpits (38: 1–13). For the last time the desperate king then consulted the prophet, and was again advised to save the city, and his own life, by surrender to the Babylonians (38: 14–28).

Zedekiah continued irresolute to the extremely bitter end. The siege of Jerusalem lasted from December 589 to June 587 B.C. At last, when the food supply was completely exhausted, a breach was made in the city walls (52: 6, 7). Zedekiah tried to escape in the direction of the Jordan, but he was overtaken near Jericho and captured by the Chaldean soldiers. He was taken to Nebuchadrezzar at Riblah. When his sons had been butchered before his eyes, he was blinded and led off in fetters to Babylon (39: 4–7). Nebuchadrezzar sent a high official, Nebuzaradan, to dismantle the captured city. He tore down the walls; he destroyed the houses, the palace, and the Temple with fire. The urban, though not the rural, population was deported. The Davidic monarchy was brought to an end, and the former state of Judah became a province of the Babylonian empire.

Gedaliah, a Judean, was appointed to administer this, and set up his headquarters at Mizpah. On the orders of Nebuchadrezzar, Jeremiah was released from confinement (39: 11–14). Perhaps by mistake, he was led off with the other captives destined for Babylonia; but he was recognized at Ramah and set free by Nebuzaradan. Would he prefer to accompany Nebuzaradan to Babylon or stay where he was? Given this choice, 'Jeremiah went to Gedaliah the son of Ahikam at Mizpah and dwelt with him among the people who were left in the land' (40: 1–6). After only two months, Gedaliah was murdered by a group of fanatics led by one Ishmael, acting at the instigation of the king of Ammon. Fearing the wrath of Nebuchadrezzar, the Judean military leaders, after seeking and then disregarding the counsel of the prophet, fled to Egypt. They compelled Jeremiah and Baruch to go with them. There we catch a last glimpse of him rebuking the Jews for their idolatry (chapter 44). According to tradition, Jeremiah was stoned to death in Egypt.

THE CONFESSIONS OF JEREMIAH

The story of Jeremiah has now been told and his messages studied in the context of events. There are, however, many transmitted words of the prophet concerning which we have little or no knowledge of the occasions on which they were spoken. To these we now turn, beginning with that remarkable series of autobiographical passages which are usually referred to as the Confessions of Jeremiah.[1] Reading these intimate poems is like looking through a window into the prophet's heart. The other prophets, like Jeremiah, were concerned with the interpretation of external events; unlike him, they rarely lifted the veil which hides the inner life of the interpreter himself. Here, as in no other prophecy, through these outpourings of his heart the prophet himself is revealed. In this respect the book of Jeremiah may be compared with the Second Letter to the Corinthians, in which the personality and contending emotions of Paul are so clearly revealed. Like the *Confessions* of St. Augustine, the *Journal* of Amiel, the *Thoughts* of Pascal, it is a mirror of the interior life, a treasury of personal experience. Here Jeremiah tells the story of his struggle with men and with God.

With men: for throughout the course of his public ministry, Jeremiah was in conflict with his fellows. It was not a conflict of his own choosing, for it ran counter to his desires. He was a man of intense sympathy and tenderness of heart, who longed for the love and companionship of others. Yet he was denied the affection and goodwill he so ardently desired. Because of the impending crisis, he was forbidden by God to marry and have children

[1] 11: 18–23; 12: 1–6; 15: 10–21; 17: 9–18; 18: 18–23; 20: 7–18.

(16: 1–4). His mission led him into head-on collision with his fellow-men. 'Woe is me, my mother, that you bore me, a man of strife and contention to the whole land!' (15: 10). Moral indignation, and the constraint of God upon him, set him apart from human enjoyment, and condemned him to a life of loneliness. 'I did not sit in the company of merrymakers, nor did I rejoice; I sat alone, because thy hand was upon me, for thou hadst filled me with indignation' (15: 17). He was the target for the sarcasm and ridicule of the populace. He had foretold disaster, but it had not arrived; the people were sceptical and scornful. 'Where is the word of the Lord? Let it come!' As if the prophet had found any pleasure in predicting the destruction of the nation he loved! He had simply been faithful in proclaiming the word God had given him (17: 15, 16). As at the crucifixion of Christ, the spiritual leaders joined in this mockery and ridicule. The priests, the wise men, and the prophets reacted to trenchant criticism by attempting to entangle the prophet in his own words. ' "Come on", they said, "let us concoct a plot against Jeremiah; the priest will not run short of instruction without him, nor the sage of advice, nor the prophet of the word" ' (18: 18).[1] The nation would continue to have adequate guidance without the agitator! Jeremiah found it hard to bear this contempt and ridicule. 'I have become a laughingstock all the day; everyone mocks me . . . the word of the Lord has become for me a reproach and derision all day long' (20: 7, 8). The people picked up a sentence from his preaching—'Terror is on every side'—and repeated it in mockery. His 'familiar friends' denounced him and waited eagerly for his downfall (20: 10). This persecution and enforced loneliness, this ridicule and cruel malice, was an intolerable burden for the sensitive prophet, and in anguish of heart he prayed to God for vengeance (11: 20; 17: 18; 18: 21–23). These occasional outbursts of resentment and vindictiveness are ugly blots on the character of Jeremiah. They stand in contrast to the magnanimity of Christ and of the first Christian martyr (Luke 23: 34; Acts 7: 60). It is unjust, however, to judge a servant of God who lived before Christ, by a standard applicable to those who live after the time of Christ.

In addition to this outward conflict with men, Jeremiah was also engaged in a struggle with God. He was torn by an inner conflict between obligation and inclination, between his stern

[1] *The Jerusalem Bible.*

prophetic task and his natural human desires. Initially, the word of God had been to him a fount of gladness, a source of strength. 'Thy words were found, and I ate them, and thy words became to me a joy and the delight of my heart' (15: 16). Yet that word, sweet as honey, also burned like fire; along with the joy of communion with God went the inner compulsion to proclaim his judgment upon the nation. That judgment, however, was tardy in its arrival, with the result that he who had announced 'violence and destruction' was discredited, ridiculed, and scorned (20: 8). In almost blasphemous words Jeremiah accuses God of overpowering and misleading him. 'O Lord, thou hast decived me, and I was deceived; thou art stronger than I, and thou hast prevailed' (20: 7). His pain is unceasing, his wound is incurable, refusing to be healed. He is like a traveller who finds that the brook, where he hoped to quench his thirst, has dried up. God has failed him (15: 18). In many a rebellious mood he had thought of giving up the ministry, of speaking no more in God's name. Yet he found it impossible to keep quiet, for the constraint of the word was irresistible. 'If I say, "I will not mention him, or speak any more in his name," there is in my heart as it were a burning fire shut up in my bones, and I am weary with holding it in, and I cannot' (20: 9). In a bitter lament, the prophet curses the day on which he was born. Would that his mother's womb had been his tomb! 'Why did I come forth from the womb to see toil and sorrow, and spend my days in shame?' (20: 14–18).

These unrestrained outpourings reveal imperfections in the character of Jeremiah—self-pity and impatience, doubt and despair, vindictiveness toward man and irreverence toward God. Jeremiah was aware of these sins, and was challenged by God to act upon the truth he had so assiduously preached to others. If he was to continue in the Lord's service, he too must repent. 'If you return, I will restore you, and you shall stand before me.' The grain must be winnowed, the wheat separated from the chaff. 'If you utter what is precious, and not what is worthless, you shall be as my mouth.' If he repents and resolves henceforth to speak only the words that are given to him, God will strengthen him to overcome all his human enemies (15: 19–21). 'We can scarcely be wrong in thinking that this illumination which comes to Jeremiah in answer to prayer, marks a turning point in his life.'[1]

[1] J. Skinner, *Prophecy and Religion*, 214.

The intimate words of these autobiographical passages were not addressed to the public. Why then did Jeremiah record them and pass them on to Baruch? Perhaps it was for the same reason that Jesus told the apostles about his temptations in the wilderness. 'For whatever was written in former days was written for our instruction' (Romans 15: 4). It was the intention of the prophet that his own dark experiences and painful struggles should be used by God to help others. It is encouraging to know that it was not all plain sailing on the voyage of life, for even the greatest of the Hebrew prophets. 'They wrestled hard as we do now, with sins and doubts and fears.'[1] For us, as for them, life is warfare, a ceaseless struggle with foes without and within.

It is of abiding significance that Jeremiah overcame through prayer. Most of these autobiographical lyrics are dialogues between the prophet and the Lord. Jeremiah did not wrestle with his problems alone; he took them to God and talked to him about them with a startling directness and frankness. He asked for what he needed—healing, help, vindication. 'But to Jeremiah prayer is more than petition. It is intimate converse with God, in which his whole inner life is laid bare, with its perplexities and struggles and temptations; and he unburdens himself of the distress which weighs down his spirit, in the sure confidence that he is heard and understood by the God to whom all things are naked and open.'[2] Not only the call, but the subsequent ministry of Jeremiah was a dialogue with God. It is a story of personal encounter and conversation, of revelation and response, of God's word uttered within the prophet's heart and of his answer in prayer. The piety and prayers of Jeremiah had a profound influence upon the Psalmists and upon the devotion of the Jewish and Christian Churches.

GOD AND MAN

From the autobiographical passages just cited, it is evident that Jeremiah's knowledge of God was not theoretical and abstract, but experiential and personal. It was the outcome of revelation and response, of personal encounter and direct relationship. His prophecy is not a book of systematic theology, and we look here in vain for new or original conceptions of God. He was heir to the Mosaic tradition in making the great affirmation, 'the Lord is the true God; he is the living God and the everlasting King' (10: 10). That which had been revealed to Amos

[1] Isaac Watts.   [2] J. Skinner, ibid., 213.

about the righteousness of God, to Hosea about his love, to Isaiah about his holiness, Jeremiah inherited. Like the prophets who came before him, he believed that God was the Creator of the universe and the Lord of history. 'It is I who by my great power and my outstretched arm have made the earth, with the men and animals that are on the earth, and I give it to whom ever it seems right to me' (27: 5). All these convictions and insights the prophet shared with his predecessors.

The new factor was the quality and intimacy of his fellowship with God. His unique contribution to Israel was not new knowledge *about* God, but deeper knowledge *of* God. This personal knowledge of God is the supreme good, and the right ground for man's glorying. 'Let not the wise man glory in his wisdom, let not the mighty man glory in his might, let not the rich man glory in his riches; but let him who glories glory in this, that he understands and knows me' (9: 23, 24). This knowledge of the living God, who loves and practices kindness, justice, and righteousness, is revealed to the heart of the man who responds to him in trust and obedience. Such a man is truly blessed. 'He is like a tree planted by water, that sends out its roots by the stream, and does not fear when heat comes, for its leaves remain green, and is not anxious in the year of drought, for it does not cease to bear fruit.' On the other hand, he who trusts in man and turns away from the Lord, is without resources like a stunted shrub in the desert (17: 5–8).

Taught by experience, Jeremiah recognized that the people did not trust in the Lord, and were devoid of the true knowledge of him. Such faithlessness, ignorance, and disobedience were to the prophet a monstrous perversion of the created order. He contrasts men and birds. At the season of migration stork, turtle-dove, swallow, and crane return, mysteriously directed on their way. They act in obedience to innate instinct, to an inner knowledge which is the gift of the Creator. Yet the people, unlike the migratory birds, neither know nor follow the way of the Lord. Every one turns to his own course, like a horse plunging headlong into battle' (8: 6, 7). This persistent rejection of the way of the Lord in the past, had resulted in an almost complete impotence of the will in the present. By custom and habit the people had become hardened in sin. 'The sin of Judah is written with a pen of iron; with a point of diamond it is engraved on the tablet of their heart' (17: 1). They were now virtually unable to do good. 'Can the Ethiopian change his skin or the leopard his spots? Then also you can do good who are accustomed to do evil' (13: 23). Such is the power of sin to enslave (John 8: 34). 'Could the young but realise how soon they will become mere walking bundles of habits, they would give more heed to their conduct while in a plastic state. We are spinning our own fate, good or evil, and never to be undone.'[1]

A change in the human heart can be brought about not by the unaided effort of man, but only by the re-creative power of God, who in his loyal love suffers with and for his people. Insight into that divine suffering for sin was given to Baruch the scribe, in a message which he appended to his biography of the prophet. Having complained of the hardships and frustrations he was enduring in the service of Jeremiah, the far greater sorrows and sufferings of God were revealed to him. Was it a time for personal ambition when the Lord himself was being compelled to break down the nation he had built up, to uproot, through Nebuchadrezzar of Babylon, the people he loved so much? (chapter 45). 'There is hardly a passage in the Old Testament which gives us a more impressive glimpse of the eternal cross in the heart of God, the bitterness of his disappointment with man.'[2]

This patient love of God for his sinful people was revealed to Jeremiah himself through a commonplace incident. In obedience to divine impulse he visited a workshop and watched a potter turning with his feet a large lower stone or disc, and shaping with his hands the clay which rested on the upper stone. The potter was not always successful *first time* in shaping the clay into a vessel in accordance with the pattern in his own mind. He did not on that account throw the clay away. Rather, he would squeeze it into a formless mass, and start all over again, until the shape envisaged at the outset had been attained. Interpreting the commonplace incident, the prophet saw that the sovereignty of God over his people was absolute—although in his omnipotence he made room for the freedom and response of men. 'The house of Israel' was like clay in the hands of the divine potter who makes and shapes his people according to his definite plan and foreknowledge. A flaw in the human material, whether the passive failure of the people to respond, or their active and wilful disobedience, would not cause the Lord to abandon his plan and his people. He would indeed crush the

[1] William James, *The Principles of Psychology*, Vol. I, chapter 4.
[2] H. Wheeler Robinson, *The Cross in the Old Testament*, 185.

nation through the instrumentality of Babylon, but that would not be the end. The spoiled vessel would not be thrown away but reworked into another vessel. The destruction was with a view to reconstruction (18: 1–11). The former, however, had to precede the latter. That was why so many of the oracles of Jeremiah, before the fall of Jerusalem, were proclamations of impending judgment.

That judgment was not announced to Israel alone, for her destiny was bound up with that of her neighbours. From the beginning, Jeremiah was appointed 'a prophet to the nations' (1: 5; 25: 15). His utterances against foreign nations are collected in the closing part of the book (chapters 46 to 51). The oracle against Egypt has a two-fold reference—to the defeat inflicted upon her by Babylon at Carchemish in 605 B.C., and to a predicted later invasion of that country by Nebuchadrezzar (chapter 46). After the battle of Megiddo, Pharaoh Necho overran Gaza; probably that event was the occasion for the message against Philistia (chapter 47). The three neighbours of Judah to the east of Jordan—Moab (chapter 48), Ammon (49: 1–6), and Edom (49: 7–22)—were to be destroyed, from without, by military invasion; from within, by moral corruption. Further oracles announced the downfall of more distant peoples, of Damascus to the north-east (49: 23–27), of the Arab tribes of the desert (49: 28–33), and of Elam east of Babylonia (49: 34–39). The long collection of oracles concerned with the collapse and destruction of Babylon and the return of the Jewish exiles to Jerusalem, are generally regarded as later than the time of Jeremiah (50: 1 to 51: 58). Read in isolation, these various oracles are harsh, stringently moral, revelations of the austerity and indignation of God. They must not be read in isolation, for the divine potter crushes in order to remake. The destructive mission is with a view to reconstruction. 'See, I have set you this day over nations and over kingdoms, to pluck up and to break down, to destroy and to overthrow, to build and to plant' (1: 10).

THE FUTURE

Jeremiah was a foreteller as well as a forthteller; he was concerned not only with contemporary events but also with the future of the nation. He was not alone in that respect. Throughout the course of his ministry his predictions were in conflict with those of false prophets, of whom Hananiah of Gibeon was a conspicuous representative (chapter 28). Since there was no difference in the *form* of the messages and all alike were delivered with conviction, how were the people to distinguish the true from the false prophets? This problem confronts God's people in all ages, for not all those who speak in his name do so by his authority. How then is the grain to be separated from the chaff (23: 28)? Two criteria are offered in the Book of Deuteronomy. The oracles of the genuine prophet are in accordance with what God has already revealed and commanded in the past and they are verified by the course of events (Deuteronomy 13: 1–5; 18: 22).

Further guidance on this difficult problem is given by Jeremiah himself in a collection of oracles headed 'concerning the prophets' (23: 9–32). There is the *moral* test. Prophets who 'commit adultery and walk in lies . . . strengthen the hands of evil-doers, so that no one turns from his wickedness' are not servants of the Holy One of Israel (23: 9–15). 'Thus you will know them by their fruits' (Matthew 7: 20). The *content* of the message also distinguishes the true from the false prophet. For a nation impenitent, disobedient, hardened in sin, the genuine prophets predicted judgment and doom (28: 5–9). To those same impenitent sinners the phoney prophets declared 'it shall be well with you'. Men of shallow optimism and wishful thinking, they ignored the serious and inevitable consequences of sin (23: 16–17). Furthermore, the message of the true prophet has its *origin* in God and is not self-induced. The deluded false prophet is unable to distinguish his own dreams and imaginings from that word of the Lord which is 'like fire . . . like a hammer which breaks the rock in pieces' (23: 25–32). The true prophet is not guilty of 'palliness with the Deity',[1] but stands in awe of the transcendent, all-knowing, all-present Majesty. 'Am I a God at hand . . . and not a God afar off? Can a man hide himself in secret places so that I cannot see him? . . . Do I not fill heaven and earth? says the Lord' (23: 23, 24). Jeremiah had stood in the council of this exalted and glorious God, and had been sent to speak his word to the people (23: 22). 'This immediate consciousness of having the mind of God is the ultimate secret of true prophetic inspiration.'[2]

Looking back, we can now see that the course of events verified the messages of Jeremiah. Contrary to the predictions

[1] Dr. H. H. Farmer's phrase.
[2] J. Skinner, *Prophecy and Religion*, 195.

of the false prophets in Judah, the state was destroyed by Nebuchadrezzar; contrary to the predictions of the false prophets among the exiles, there was no speedy return from Babylonia. It would be a mistake, however, to suppose that all the oracles of Jeremiah were predictions of judgment and doom, although the use of the word 'jeremiad' is evidence of such a widespread misunderstanding. If, unlike the false prophets, he predicted judgment and destruction as the consequence of national apostasy, yet he also saw beyond the dark night to the bright day of restoration and salvation. In Judah's darkest hour, he made a significant venture of faith. The land was then in the possession of the Chaldeans and Jerusalem was under siege. The prophet's cousin, Hanamel, came and invited him to buy a field, part of the family property at Anathoth up for sale. Jeremiah signed the deed and paid down the full price for the field, and thereby declared his faith in the future of his nation. 'Houses and fields and vineyards shall again be bought in this land' (32: 1–15).

While discouraging the false hopes aroused by prophets in Babylonia of an *early* return to Zion, Jeremiah did not leave the exiles without 'a future and a hope'. After an indefinite period ('seventy years') in Babylon, the Lord would visit his people. 'I will fulfil to you my promise and bring you back to this place' (29: 10–14). This reversal of fortunes would not be confined to those exiled from Judah by Nebuchadrezzar of Babylon. The oracles in 'the Book of Comfort' (30: 1 to 31: 40), some of which are Jeremiah's, some from later periods, describe the restoration of those exiled from the former Northern Kingdom. Rachel, ancestress of those northern tribes, ceaselessly weeping over the loss of her exiled children, is comforted with the promise of their restoration. 'Your children shall come back to their own country' (31: 15–17). This return of the exiles would be even more glorious than the ancient Exodus from Egypt (23: 7, 8). Restored Israel and Judah would then live in security under the rule of an ideal king. 'I will raise up for David a righteous Branch, and he shall reign as king and deal wisely, and shall execute justice and righteousness in the land.' In contrast with the weak contemporary, King Zedekiah (whose name means 'The Lord is my righteousness') the future king, the Messiah, would be called 'The Lord is our righteousness' (23: 5, 6).

In those days, the Lord would make a new covenant with his people. For the old covenant made at Sinai had been broken.

The binding contract between the two parties had been annulled by the faithlessness of Israel. Josiah's noble attempt at reformation and renewal had failed. The external law, written in a book, had been ineffective, because the heart of man was 'deceitful above all things, and desperately corrupt' (17: 9). The new covenant would be new in kind. The new age would be a time, not of reformation, but of regeneration. The Spirit of God himself would transform the heart of man from within. Like the old, the new covenant would also be made between the Lord and the people—'with the house of Israel and the house of Judah'. Life to the full is possible only within the renewed community. Yet, unlike the old, which was external, written on tablets of stone or in a book, the new covenant would be inward, written upon the heart. The creative power of God would effect such a change within his people, that henceforth they would have both the desire and the power to do his will. 'I will put my law within them, and I will write it upon their hearts.' The knowledge of God, in which men may rightly glory, would then be universal. Jeremiah himself had known God directly, intimately, personally; in the new age that knowledge would be the possession of every man. 'They shall all know me, from the least of them to the greatest.' The fellowship between God and his people, ruptured by the breaking of the old covenant, would be restored. 'For I will forgive their iniquity, and I will remember their sin no more' (31: 31–34). Jeremiah's prophecy of the new covenant was in the mind of the Lord Jesus Christ on the night when he was betrayed. At table in the Upper Room, he took the cup, gave thanks to God and said 'this cup is the new covenant in my blood' (I Corinthians 11: 25). The blessings of the new covenant foreseen by Jeremiah —obedience from the heart, personal knowledge of God, restoration of fellowship through forgiveness—are made available to the People of God 'through the offering of the body of Jesus Christ once for all' (Hebrews 10: 8–18). From Jeremiah we derive the name of our Christian scriptures—the New Testament. (Taken from the Latin Bible, the Vulgate, the word 'testament' means 'covenant'.) It is a further indication of the greatness of the prophet, that some of the contemporaries of Jesus identified him with Jeremiah (Matthew 16: 14).

X

Ezekiel

The Book of Ezekiel is probably the most neglected part of the Bible. There are many reasons for this. In an age of digest books, it seems excessively long, with many needless repetitions. Much of the subject matter has nothing to do with our contemporary concerns and problems. Of what interest to us, for example, is the fate of ancient Tyre or the architecture of the ideal Jewish Temple? Symbols and allegories abound, and puzzle and confuse the reader who may be without clue or commentary. The language of the prophet is sometimes crude and offensive to modern ears, and his actions appear to be weird and childish. The atmosphere of the first half of the book, with its messages of 'lamentation and mourning and woe' is one of almost unrelieved gloom. The stern and austere prophet portrays the severity rather than the kindness of God, his judgments rather than his mercies.

These first impressions, however, should not be allowed to mislead or deter the reader, who must come to this book as to 'a mine for silver and a place for gold'. Come prepared to search and to dig, for great treasures lie hidden in the visions and symbols, the parables and allegories of this prophecy. Many of them reappear in the New Testament—God on his throne, the good shepherd, the vine, the life-giving Spirit, the river of life, the new Jerusalem. Much of the teaching of the prophet—on, for example, sin and judgment, the responsibility of the individual, the function of the true pastor, the need for a change of heart, the work of the Spirit, the sovereignty of God over all nations— speaks directly to our own situation. In his own person Ezekiel combines the prophet and the priest, and his ministry is like a bridge spanning the gulf between the Jewish state and the Babylonian exile. He both conserves and originates.

Fortunately the difficulties of the book are to some extent offset by its orderly arrangement. There are four main divisions. (i) Chapters 1 to 24. Prophecies concerning the doom of

Jerusalem and Judah. These were delivered before the fall of the city and the state in 587 B.C. (ii) Chapters 25 to 32. Prophecies concerning foreign nations. (iii) Chapters 33 to 39. Prophecies of restoration and hope. These were delivered after the fall of the city and the state in 587 B.C. (iv) Chapters 40 to 48. Prophecies concerning the new temple and the restored community.

THE HISTORICAL BACKGROUND

As will be seen from the divisions of the book, 587 B.C. is the decisive date. For the fall of the city of Jerusalem that year is like a continental watershed, separating the messages of judgment and doom from those of restoration and hope. To get a clear picture of the background of Ezekiel's ministry, let us here recall the main events. Nebuchadrezzar, king of Babylon, deported the Hebrews into exile in two stages—first in 598 and then in 587 B.C. The first exile was the outcome of the foreign policy of Jehoiakim, the tyrannical and misguided son of good King Josiah. After accepting the sovereignty of Babylon for three years, Jehoiakim rebelled. He himself did not live to face the consequences. His son, Jehoiachin, had reigned only three months when the armies of Nebuchadrezzar came and besieged the city. Forced to surrender, Jehoiachin was deported to Babylonia, together with a large number of the leaders and influential citizens. 'He carried away all Jerusalem, and all the princes, and all the mighty men of valour, ten thousand captives, and all the craftsmen and the smiths; none remained, except the poorest people of the land' (II Kings 24: 14).

In place of Jehoiachin, who was well treated in exile, his uncle Zedekiah was set on the throne of Judah by Nebuchadrezzar. After about eight years this weak and vacillating king broke his oath of allegiance. With the support of Egypt he revolted against Babylon. Nebuchadrezzar then advanced and attacked the cities of Judah, and soon afterwards invested Jerusalem. The terrible siege, accompanied by all the horrors of famine, disease, and bloodshed, dragged on for two and a half years. The city fell in July 587 B.C. Zedekiah was captured and taken to Nebuchadrezzar at Riblah on the Orontes; his sons were killed in his presence, and his own eyes were put out. He was exiled to Babylon. The city of Jerusalem, including the Temple and the palace, the large houses and the walls, was dismantled and destroyed. A second deportation of captives now took place. Ezekiel prophesied *between* the first and the second deportations (the first twenty-four chapters), and *after* the second deportation (most of the second twenty-four chapters.)

THE MAN

Not very much is known about the personal life of Ezekiel, whose name means 'God strengthens'. The son of Buzi, a Zadokite priest, he probably lived near the Temple at Jerusalem; he was certainly familiar with its architecture and worship. He was married, but lost his wife suddenly on the very day the first siege of Jerusalem began. The Babylonians must have considered Ezekiel to be a person of some importance, for he was included among the nobles, warriors, and craftsmen, the cream of the population, carried away into exile in 598 B.C. He settled in Babylonia with fellow-exiles at a place called Tel-abib (after which the Tel-aviv of today is named). There he lived in a house of his own. About his first four years in Babylonia nothing is known; but in 'the fifth year of the exile of King Jehoiachin' he received his call and commission to be a prophet of God (1 : 2). Many scholars believe that some time after this call Ezekiel returned to Jerusalem, and lived and preached in that city until shortly before its fall in 587 B.C.

The traditional view, however, is that the prophet remained in Babylonia during the whole of his ministry, which lasted for about twenty-two years. In that case, Ezekiel must have been endowed by the Spirit of God with remarkable mental powers. For while in Babylonia, he could nevertheless see clearly what was happening in Jerusalem. He could visualize distant places, events, and people as if he were actually present; he was endowed with 'the faculty of seeing mentally what is happening or exists out of sight'.[1] Even if we accept the other view, that Ezekiel actually went to Jerusalem to deliver his messages against that city, he still stands before us as a man of remarkable mental powers. Like 'the lunatic, the lover, and the poet' he was 'of imagination all compact'. As a poet he 'bodies forth the forms of things unknown' in vision and symbol, in parable and allegory. His word pictures, often painted with minute detail, show him to be a man of great imaginative power. He was also a man of great strength of will and purpose. His character is well portrayed in the words addressed to him by God at the outset of his ministry. 'Like adamant harder than flint have I made your forehead' (3 : 9). Of indomitable courage and steadfast

---

[1] Definition of 'clairvoyance' in the *Oxford Dictionary*.

purpose, this man of adamant was stronger than the 'rebellious house', more persistent and resolute than the obstinate and disobedient people. Just and faithful, grim and austere, Ezekiel was the embodiment of the four military virtues—courage and endurance, discipline and obedience.

CALL AND COMMISSION

When he had been in exile for about five years, in the year 593 B.C., Ezekiel received his call to the prophetic ministry. It was preceded by a vision of the chariot-throne of God. 'I was among the exiles by the river Chebar, the heavens were opened, and I saw visions of God' (1 : 1). In a state of trance, Ezekiel saw a bright storm-cloud approaching from the north, out of which lightning was flashing forth continually. In this cloud, he was able to discern four living creatures, each one of which had four faces—of a man, a lion, an ox, and an eagle. Alongside these four-winged living creatures were four vast wheels, the rims of which 'were full of eyes round about'. These wheels were such that the chariot-throne they supported could move in any direction. Although distinct from the living creatures, yet there was perfect accord between them, 'for the spirit of the living creatures was in the wheels'. Both creatures and wheels supported a solid platform 'shining like crystal', on which was a throne. A majestic Figure of indescribable brightness and splendour was seated thereon. Overwhelmed by the majesty and glory of God, Ezekiel prostrated himself, only to be set on his feet again by the power of the Spirit of God.

In an outstretched hand he now saw a scroll, on both sides of which were written 'words of lamentation and mourning and woe'. He was commanded to eat the scroll, and to proclaim the words of judgment written thereon to the house of Israel (chapter 2 and 3: 1–3). By means of these symbols it was revealed to Ezekiel that the throne of God was not fixed in one place. It was of vital importance that the Hebrews exiled in Babylonia should realize that the living God was not confined to the Promised Land, or to the Holy of Holies of the Jerusalem temple. He was mobile and could and would be with them in their captivity. The eyes in the rims of the wheels indicated that he is omniscient as well as omnipresent—he sees and knows everything. This vision is Psalm 139 in picture language.

The sovereignty of God over men and animals is represented by the four living creatures beneath his throne. Their faces may also portray four attributes of God: the man, reason; the lion, majesty; the ox, strength; the eagle, swiftness. Only with the utmost reserve does the prophet make any attempt to describe God himself, and in doing so he makes use of the words 'likeness' and 'appearance'. He is aware that the symbol is not the reality. Picture language, the only language we have here on earth, goes only a little way towards describing God as he is in himself. 'For now we see in a mirror dimly' (I Corinthians 13: 12). Even when he reveals himself to us, he still remains far beyond all our understanding. This is the supreme value of Ezekiel's vision; the symbolical language conveys his awareness of over-whelming majesty and mystery.

It is also significant that the words of God communicated to the prophet are seen by him as *written* on a scroll (cf. Jeremiah 1: 9). About 621 B.C., the discovery of the written law (the kernel of our Book of Deuteronomy) in the Temple had resulted in a reformation of worship and life under King Josiah. This steadily increasing importance of the *written* word in the life of Israel is symbolized by the scroll which the prophet is ordered to eat. The man of God must assimilate, must take into himself, must 'inwardly digest' the communications of God. For the true prophet does not speak his own mind; by the inspiration of the Spirit he receives his messages from God. To receive these messages gives profound inner joy and satisfaction to the messenger—'it (the scroll) was in my mouth as sweet as honey'. This inner satisfaction does not depend on outer success—indeed Ezekiel was warned not to expect that. 'The house of Israel will not listen to you; for they are not willing to listen to me' (3: 7). But the messages must be delivered whether the people accept or reject them. The man of God is not ordered to be successful, but to be faithful. Thus it was that Ezekiel, like Isaiah before him, 'saw the Lord', heard his call, and received his commission.

AN UNSOLVED PROBLEM

What was the setting for the first part of the prophetic ministry of Ezekiel—Jerusalem or Babylonia? There is no doubt that he was in Babylonia when he delivered the later prophecies of restoration and hope. But where was he when he spoke the words recorded in chapters 1 to 24? There are serious objections to the traditional view that he received his call in Babylonia, and delivered *all* his oracles to the community in exile at Tel-abib. For the messages in chapters 1 to 24 are obviously addressed to the people in Palestine before the fall of Jerusalem in 587 B.C. Could the prophet have preached to them effectively in his absence? Could he have known with such accuracy and detail what was happening in Jerusalem from a distance of many hundreds of miles? Furthermore, the prophet was commanded by God to perform certain symbolical actions portraying the impending destruction of Jerusalem and the exile. These 'action sermons' were addressed to the people in Palestine before 587 B.C. and could not have communicated God's word effectively unless performed in their presence. In reading the first half of the book the reader has the impression that Ezekiel was in Jerusalem, and that his words were spoken to the people there. How, for example, did it come about that Pelatiah, who lived in Jerusalem, died while Ezekiel was prophesying against him? As with all the other prophets, is it not here taken for granted that Ezekiel addressed his audience directly? These are some of the reasons why many scholars take the view that the prophet was in Jerusalem when he delivered the oracles recorded in chapters 1 to 24. He may have received his call in Babylonia, but he subsequently returned to Jerusalem, and prophesied in or near that city until shortly before its destruction in 587 B.C.

On the other hand, the traditional view is based upon the clear statements of the book, as it has come down to us, that Ezekiel addressed his messages, including those intended for the people still in Palestine, to the exiles at Tel-abib. On this view it is maintained that his visits to the city of Jerusalem were not literal journeys: he was transported by the Spirit. It was not with his physical eyes that he beheld the doomed city: he saw visions. Of course, that which he knew about Jerusalem before he became a captive, together with information brought by travellers about current conditions and events in the city, was taken up into his visions. God made use of the information the prophet had acquired through the usual channels, and of his unusual mental powers, akin in some respects to telepathy and clairvoyance. But it was by the inspiration of the Spirit that he 'saw' and 'heard' what was going on in Jerusalem. Furthermore, his messages concerning the doom of the city, whether spoken or enacted, were intended both for the exiles in Babylonia and for the people still in Palestine. For the former were in danger of being deluded by false hopes of a speedy return to the homeland. To the latter, the messages of the prophet would be conveyed by travellers from Babylonia to Jerusalem.

Such in outline are the alternatives. Since the experts differ, it would be unwise to be dogmatic on this question of locale. It is better to be aware of the reasons for the alternative views, and to regard it as an unsolved problem.

THE STATE OF THE NATION

Let us now look at the situation of the people to whom the messages in chapters 1 to 24 were addressed. What was the state of affairs in Judah and Jerusalem under King Zedekiah after the first deportation in 598 and before the fall of the city and the state in 587 B.C.? Whether he saw it with his eyes or in spiritual vision, Ezekiel paints the picture of the nation in lurid colours. The reformation of religion and morals carried through by King Josiah had been followed by a reaction. Idolatry was rampant in the land and was represented even within the precincts of the Temple itself. Near the north gate of the Temple was an image, perhaps of the goddess Ashera, consort of Baal, which provoked the indignation or jealousy of God (8: 5, 6). On the walls of one of the rooms of the gateway were carved figures of reptiles and animals, before which seventy elders were secretly burning incense. This animal worship may have been introduced from Egypt (8: 7–13). Near the northern gate, women were weeping for the god Tammuz, whose death was associated with the annual decay of the spring vegetation caused by the heat of the summer (8: 14, 15). Standing between the Temple and the altar, their backs turned disrespectfully to the shrine of God, twenty-five men with faces turned to the east were worshipping the sun (8: 16–18). These are typical examples of what was happening all over the land. Having 'exchanged the glory of the immortal God for images resembling mortal man or birds or animals or reptiles' (Romans 1 : 23), they were guilty of every kind of personal and social sin.

So many had been done to death by the wicked rulers, that Ezekiel described Jerusalem as 'the bloody city'. Contempt for parents; the ruthless oppression of the fatherless, the widow, and the sojourner; lying; sexual immorality of many kinds; taking bribes and extortion—these are among the many evils denounced (22: 1–12). The prophets, as well as the people, are castigated. While claiming to speak the word of God, they 'prophesy out of their own minds' and 'follow their own spirit'. Blind to the sorry state of the nation and unaware of the coming judgment, they are like men who hide the weaknesses in a mud-brick wall by daubing it over with whitewash. Self-deceived, they mislead the people, and encourage a facile optimism, 'saying, "peace", when there is no peace' (13: 1–16). The whole community is so corrupt that 'even if these three men, Noah, Daniel, and Job, were in it, they would deliver but their own lives by their righteousness' (14: 14). Looking back during the exile to the former rulers of the nation, the prophet describes them as bad shepherds; they had cared only for themselves and not at all for the sheep. They had ruled 'with force and harshness', domineering over those in their charge. It was owing to their misrule that the flock was left defenceless, and the sheep were scattered 'over all the face of the earth' (34: 1–6).

For people, prophets, and rulers, Ezekiel has, at this period of his ministry, no word of hope. The sword of the Lord is about to be drawn, and both the righteous and the wicked will be cut off (21: 1–5). This sword is the king of Babylon, who is depicted standing at the parting of the ways, casting lots to decide whether Jerusalem or Rabbah of Ammon is to be crushed first. Nebuchadrezzar takes the road to Jerusalem (21: 18–23). He captures the city and punishes the 'unhallowed wicked one', King Zedekiah, who had treacherously broken his oath of allegiance to Babylon. He destroys the city, and thus carries out the just judgment of God. 'A ruin, ruin, ruin I will make it; there shall not be even a trace of it until he comes whose right it is; and to him (the ideal king) I will give it' (21: 24–27).

SYMBOLIC ACTS

The downfall of the city and state which is the main theme of the first part of this prophecy, is depicted by a number of symbolic acts. We have already had examples of these in the ministries of Isaiah and Jeremiah, but they are especially characteristic of Ezekiel. He was commanded by God to take a brick or slab of clay, to outline the city of Jerusalem on it, and to depict mimic siegeworks around it. Taking the part of the Babylonians, he was then to 'press the siege against it'—thus enacting God's purpose to overthrow the city (4: 1–3).

On another occasion, the prophet was directed to lie on his left side for 390 days, and on his right side for 40 days. These numbers added together represent the duration of the siege of Jerusalem. The days also correspond to the years of the captivity of Israel (beginning perhaps with the revolt of the Ten Tribes under Jeroboam), and the captivity of Judah (4: 4–8).

Ezekiel was also commanded to prepare cheap and coarse bread, baked by using unclean fuel. He was to eat this scanty portion and to drink a little water, once each day. For rationing would be imposed during the siege, and in the ensuing exile food would have to be eaten in a foreign (i.e. unclean) land (4: 9–17).

After cutting off the hair of his head and beard with a sword as sharp as a barber's razor, the prophet divided it into three parts. The first part was burned, the second part was struck with a sword, the third part was scattered to the winds. These actions depicted the fate of the people of Jerusalem; many would die of disease and famine, some would be slain, others would be scattered in exile (5: 1–12).

Shortly before the downfall of the city, Ezekiel received the order 'prepare for yourself an exile's baggage'. He was then to dig a hole through the wall of his house at night, and pass through it, carrying his few salvaged belongings on his back. Thus he symbolized both the going forth of the people into exile, and King Zedekiah's attempt to escape by night from the doomed city (12: 1–16).

On the very day the siege began, Ezekiel's wife died in the evening. In those days it was customary for people to give spontaneous outward expression to inner emotion. But although Ezekiel was deeply devoted to his wife, he suppressed his grief and made no use of the traditional signs of mourning. As intended, his extraordinary conduct attracted attention and invited comment. It was a symbol and sign to the people. At the fall of Jerusalem, the grief of the captives would be too deep for cries and tears; overwhelmed by the catastrophe, they would be stunned into silence (24: 15–27).

It will be observed that almost all (for an exception see 37: 15–23) the symbolic acts of Ezekiel have to do with the impending fall of the city of Jerusalem. 'Actions speak louder than words.' By means of these dramatic demonstrations, engaging the eyes as well as the ears of the people, the message of God was driven home. That which the prophet had proclaimed in words was expressed and embodied in actions. It would be a mistake, however, to regard these symbolic acts as little more than 'visual aids' to a deeper understanding of the truth. 'Like the spoken word, they are instrumental acts, helping to bring about that which they signify. They are part of the divine activity, that part which the prophets initiate.'[1] They are the

[1] H. Wheeler-Robinson, *Redemption and Revelation*, 250.

Old Testament forerunners of the gospel sacraments of Baptism and the Lord's Supper. The sacraments, if rightly administered, are always accompanied by the spoken word. Yet they are far more than pictures of the truth. They convey the unseen realities they symbolize, even although they symbolize far more than they convey. Through them God acts here and now; yet they also point forward to his action in the future. God was acting through the symbolic acts of Ezekiel—and yet those acts themselves pointed to the greater action of God in history, in which they were fulfilled.

ALLEGORIES

Ezekiel embodied the word of God in stories as well as in actions. He made extensive use of allegory. This is defined as 'narrative description of a subject under guise of another suggestively similar'. The *Pilgrim's Progress*, one of the best loved books in the English language, is an extended allegory. Some of the allegories in this prophecy tell the tragic story of Israel, the people of God. There is, for example, the allegory of the vine. Among all the trees of the forest, the wild vine is worthless. Its wood cannot serve any useful purpose; not even a peg can be made of it. Jerusalem is like that—worthless, useless, fit only for the fire of destruction (15: 1–8). Christ was contrasting himself and his disciples with this symbol of faithless Israel, when he said 'I am the *true* vine . . . you are the branches' (John 15: 1, 5).

In a longer historical allegory, Jerusalem is likened to a deserted girl-child of mixed parentage. Exposed and left to die after birth, God pitied and rescued her and she 'grew up and became tall and arrived at full maidenhood'. Then God took her to be his wife, arraying her in beautiful clothes, adorning her with costly ornaments, and establishing her in 'regal estate'. But she was disloyal to her husband, and played the harlot, offering herself to every passer-by. These same lovers, however, would become her worst enemies and bring about her humiliation and downfall. Nevertheless God would not abandon her; in loyal love he would establish and restore her (chapter 16). The allegory of the two unchaste sisters is similar. Oholah (Samaria) and Oholibah (Jerusalem) were both espoused by God and both were unfaithful to him. Samaria was destroyed by her lovers, the Assyrians. But her fate has been disregarded by her sister, Jerusalem, who has now turned from the Babylonians to the Egyptians. She will suffer destruction at the hands

of the lovers she has forsaken (chapter 23). In both these allegories, the idolatrous worship adopted by Israel and Judah
from Assyria, Egypt, and Babylon is spoken of under the figure
of unchastity. As in the prophecy of Hosea, the marriage analogy
is used to set forth the relationship between God and Israel. The
apostle Paul uses it of the relationship between Christ and the
Church (Ephesians 5: 21–33). It is intended to be a relationship
characterized by intimate personal knowledge and loyal love.
In fact the ingratitude and disloyalty of his people are here contrasted with the compassion and faithfulness of God.

An allegory may also set forth in picture and story the career
and fate of a prominent individual. A lioness had a whelp. He
was captured by the hunters in a pit, and led away into Egypt.
Then the lioness 'took another of her whelps and made him a
young lion'. But the hunters spread their net over him, put him
in a cage, and brought him to Babylon. The lioness is the royal
house of Judah, and the two young lions are King Jehoahaz,
who was deported by Pharaoh Necho to Egypt, and King Jehoiachin, who was taken captive by Nebuchadrezzar to Babylon
(19: 1–9). This same symbol is used in the New Testament to
describe the majesty and regality of the true King, the risen
Lord, 'the Lion of the tribe of Judah' (Revelation 5: 5).
There is yet another foreshadowing of the Messiah in the
allegory of the two eagles (chapter 17). A great eagle (Nebuchadrezzar) broke off the topmost twig of a lofty cedar (Jehoiachin) and carried it to a city of commerce (Babylon). The eagle
then 'took of the seed of the land (Zedekiah) and planted it in
fertile soil'. But after a time this little vine treacherously turned
away from the first eagle to a second great eagle (the Pharaoh of
Egypt). Because of this disloyalty, it would be uprooted. God
would in due time take another twig of the cedar (the future,
ideal king) and plant it on a high mountain (Zion); it would
become a great and fruitful tree. Not in any literal Jewish state,
but in the kingdom of Christ, this prophecy has its fulfilment.
These pictures, poems, parables, and allegories of Ezekiel have
been taken up and applied by other biblical writers, and
continue to have a profound influence upon the thought and
devotion of the people of God. Like the parables of Jesus,
once heard—or rather seen—they are not easily forgotten.
In the familiar words of Tennyson, they are 'truth embodied in
a tale'.

'BY THE WATERS OF BABYLON'

So far we have been largely concerned with the words of Ezekiel recorded in chapters 1 to 24, relating to the situation in Jerusalem between the first deportation in 598 and the fall of the city in 587 B.C. We turn now to his messages in the second half of the book, addressed and intended for the Hebrews in exile after the fall of Jerusalem. We know a little about these exiles, their circumstances, and manner of life. They were not dispersed, but settled in colonies, and for that reason were able to maintain their identity, faith, and customs. One of these colonies was at Tel-abib by the canal Chebar, near Nippur, and one or two other places are mentioned in the books of Ezra and Nehemiah. It would be misleading to think of these 'captives' as prisoners, for they were treated leniently and had a considerable amount of freedom. They were allowed to marry, to build houses of their own, to plant gardens, and to engage in business (Jeremiah 29: 4–7). Since it had been the policy of Nebuchadrezzar to deport only the prominent citizens, there must have been men of considerable ability among them. Some became secure and wealthy, and were unwilling to return to Judea when the opportunity came. These communities had their own elders, and were free to assemble to listen to a speaker or to sing. While there were, no doubt, some apostates, the majority remained loyal to the faith of their fathers, and cherished and preserved the customs of the old religion. Because they continued to worship and serve the one true God, they maintained their identity as a people. The religious observances and customs became marks of separation from the heathen environment. It was for this reason that the rite of circumcision and the observance of the Sabbath acquired a new significance and a greater importance. Life in exile had these favourable aspects, these redeeming features.

But these positive elements were offset by the fact that for most of these Judaeans, the destruction of their own state, city, and Temple was an overwhelming disaster. Stunned and perplexed by this tragedy, they were discouraged and dispirited. The prophet reports them as saying 'our bones are dried up, and our hope is lost; we are clean cut off' (37: 11). The Psalmist depicts their nostalgia and grief. 'By the waters of Babylon, there we sat down and wept, when we remembered Zion. On the willows there we hung up our lyres' (Psalm 137: 1, 2). In this situation we find a significant change, a new note in the message of Ezekiel. Before the fall of Jerusalem he had been the austere prophet of punishment and doom. He now becomes the prophet of restoration and hope.

REVIVAL AND REUNION

The revival, restoration, and reunion of the exiled people are depicted with imaginative power in the best known vision of the prophet (37: 1–14) and in the oracle which follows it (37: 15–28). Ezekiel is transported in vision to a battlefield, where the fallen soldiers have been left unburied. The flesh of the corpses has long since decayed, the skeletons have disintegrated, and the floor of the valley is littered with the old bones. 'Can these bones live?' Challenged with this question he cannot answer, the prophet is then commanded to proclaim to the bones that by the breath or spirit of God they are to be raised to life again. As Ezekiel speaks, there is a rattling noise, and the bones move to form coherent skeletons, over which the sinews are stretched. Then the flesh and skin are restored, and each corpse is complete—but still a corpse! Ezekiel is now commanded to call upon the wind or breath. In obedience to his word, the wind sweeps up the valley and enters the corpses, transforming them into living men. 'They lived and stood upon their feet, an exceeding great host.'

The interpretation follows. The dead bones are the exiles. By his spirit God will quicken and renew the life of his people. He will raise them up from the grave of the Babylonian exile, and restore them to their own land. In the oracle which follows, the prophet is bidden to take one stick or tablet and write on it *For Judah*. On a second stick he is to write *For Joseph*—the poetical name for the Northern Kingdom, Israel. He is then ordered to join them together in his hand so that they become one. This symbolic act declares God's intention to reverse the disruption of the kingdom at Shechem, when the ten northern tribes broke away from the house of David (I Kings 12: 1–20). He will restore, not the two former kingdoms of Israel and Judah, but one people, under one shepherd-king, the greater David, the Messiah. God will give both vitality and unity.

There is a play upon the key-word in this great chapter. For the Hebrew word *ruach* may be translated 'wind' or 'breath' or 'spirit'. It is the breath or spirit of the Almighty which gives life (Job 33: 4). In the creation story, when God formed man from

L

the dust of the ground, he 'breathed into his nostrils the breath of life', and 'man became a living being' (Genesis 2: 7). So also in this vision, it is by the breath or spirit of God that the dead are made alive. This truth is reaffirmed by Jesus in his conversation with Nicodemus the Pharisee. A man must be born anew, born from above; born of that spirit which, like the wind, 'blows where it wills'. Otherwise 'he cannot see the kingdom of God' (John 3: 1–8). The Holy Spirit regenerates; in the words of the Nicene Creed, he is 'The Lord and giver of life'.

THE RESTORED COMMUNITY

When the exiles returned from Babylonia, what would life be like in Palestine? In the last nine chapters of the book (40 to 48) we have visions of the restored nation. At the heart of the new community is the Temple. Ezekiel is transported from Babylonia to the sacred mount at Jerusalem, and taken on a conducted tour by an angelic guide, who delivers to him a blue-print of the ideal Temple. It will differ from the Temple of Solomon destroyed by Nebuchadrezzar. That was adjacent to the palace and other royal buildings, and stood within a court, in which priests and people mingled. In the old, the holy and the profane were not separated. Now, as a result of the exile, there is a deeper awareness of the holiness of God. This is reflected in the plan of the new Temple, in which the sacred is rigidly separated from the profane. There are now to be two courts, not one. In the large outer court, 500 cubits square, free from all secular dwellings, surrounded by a wall with gates on the north, east, and south, the people are to assemble for worship. At the centre of this outer court, there is an inner court, 100 cubits square, to which gates on the north, east, and south give access. In the middle of this inner court stands the great altar of sacrifice. This court is for the priests only. To the west of the inner court stands the Temple. This is divided into the holy place (*hekal*), forty cubits long and twenty broad, containing a cedarwood altar, and the most holy place (*debir*), a cube of twenty cubits each way. As the ark has been destroyed, this is now an empty shrine. The separation of the holy from the common is also emphasized by means of elevation. There is an ascent of seven steps from the city to the outer court, a further ascent of eight steps from the outer to the inner court, and a final ascent of ten steps from the inner court to the Temple. There is separation, elevation, and symmetry, symbolizing the holiness, sublimity, and perfection of God. The prophet witnesses the return of the glory of the Lord to the reconstructed Temple, and describe's its altar, ministry, and worship.

His vision culminates in the account of a sacred stream. From beneath the threshold of the new Temple there issues a river. Its 'streams of living water' pass south of the altar and flow across the former barren region between Jerusalem and the Dead Sea. The further from the source, the deeper the river becomes, until it is unfordable. Evergreen trees with medicinal leaves grow on its banks and bear fruit every month. Its life-giving waters transform the Dead Sea, so that it now swarms with fish. The Hebrews knew from their experience in the desert and in the Holy Land that all life, vegetable, animal, and human, is dependent on water. The sacred stream symbolizes the life and blessing, the renewal and fruitfulness which flow from the presence of God, and from the place of sacrifice. Like the river which increases in depth, so these resources of grace never fail. But we must not over-spiritualize this vision. The prophet looks forward not only to the renewal of the community, but also to the transformation of nature. Like the two sides of a coin, spiritual renewal and material blessing are inseparable.

This fruitful land is allotted to the twelve tribes, with a sacred territory around the sanctuary and city for the use of priests and Levites. Of course the land never was subsequently divided up in this way, nor was the Temple rebuilt by Zerubbabel (520–516 B.C.) according to the pattern of this prophecy. Here we have an *ideal* picture of Temple, community, and land. Does this mean that these visions were ineffective and futile? No! In human life, even at its best, there is always a gulf between the ideal and the actual, between our highest aspirations and our best achievements. Yet our ideals, personal or communal, can profoundly and enduringly influence our conduct and achievements. Ezekiel was not primarily concerned with architecture, but with the holiness of God, and he was used to inspire and help Israel to offer worship with due reverence and awe. His vision of the restored community, the life-giving stream, and the transformed earth, taken up in the New Testament (Revelation 22: 1–5) has become part and parcel of the Christian hope of eternal life.

PROPHECIES AGAINST FOREIGN NATIONS

We have described in the imagery of the prophet the

establishment of the new Israel—the restoration of the community, the renewal of the worship, the transformation of the land. But would such a state of joy and prosperity, peace and security, be possible, if the existence of Israel continued to be threatened by powerful enemies? That is why the downfall of the surrounding pagan nations is described in a series of oracles which come between the destruction of the old and the establishment of the new Israel (chapters 25 to 32). Having gloated over the fall of Jerusalem, these nations would not be spared the punishment which had befallen God's people. The countries on her eastern frontier, Ammon (25: 1–7), Moab (25: 8–11), Edom (25: 12–14), and to her south-west, Philistia (25: 15–17), had been vindictive, malicious, revengeful, rejoicing over and taking advantage of the downfall of Judea. They were doomed to destruction.

There are several oracles against Tyre, capital of Phoenicia (chapters 26 to 28). This sea-port, centre of trade and commerce, home of brave mariners and skilled craftsmen, was renowned for its great wealth and splendour. Built on an island off the coast, it was almost impregnable, and was captured by Nebuchadrezzar only after a prolonged siege of thirteen years. During the siege, the prophet predicts the downfall of this secure and wealthy—and therefore proud and self-sufficient—city. He aptly depicts this great sea-power under the figure of a ship, constructed from the finest timber contributed by the surrounding nations, and manned by skilled sailors conscripted from neighbouring cities. Heavily laden, this ship puts out to sea and founders in the stormy waters (chapter 27). The sea destroys the ruler of the sea!

There are also oracles against Egypt and the Pharaoh Hophra (588–569 B.C.) who is depicted as a huge crocodile reclining in the canals of the Nile. Like the king of Tyre who boasts 'I am a god' (28: 2) the Pharaoh of Egypt is also guilty of arrogance and self-deification. 'The Nile is mine, and I made it' (29: 9). God will destroy the proud monarch, and after forty years of desolation, Egypt will be restored, not to her former greatness, but as 'the most lowly of the kingdoms'. The great cedar tree, pharaoh and his hosts, will be cut down by the Babylonians 'because it towered high and set its top among the clouds, and its heart was proud of its height' (31: 10). The prophet describes the descent of the Egyptians into the underworld, the land of the grave (32: 17–32). The departed, 'the shades', are conscious and speak. The ancient heroes in 'the midst of Sheol' rise to taunt the new arrivals, who are given a place not among those heroes, but among the dishonoured dead in 'the uttermost parts of the Pit'. It is significant that the cardinal sin for which the rulers of both Tyre and Egypt are denounced is that of arrogance or pride. The judgments of God on rulers and nations exemplify the principle enunciated by Christ—'Every one who exalts himself will be humbled' (Luke 18: 14).

This humiliation of her traditional foes, the nations surrounding Israel, does not, however, permanently remove all threats to the life of the restored community. For what about the barbarians who live on the edges of the world? The prophet foresees the coming of a time when the heathen, geographically remote from Israel, will be mobilized and invade her territory. The dread leader of these hordes from the far north will be one called Gog, from the land of Magog. When with all his allies, he has invaded the Holy Land, he will be destroyed by the direct intervention of God (chapters 38, 39). Gog has been identified with Gyges, king of Lydia, Alexander the Great, Antiochus Eupator and many another historical figure. Because he comes from the north (of Palestine) and because the Hebrew word for 'chief' (38: 2) is *rosh*, fanciful minds have suggested that Russia is the land of Gog! But Gog is not a person who has or will yet appear on earth, nor are these chapters a blue-print of past or future events on the stage of history. Gog is a symbol; he and his hordes represent the powers of evil in conflict with the kingdom of God. In spite of temporary victories, such as that envisaged in the restoration of Israel from exile, the powers of evil would not be completely and permanently subdued. In this present evil age, ground won from the enemy may be lost again. The triumph of good may not be permanent, and it is never absolutely secure. But this will not always be so. The tension between good and evil, the conflict between light and darkness, will not go on for ever. One day, 'the Day of the Lord', evil will be vanquished. God himself will act, and his victory will be eternal.

INDIVIDUAL RESPONSIBILITY

From the corporate to the personal—from these visions of the restored community and oracles about foreign nations, we turn to the teaching of the prophet about the individual. Distinctive of this prophecy is the stress laid on the responsibility of each

man to God. He deals with us individually. Before Jeremiah and
Ezekiel, while the idea of individual responsibility was certainly
present, it was not predominant in Hebrew thought. It was
believed that God dealt with the family or the clan, the tribe or
the nation, as a unit. Men were inseparably bound together in
the bundle of life. For the sin of one man, Achan, the whole of
his family was destroyed (Joshua 7). Furthermore, not only was
the individual one with the group, there was also solidarity
between one generation and the next. God visited 'the inquity of
the fathers upon the children to the third and the fourth generation' (Exodus 20: 5). But is this fair? Is God just if he punishes
the innocent with the guilty, or allows one generation to suffer
for the sins of their ancestors?

This problem became acute at the time of the deportations
into exile. The embittered people were quoting the proverb
'The fathers have eaten sour grapes, and the children's teeth are
set on edge' (18: 2). There are four passages in which Ezekiel
challenges and contradicts this orthodox doctrine, this overstress on the solidarity of the group (3: 17–21; 14: 12–23; 18:
1–32; 33: 1–20). Here the responsibility of the individual for his
own life and conduct is strongly affirmed. God deals directly
with each one, and will not punish one man for the sins of
another, even within the same family. 'Behold, all souls are
mine; the soul of the father as well as the soul of the son is mine:
the soul that sins shall die' (18: 4). A good father will be rewarded with life, but his goodness will not avail for his evil son. On
the other hand, if a good son has an evil father, 'he shall not die
for his father's iniquity; he shall surely live' (18: 5–18).

In thus correcting the overstress on corporate responsibility,
the prophet swings to the other extreme. In fact, 'No man is an
Island, entire of it self.'[1] We are not isolated; we can and do
receive undeserved sufferings and punishments, just as we also
receive undeserved benefits and blessings. But the prophet is not
making a balanced logical statement; he is correcting a distor-
tion. His positive affirmation is of abiding value. Each man is
responsible to God, and must bear his own burden. The past and
the present, heredity and environment, are influential factors in
every life; but they must never be made an excuse for sin or for
failure to shoulder responsibility for one's own character and
conduct. The prophet himself is a good illustration of his own
teaching. 'Son of man, I have made you a watchman for the

[1] John Donne, *Devotions*.

house of Israel; whenever you hear a word from my mouth, you shall give them warning from me' (3: 17). If he fails to speak the inspired word of warning, he will be held responsible for the death of the wicked; if he speaks the word faithfully, whether the message is received or rejected, his responsibility is discharged. Since all Christians are called to bear witness, it is not only preachers and teachers who should take this challenge to heart.

This strong emphasis on individual responsibility is one side of the coin; the other side is the message of spiritual regeneration. Certainly the prophet did not believe in salvation by trying! He did not assume that each individual was able by his own efforts to will and to do that which he ought. Nothing less than a change of heart was needed, and could be brought about, not by the effort of man, but by the activity of God. 'A new heart I will give you, and a new spirit I will put within you; and I will take out of your flesh the heart of stone and give you a heart of flesh' (36: 26). The perverse and wilful, the hard and sinful heart of man can be changed by the life-giving spirit of God. Rebirth and renewal, described in chapter 37 in terms of the whole nation, must take place within the life of each individual. Responsibility, as the word implies, is *response* in repentance, faith, and obedience to this prior activity of the Spirit of God. 'Work out your own salvation with fear and trembling; for God is at work in you, both to will and to work for his good pleasure' (Philippians 2: 12, 13).

PORTRAYAL OF GOD AND THE MESSIAH

'Note then the kindness and the severity of God' (Romans 11: 22). Ezekiel portrays the severity rather than the kindness. His conception of God is stern and austere. He challenges the popular illusion that the city of Jerusalem is inviolate because God dwells in her Temple. His throne is not fixed, but mobile; his heavenly chariot equipped with wheels and wings can move in any direction, at any time, to any place. He is where he wills to be. Exalted above the world, Lord of all nations, he is not confined to the Promised Land, but uses Babylon as his instrument, brings down Tyre and Egypt to destruction, and controls barbarian nations afar off. 'You shall know that I am the Lord'. This expression, used dozens of times, is indicative of the stress the prophet places on the honour of God. He acts to vindicate his name. This does not mean that God, like a self-centred human being, is concerned only with his own reputation. In Hebrew thought 'name' means 'revealed nature'. God acts in the world in order to make known his true nature to men. Indignation against sin in all its forms, is an essential part of his nature. This is what the prophet means by the jealousy of God—it is his righteous anger against all unrighteousness, the zeal of his indignation against the faithlessness of man. The circumstances of his ministry made it necessary for the prophet to stress this aspect of indignation and sternness, of austerity and judgment. Yet in portraying the severity, he does not overlook the kindness of the God who has 'no pleasure in the death of the wicked, but that the wicked turn from his way and live' (33: 11).

There are several ways, in addition to those already mentioned, in which Ezekiel foreshadows the person and work of our Lord Jesus Christ. As distinct from the selfish and tyrannical rulers of Jerusalem and Judah, God is the good shepherd who feeds, guides, and protects his flock. 'I myself will be the shepherd of my sheep . . . I will seek the lost, and I will bring back the strayed, and I will bind up the crippled, and I will strengthen the weak' (34: 15, 16). This pastoral care of God is to be exercised through a human shepherd-king. 'And I will set up over them one shepherd, my servant David, and he shall feed them' (34: 23). Under him, there will no longer be two kingdoms, Israel and Judah; he will rule over one united people of God (37: 22). These predictions of Ezekiel are taken up by our Lord in John 10: 1–39. It is also significant that the title which now means so much to Christians—the Son of Man —is used nearly one hundred times in this prophecy. This is the title by which God addresses the prophet. Ezekiel is simply one man among others, an ordinary man, frail, weak, and mortal. What meaning did Jesus give to this title when he deliberately used it of himself? Was he referring to the heavenly 'Son of Man' who appears in the visions of Daniel and Enoch? Perhaps so. But he also used it, as it is used in this prophecy, to emphasize his oneness with us, his share in our common humanity. He too was weak, frail, mortal man, the servant of God who suffered and died for us.

There is yet another way in which the personality of Ezekiel points to Jesus Christ. He was both prophet and priest. Commissioned to declare the word of God to the people, Ezekiel was also concerned with the rebuilding of the Temple, the renewal of the priesthood, and the offering of sacrifice. Christ fulfils the prophetic office and ministry, for he not only declared the word, but is the Word, sent forth by God in judgment and mercy. He is also the 'high priest of our confession' (Hebrews 3: 1). Himself both Victim and Priest, he offered himself once and for all, and lives for ever to make intercession for us. Shepherd and King, Son of Man, Prophet and Priest—he is also Immanuel, God with us (Matthew 1: 23). He dwelt among us full of grace and truth. He is with us always, to the close of the age. This is Ezekiel's final vision for the new community in the restored land. This, we are told in the last two Hebrew words of the book, is to be the name of the new Jerusalem—'The Lord is there' (48: 35).

XI

Second Isaiah

THE BOOK OF CONSOLATION

For well over 2,000 years, the oracles in chapters 40 to 55 of the Book of Isaiah were attributed to the prophet of that name. It was believed by Jews and Christians that Isaiah of Jerusalem (whose ministry extended from 740 to about 681 B.C.) was inspired by the Spirit of God to see into the distant future. Over 150 years in advance, he was given messages of consolation for the exiles in Babylonia. This view was prevalent among the Jews at least as early as the second century B.C. Writing about 190 B.C. the Jewish author, Ben Sira, attributed the oracles of comfort to Isaiah the prophet. 'In the power of the spirit he saw the last things, he comforted the mourners of Zion, he revealed the future to the end of time, and hidden things long before they happened' (Ecclesiasticus 48: 23–25).[1] This traditional view was accepted by the first Christians. There are nearly forty quotations from Isaiah chapters 40 to 66 in the New Testament, and in eleven instances the passage quoted is expressly attributed to Isaiah the prophet.[2] (See Matthew 3: 3; Acts 8: 27–35.)

Both Jewish and Christian scholars continued to believe in the unity of the Book of Isaiah, until towards the end of the eighteenth century.[3] The traditional view, then first seriously questioned, has been abandoned by many scholars—Protestant, Roman Catholic, and Jewish. It is now widely accepted that the oracles in Isaiah 40 to 55[4] are the utterances of a prophet of the sixth century B.C. who lived among the exiles in Babylonia. He addressed his words of consolation and hope to his fellow-Israelites shortly before the fall of Babylon to Cyrus the Persian (539 B.C.). This anonymous prophet is usually designated

---

[1] *The Jerusalem Bible.*   [2] E. J. Kissane, *The Book of Isaiah*, Vol. 2, XII.

[3] An exception was Iben Ezra, who in the twelfth century expressed doubts about the unity of the book.

[4] The reasons for assigning the material in chapters 56 to 66 to a still later period are set forth on pages 203–204 of this book.

Second Isaiah or *Isaiah of Babylon*, because his oracles were sub-sequently added to the scroll on which those of Isaiah of Jeru-salem were written.

Three main reasons, having reference respectively to differ-ences in historical situation, language and style, and theological ideas, are advanced in support of this conviction. Isaiah of Jerusalem, whose name nowhere appears in these chapters, was preoccupied with Assyria, and with the independent king-doms of Israel and Judah. In chapters 40 to 55, it is evident that both Hebrew kingdoms no longer exist, Jerusalem and the Temple are in ruins, and the exile is an accomplished fact. Cyrus the Persian has already embarked on his career of con-quest, and the fall of the Babylonian empire is imminent. There are also considerable differences in language and style, which cannot be accounted for simply by the differences of subject matter. The style of Isaiah is terse and compact, that of Second Isaiah profuse and flowing; the former is grave and restrained, the latter gives free expression to emotion and often breaks out into song. There are both similarities and differences in theo-logical outlook. The implicit monotheism of Isaiah is here fully explicit. The doctrine of God as the Creator of the world, as the Ruler of history, as the Redeemer of Israel, is more highly developed. Second Isaiah's portrait of the Servant is in marked contrast to Isaiah's portrait of the Messiah.

It is not suggested that God could not have revealed to Isaiah of Jerusalem events which were to take place over a century and a half later. Whether or not we believe that he did so will depend upon our understanding of revelation as a whole, and upon our general interpretation of Hebrew prophecy. The prophets did foretell, but their predictions were usually made from the standpoint of the situations and times in which they lived, and had relevance to the needs of their contemporaries.

Nothing is known about the life of Second Isaiah. While not certain, it is highly probably that, like Ezekiel before him, he lived among the exiles. His knowledge of life in Babylonia is that of an eyewitness. On what occasions and to what audiences he delivered his messages is also unknown. The origin of the synagogue has been traced back to the exile, and it is possible that they were delivered to worshippers on the Sabbath. Some scholars believe that the written prophecy consists of what were originally some fifty or more separate units; if so, they were subsequently arranged in an impressive sequence which expresses the unity and continuity of the author's thought. He was not only a great prophet; he was also a superb poet. The depth of his thought and the intensity of his feeling is expressed in exalted language of great power and beauty. He is a lyrical poet. As he contemplates the activity of God in creation, in history, in redemption, he breaks out again and again into songs of praise. His great themes are presented with dramatic power and with a wealth of visual imagery. He does not himself appear in the book, which unlike *Isaiah* or *Jeremiah* has no biographical or autobiographical material. The personal pronoun, the 'I' used throughout, almost always stands for God himself. He is speaking through the lips of his prophet, who is to be numbered among those 'who hide their own, to serve another's glory'.[1]

CYRUS OF PERSIA

After Nabopolassar of Babylonia and Cyaxares of Media had captured Nineveh in 612 B.C., they divided the former Assyrian empire between them.[2] The Babylonians took possession of the Fertile Crescent, and the Medes of the highlands to the north and as far west as central Asia Minor. In the south-east, even before the downfall of Assyria, the Medes had already subjected the Persians to their rule. But the tables were turned when in 553 B.C. Cyrus, the Persian ruler of the little Elamite principality of Anshan, revolted against his overlord, Astyages, king of Media. The struggle went against Cyrus at first, but after three years he defeated Astyages, and took possession of his empire. The king of Babylon, Nabonidus, then entered into alliance with Egypt and Lydia (a kingdom of western Asia Minor) in order to resist the Persian menace. Cyrus continued his conquests westwards, and in the year 546 B.C. defeated Croesus, king of Lydia. The fabulous wealth of Croesus hoarded at Sardis fell into the hands of Cyrus (45: 3), whose vast empire now extended from the head of the Persian Gulf to the Aegean Sea. Babylonia alone now lay in the conqueror's path to dominion over the whole Near East. For some years Nabonidus had been living at Tema in Edom, leaving his son Belshazzar as regent in Babylon. He had deeply offended the priests of the god Marduk by ignoring the official cult, and by building a sanctuary to the moon-god Sin at Harran. Nabonidus now returned to defend Babylon. Shortly afterwards, the Persians fought a great

[1] From the hymn on St. Luke by J. R. Darbyshire.   [2] See pages 109–110.

battle with the Babylonians at Opis by the river Tigris. The Babylonians under Belshazzar were decisively defeated, and a few weeks later, and without further struggle, the victorious Cyrus entered Babylon (539 B.C.). That was the end of the neo-Babylonian empire, and for the next 200 years Cyrus and his successors were the rulers of 'all the world' (539–333 B.C.).

On the Cylinder of Cyrus we have his own account of the conquest of Babylon. He attributes his victory to the state god of Babylon, who was very angry with Nabonidus for ignoring his temple. Marduk 'scanned and looked (through) all the countries, searching for a righteous ruler willing to lead him' (i.e. Marduk, in the annual procession on New Year's Day), ' . . . he pronounced the name of Cyrus, king of Anshan, declared him the ruler of all the world . . . he made him set out on the road to Babylon going at his side like a real friend.'[1] The Cylinder further records that Marduk was pleased with Cyrus for the kindly and humane manner in which he treated the subject-peoples. Formerly, the Assyrians and the Chaldeans had secured the subjection of a conquered nation by deporting the upper classes into exile, replacing them with people from other parts of the empire. This ruthless policy was reversed by the humane Cyrus, who respected and protected the traditions and religions of the subject peoples. He rebuilt ruined sanctuaries, restored sacred images, and both permitted and encouraged displaced people to return to their own lands.

Cyrus' career of conquest was already well advanced when Second Isaiah began his ministry, but Babylon had not yet fallen. The references to Cyrus in the prophecy are at first indirect. The nations are summoned as to a court of law and questioned by the Judge. Who has raised up one from the east, who is victorious over rulers and nations, who moves with incredible speed? This has been 'performed and done' by the Lord who 'from the beginning' has directed the course of events in accordance with his wise and mighty purpose (41 : 1–4). The so called gods of the heathen neither know nor do anything at all, and their worshippers are without insight into the events of history. But the living God can predict the future through his prophets and has 'stirred up one from the north, and he has come, from the rising of the sun' (41 : 21–29.) Later in the prophecy, Cyrus is mentioned by name. The Creator of Israel and of the universe frustrates the vain predictions of the Babylonian

[1] J. B. Pritchard, *Ancient Near Eastern Texts*, 315.

diviners and astrologers, but confirms the word of his servant Israel and brings to fulfilment the prophecies of his messengers. He has chosen Cyrus to be his shepherd, and through him will carry out his purpose to rebuild the cities of Judah, Jerusalem, and the Temple (44: 24–28). The Persian conqueror is then designated by the title, used elsewhere in the Old Testament of Hebrew kings, prophets, priests, and patriarchs. He is the Lord's anointed, his Messiah, his vice-regent on earth. God upholds him, subdues nations before him, enables him to capture strong cities, and delivers the treasures of Sardis and Babylon into his hand (45: 1–3). He does this not only for the sake of his people Israel, but in order that all mankind may know that he alone is God, responsible for everything in the whole universe (45: 1–7). The prophet suspects that the exiles will be offended by his announcement that the Lord is about to deliver them through a *foreign* conqueror, that his anointed is a *Persian* king. Yet they have as little right to question the strategy of God as clay to challenge the design of the potter. In raising up Cyrus, God has a firm purpose in mind—'he shall build my city and set my exiles free' (45: 9–13).

Cyrus, as recorded on his Cylinder, ascribed his conquests to Marduk; Second Isaiah ascribed them to the God of Israel. The prophet was fully aware that Cyrus, at the time, did not know that he was the agent of the only true God, the Ruler of history. 'I call you by your name, I surname you, though you do not know me . . . I gird you, though you do not know me' (45: 4, 5). In the furtherance of his own plans and ambitions, and all unknown to himself, a man may nevertheless be greatly used to advance the cause and purpose of God. It is even affirmed of Cyrus, who so far as we know never became a worshipper of the one true God, that 'he shall call on my name' (41: 25). 'For monotheistic faith all active enterprise is service of the one God, even though the human instrument is not fully conscious of the significance of what he is doing.'[1] After the fall of Babylon, Cyrus did know what he was doing, when he permitted and encouraged the exiled Hebrews to return to the homeland and rebuild Jerusalem and the Temple. This was in accordance with his general policy towards all deported peoples. His edict concerning the return of the exiles to Judah is found in the Book of Ezra (1: 1–4; 6: 1–5). While it has no doubt been reworded in accordance with the faith of Israel, it is an authentic record of

---

[1] C. R. North, *Isaiah 40–55*, 58.

the policy of the astute and benevolent conqueror. In his interpretation of the rise and conquests of Cyrus of Persia, Isaiah of Babylon declares his faith that God is the Ruler of all nations and that all events are under his control. 'No blind caprice or fortuitous succession of events; no hidden mysterious force within the nature of things; no view of self-fulfilling history explains the coming of Cyrus, but only a divine government with a steadfast and consistent purpose.'[1]

THE PORTRAIT OF GOD

Isaiah of Babylon was commissioned to announce the advent of God on the stage of world history. The prophecy opens with a session of the heavenly council, at which the command is given to speak consolingly and tenderly to the exiles. For Israel's period of hard service is over and her guilt is expiated. A second command is heard—prepare in the desert a highway for the Lord, whose glory is to be revealed to all mankind. The prophet himself is then given a message for the despondent exiles. The power and glory of man is as frail and transient as vegetation scorched by the hot desert wind; but the word of God lives and abides for ever. Zion the herald, the ruined city of Jerusalem, is then commanded to proclaim to all the devastated cities of Judah the coming of the Lord. He is coming, the mighty king and conqueror, carrying the booty won from Israel's enemies, and bringing the exiles back to Zion like a gentle shepherd leading his flock to pasture (40: 1–11).

The Redeemer who is coming is the Creator of the world, and so the prologue is followed by a description of his incomparable power and greatness in creation. He made the seas, the heavens, the earth, the mountains—without helper or counsellor (40: 12–14). Great nations are as nothing before him, and the forests and beasts of Lebanon would not suffice to make a worthy sacrifice (40: 15–17). Unlike anything the mind of man can conceive or his hands fashion, exalted above the universe in which his power is manifested, he is also the ruler of history, the disposer of men and nations (40: 18–24). Since he knows and controls the myriads of stars he has created, he is not without knowledge of the plight of the exiles or without power to help them (40: 25–27). Lord of all time, unlimited in power and wisdom, he is the unfailing source of renewal and strength to all those who wait patiently for him (40: 28–31).

[1] J. Muilenburg, *Isaiah in The Interpreter's Bible*, Vol. V, 520.

Here and elsewhere the prophet moves on from the work of God in creation to his activity in history. He who formed his people, Israel, has now raised up Cyrus to carry out his purpose (44: 24–28). He who created the universe is active in contemporary events (45: 12, 13). One purpose is to be seen in both realms. He did not make the world for chaos but to be inhabited, and he has now declared his purpose for his people through the prophets (45: 18, 19). It is from the standpoint of history, and in order to emphasize what God is doing in contemporary events, that Second Isaiah describes the activity of the Creator. One magnificent poem celebrates the activity of the Creator *and* of the Redeemer. 'Awake, awake, put on strength, O arm of the Lord; awake, as in days of old, the generations of long ago.' In this passionate cry for deliverance, God is urged to repeat his mighty acts of old, in both creation and history. The creation of the universe was the outcome of a combat between the Creator and the original chaos, here represented in mythological terms as Rahab, the Dragon, the great deep. This primitive creation story, which was widely known in the ancient world, is historicized, reinterpreted by the prophet in terms of the Exodus from Egypt. The Creator who triumphed over the waters of chaos is the Redeemer who triumphed over the waters of the Red Sea. In the beginning the Victor created the world; in the Exodus, he created Israel. 'Was it not thou that didst dry up the sea, the waters of the great deep; that didst make the depths of the sea a way for the redeemed to pass over?' (51: 9–11). Yet great as were the wonders of that deliverance, when the Lord destroyed 'chariot and horse, army and warrior', the exiles are commanded to remember the Exodus no more. For 'the former things' are about to be surpassed in splendour by 'a new thing' —the deliverance of the exiles from Babylon and their return to the Promised Land. The journey, following this new Exodus, would be through a wilderness transformed into paradise, with mountains, trees, and beasts joining in the united chorus of praise to God (43: 15–21; 55: 12, 13).

The work of the Redeemer is also described in imagery drawn from the social life of Israel. If a man had been sold into slavery, it was the duty of the nearest male relative, the redeemer, to buy him back. God loves the exiles so much, that he is prepared to pay a great price for their redemption. To the Persian conqueror, he intends to hand over the peoples of Africa, as the price of Israel's emancipation. 'I give Egypt as your ransom,

Ethiopia and Seba in exchange for you. Because you are precious in my eyes, and honoured, and I love you.'

The Redeemer who speaks these words describes himself as 'the Holy One of Israel, your Saviour' (43: 3, 4). Second Isaiah, who uses this title eleven times, transmits and develops the teaching of his master, Isaiah of Jerusalem, on the holiness of God. Exalted above and other than man, the mysterious God, terrible in majesty, had nevertheless entered into a covenant with Israel. The holiness of the people was derived from the holiness of God. 'Your redeemer is the Holy One of Israel' (41: 14). He who delivers and liberates his people, also teaches and leads them in the way of holiness (48: 17).

Finally, the coming Lord, the Creator, the Redeemer, the Holy One of Israel, is 'the God of the whole earth' (54: 5). All powerful to achieve his purposes, nothing is excluded from his sovereignty. He has no rival, and the whole of creation and history are under his control. 'I form light and create darkness, I make weal and create woe (calamity), I am the Lord, who do all these things' (45: 7). The belief that God 'is one, and there is no other but he', the monotheism implicit in the earlier prophets, is here explicit and militant. There are several passages in the prophecy which satirize the manufacture and worship of idols. Perhaps some of the exiles in Babylonia, impressed by the pagan ritual or the statues of the gods, were in danger of being seduced. The prophet was evidently well acquainted with the processes by which the idols were manufactured. He writes sarcastically of the labours of the ironsmith who exhausts himself making a god (44: 12). With one part of a tree the carpenter 'kindles a fire and bakes bread . . . and the rest of it he makes into a god, his idol; and falls down to it and worships it' (44: 13–17). How ridiculous to suppose that the art and imagination of man can fashion a true representation of the incomparable God (40: 18–20; 46: 5–7)! In imagination, the prophet sees the gods of Babylon, Bel (Marduk) and Nebo, loaded on weary pack-animals. Far from being able to rescue their worshippers, they have to be carried into safety at the approach of Cyrus the conqueror! The false gods are a burden; the true God is a burden-bearer. 'I have made, and I will bear; I will carry and will save' (46: 1–4).

The pagan nations and their gods are summoned, as to a court of law, and challenged—'Set forth your case . . . bring your proofs.' Which of them had ever predicted historical

M

events and seen those predictions verified? Which of them had foretold the career of Cyrus and could now interpret the significance of contemporary events? They know nothing at all and are powerless to influence the course of history. But the true God, the Lord of history, announces events in advance, interprets them through his prophets, and by his mighty power brings them to fulfilment (41: 21–29). Second Isaiah's portrait of God is painted on a large canvas. He is the prophet of the 'first things' and of the 'last things' and of the history which lies between the beginning and the end. Creation, history, revelation, redemption—he sees the various parts of the work of God as one interrelated whole, as successive acts in the one great drama. He is the prophet of the Lord of the beginning and of the end. 'I am the first and I am the last; besides me there is no god' (44: 6). In the end, all creatures will acknowledge him, the majestic and exalted Creator, Redeemer, and King (45: 22, 23). 'Source, Guide, and Goal of all that is—to him be glory for ever!' (Romans 11: 36).[1]

THE PEOPLE OF GOD

The eternal God, whose nature is disclosed in his activity in creation and history, has entered into a close and bonded relationship with his people. He is 'the Holy One *of Israel*'. According to the prophet, this covenantal relationship, the sole basis of which is the unmerited love of God, goes back to the election and call of Abraham. He appeals to his compatriots to learn a lesson from the story of their ancestor. 'Look to Abraham your father and to Sarah who bore you; for when he was but one I called him, and I blessed him and made him many' (51: 2). Let the despondent captives, few in number, take courage; for by the blessing of God, the patriarch, when old and childless, became the father of many nations. They share that blessing, for all Israelites are like so many stones quarried from one and the same rock (51: 1). Because of this solidarity, Israel is heir to the promises made to Abraham. As the servant of God and the offspring of his friend Abraham, Israel is given the assurance—'I have chosen you and not cast you off' (41: 8, 9). Her election has not been annulled by the exile; the divine husband has not put into the hand of his wife, Israel, a 'bill of divorce' (50: 1, 2). The separation was only 'for a brief moment' and would be followed by a restoration of the

[1] *New English Bible.*

marriage relationship. The renewed bond would be permanent and unbreakable, like the covenant of preservation made with Noah after the flood. 'For the mountains may depart and the hills be removed, but my steadfast love shall not depart from you, and my covenant of peace shall not be removed, says the Lord, who has compassion on you' (54: 4–10).

While the prophet makes no explicit reference to the covenant at Sinai, he does mention the promise made by God to David (II Samuel 7: 1–29). The covenant made with David, ensuring the perpetuity of his throne or dynasty, would be fulfilled in Israel's life and history (55: 3; cf. Luke 1: 32, 33). This covenantal relationship, presupposed throughout the prophecy, is affirmed in the opening words, 'Comfort, comfort *my people*, says *your God*' (40: 1). The messages of the Book of Consolation are addressed to a people chosen and loved, bound and united to the Lord. This covenant love is affirmed in the many promises and assurances given to Israel: 'I am your God', 'I will strengthen you', 'I will help you', 'I will uphold you', 'I will comfort you', 'I have redeemed you', 'I will save'. Unlike the gods of the pagans, who have to be carried by their worshippers, he has carried his people 'from the womb . . . to gray hairs' (46: 3, 4). When they pass through the waters and the fire, through the perils and confusion attending the downfall of Babylon, they are assured of his protection (43: 2). This loving-kindness of God is entirely unmerited, for his servant Israel is both blind and deaf, without insight into the unique revelation given through Moses and the prophets (42: 18–21). Yet in spite of past failures God will have mercy on his people, for his love is stronger than the deepest human love. Even a mother may forget her child, but the name of Jerusalem is tattooed on the hands of her God (49: 15, 16).

This mighty love was about to be revealed in action, in the emancipation of the captives through Cyrus his anointed. From every quarter, east and west, north and south, the dispersed exiles would return to Zion (43: 5–7). With kings as guardians and queens as nurses, the foreign nations would expedite their journey and pay homage (49: 22, 23). Their return in such large numbers would make it necessary for mother Zion to enlarge her tent. Deserted by her husband and bereaved of her children during the exile, she would now have more children than ever before (54: 1–5). In the act of emancipation the glory of the Lord would be revealed to all nations, and the ancient enemies of Israel would come and do homage. Turning from idolatry, they would acknowledge the Lord. 'God is with you only, and there is no other, no god besides him' (45: 14). The action of God the Redeemer, and the presence of the redeemed and holy people would in itself be sufficient to bring about the conversion of the heathen. 'The prophet does not invite Israel to scour the globe in order to call the heathen to conversion . . . the Chosen People's business is to exist.'[1] It has become traditional in the Christian Church to think of the mission of the People of God primarily in terms of activity; the Church is apostolic, sent into the world to preach the gospel. Yet, in truth, *being* is prior to *doing*, and in God's purpose it is the holy community which is the sent community. Effective mission depends upon the existence of a people created by God the Redeemer, present in the world with a distinctive quality of life, personal and communal. 'According to the prophet of the exile, Israel does not have to engage in any activity in order to convince the heathen nations of the superiority of its religion; it has to live in the sight of those nations and, by so doing, testify to the merciful and efficacious greatness of its God.'[2]

THE SERVANT OF THE LORD

The teaching of Isaiah of Babylon rises to a climax in the Songs of the Suffering Servant (42: 1-4; 49: 1-6; 50: 4-9; 52: 13 to 53: 12). Some scholars have denied to the prophet the authorship of these four poems, on the ground that their portrayal of the Servant differs from that found in the prophecy as a whole; but the majority view is that they were composed by Second Isaiah. The speaker in the first Song is God, who introduces his chosen and beloved Servant. Endowed with the divine spirit, the Servant's task is to bring forth true religion to the nations. Unlike Cyrus the renowned conqueror, he will quietly and unobtrusively exercise a ministry of sympathy and encouragement. Undiscouraged by difficulties, he will persist until his task of establishing true religion in the earth is accomplished (42: 1-4).

The second Song is a dialogue between the Servant and the Lord. It is opened by the Servant telling his story to the nations. The Lord called him from the womb, named him at birth, equipped him with that divine word which is like 'a sharp sword' and 'a polished arrow', and kept him in readiness until

[1] Martin-Achard, *A Light to the Nations*, 31.   [2] Ibid.

the appointed time for his ministry. 'And he said to me, "You are my servant, Israel, in whom I will be glorified."' In reply to this declaration of God's purpose for him, the Servant confesses his failure to achieve it; yet although his work appears to have been in vain, he is content to leave the outcome in the hands of God. The voice of the Lord is then heard a second time. The Servant is strengthened with the assurance that God has a greater purpose for him than the restoration of the nation Israel, crushed by the Babylonian exile. His mission is universal. 'I will give you as a light to the nations, that my salvation may reach to the end of the earth.' It should be noted that in this poem the Servant is first identified with and then distinguished from the nation, Israel (49: 1–6).

In the third Song, the Servant is the speaker. He declares that God has endowed him with the gift of eloquence and has thus enabled him to encourage the despondent. He is able to speak effectively for God because at the beginnings of each day he listens attentively to God, and in spite of the suffering involved, he has not turned aside from the task entrusted to him. In obedience to his calling, he has been subjected to harsh physical violence and gross personal insult, but he has set his face like flint, having unshakeable faith in God his helper and vindicator. Using the figure of a court of law, the Servant then asks three questions, the answers to which are self-evident. No adversary will triumph over him, because his Judge and Advocate will defend and vindicate him, and his enemies will be gradually but completely destroyed (50: 4–9).

In the fourth Song, the Lord speaks at the beginning and again at the end; in between, the rulers and people of the world also take part in the dialogue. At the beginning, God announces the impending victory and exaltation of his Servant. Many had recoiled from him in horror because he had been so disfigured by suffering; they would be amazed when they saw his triumph. Startled by the great reversal, and overwhelmed with awe, the rulers would be silent before him. The rulers of the nations then speak expressing amazement that the Lord should have accomplished his purpose through one they had utterly despised. For like a shrub in the desert, his external appearance had been unattractive and repulsive and he had been despised and shunned by men. From this man of sorrows and sickness, as from a leper, they had recoiled with loathing. They had then believed that the sufferings of the Servant were the due punishment for his own sin. They now realise that his sufferings were vicarious; he had carried their sorrows, been wounded for their sins, and chastised to make them whole. They had all gone astray like sheep, and on him all their sins had been laid by God. Treated harshly, he had endured humbly and silently, without protest or retaliation. Condemned unjustly, with no-one to reflect on his fate, he had been done to death for the sins of others. Although absolutely innocent in deed and word, he had been buried with criminals. God who began the dialogue now concludes it. He himself has been active in the career of the Servant, and the events the rulers have described were in accordance with his purpose. The sufferings of the Servant would take away the guilt of the nations, and he would be rewarded with many children, and with the victorious restoration of his own life. Seeing the outcome of all his sufferings for others, the Servant would be satisfied with the knowledge that he had made many to be accounted righteous. Raised from the dead, he would receive a bountiful reward, because by the shedding of his life-blood and his identification with evil men, he has carried the sin of many and made efficacious intercession for transgressors (52: 13 to 53: 12).

There has been and is great diversity of conviction among scholars concerning the identity of the Servant of the Lord so impressively portrayed by the prophet in these four Songs. Interpreting the four passages collectively, some believe that the Servant is the nation, Israel. This identification is made explicitly in the second Song. 'And he said to me, "You are my servant, Israel, in whom I will be glorified" ' (49: 3). Weighty evidence for this collective interpretation is to be found in the many striking similarities between the portrayal of the Servant in the Songs, and the descriptions of the Servant, Israel, in the other poems of Second Isaiah. In both the Songs and the poems, the Servant is said to be chosen, formed, upheld, and honoured by God, hidden in his hand and endowed with his spirit. In both alike he gives *torah* and justice to the nations, to whom he is himself given as a light; and in him God is glorified.[1] Since it is beyond question that the Servant in the prophecy as a whole is the nation Israel, we are led by these similarities to the conclusion that the Servant in the four Songs is also the nation Israel. This conclusion is confirmed when we take into account

[1] I owe this list of likenesses to Bernhard W. Anderson, *The Living World of the Old Testament*, 419.

the momentous character of the work of the Servant in the Songs. His mission, universal and vicarious, could hardly be discharged by any one individual, however great. Furthermore, in the fourth Song the Servant is raised by God from the dead. While a prophet in Babylon could portray the resurrection and restoration of the *nation* from the grave of exile (Ezekiel 37: 1–14), there was as yet in Israel no doctrine of the resurrection of the individual. It is true that in reading the four Songs we receive a powerful impression that the prophet is painting the portrait of an individual. Yet we also have this same impression when we read what he says about the *cities*, Babylon and Zion. Imperial Babylon, soon to be overthrown, is portrayed first as a 'tender and delicate' virgin in robes seated on a throne, and then as a naked slave girl grinding at the mill (47: 1–4). The ruined city of Zion is personified as a solitary, childless widow, deserted by her husband—and as a beloved wife compelled to enlarge her tent to accommodate her numerous children (54: 1–8). The group is personified. In like manner, the nation Israel is portrayed by the prophet as an individual with definite characteristics.

On the other hand, there are grave difficulties in the unqualified acceptance of the collective interpretation. For one thing, there are important differences, as well as likenesses, between the portrayal of the Servant in the Songs and in the other poems. Outside the Songs the Servant, Israel, despairs, is rebellious and sinful, blind and deaf, suffers unwillingly for his own sins, and is to be redeemed. Contrast this with the Servant in the Songs who is undiscouraged, not rebellious, responsive, suffers patiently and willingly for the sins of others, and whose mission is to redeem Israel.[1] Furthermore, in the second Song the Servant has a mission *to* Israel, and is therefore distinguished from the nation as a whole (49: 5, 6). Most important of all, the nation Israel, as known to us in history, was not in fact a light to all nations, nor did her sufferings in and restoration from exile result in the conversion and salvation of mankind.

Having rejected the collective interpretation, some scholars have sought to identify the Servant with some individual in the history of Israel.[2] Moses, the kings Uzziah, Hezekiah, Josiah, Jehoiachin, Prince Zerubbabel and his son Meshullam, and the

---

[1] Bernhard W. Anderson, ibid.

[2] A full account of these individual interpretations is to be found in *The Servant of the Lord*, H. H. Rowley, 3–32.

prophets Isaiah, Jeremiah, and Second Isaiah have all been suggested. It is indeed likely that the lives of the great prophets, and especially the sufferings of Jeremiah and Isaiah of Babylon, have influenced the portrayal of the Servant of the Lord. Yet all these attempts to identify the Servant with an outstanding individual of the past or with a contemporary of the prophet, meet an insuperable difficulty. No person known to us did or could have done what the Servant in the Songs is represented as doing.

We conclude this survey by stating three principles to be kept in mind in interpreting the four Songs. First, we do not have to choose between the collective and the individual interpretations, for it is not a case of either/or, but of both/and. The antithesis we make between the individual and the group was foreign to the Hebrew conception of 'corporate personality' which 'allows rapid transition from the whole group to any single or representative member of it'.[1] Because of this transition from the many to the one and from the one to the many, easy and natural to the Hebrew mind, we must beware of over-simplifying the prophet's conception of the Servant. He is portraying the vocation of Israel the nation, *and* of the faithful remnant within Israel *and* of one outstanding individual. First one aspect and then another may be predominant in his mind as his thought oscillates between the individual and the group.

Secondly, in identifying the Servant, we do not have to choose between the past, the present, and the future, for the activity of God through his Servant transcends these distinctions within time. The sufferings of Jeremiah and of other great men in the past, the contemporary experience of the exiles and of Second Isaiah himself, and the work of the Servant in the new age heralded by the prophet, are all part of the portrait.

Thirdly, and as a consequence of the two principles mentioned, we do not have to force one and the same interpretation on all four Songs. Since the mind of the prophet transcends past, present, and future and moves to and fro between the many and the one, 'we may therefore reasonably ask whether there is not some development in his thought of the mission of the Servant, and whether what began as a personification did not become a person'.[2] Thus from the first Song, unmistakably collective, we pass to the conception of the faithful Remnant in the second; in

[1] H. Wheeler-Robinson, *The Old Testament: Its Making and Meaning*, 111.
[2] H. H. Rowley, *The Servant of the Lord*, 51.

the third Song, the Servant can be understood both individually and collectively, and in the fourth, he is unmistakably individual. This progression from the collective to the individual, however, is one of emphasis. For the collective is never left behind. The prophet's vision of the Servant of the Lord is of the One who includes the many; the One who is the Remnant and who is Israel.

THE FULFILMENT

To what extent were the predictions of the prophet fulfilled in the period following the downfall of Babylon and the rise of Persia? He was expecting the advent of the Lord and the establishment of his kingdom. He had announced that Babylon was about to fall to Cyrus, and that the Jewish exiles would be set free to return to the homeland. Along a prepared triumphal way, the Lord himself would lead the liberated captives, directly across the desert from Babylonia to Palestine. The valleys would be exalted, the hills levelled; rivers would flow and trees grow in the desert. For this new Exodus nature would be transformed. The heathen nations, beholding the glory of the Lord and the complete reversal of the fortunes of Israel his servant, would be converted and acknowledge the one true God. Such, in brief, is what the prophet predicted.

What actually happened? Babylon fell and Cyrus attributed his victory, according to the Cyrus Cylinder, to Marduk; according to the Chronicler, to 'the God of heaven' (Ezra 1 : 2). The statements can be reconciled only on the supposition that the supreme god acknowledged by the Persian was identified with the God of Israel. The Jewish exiles were included in the general permission given by Cyrus to deported peoples to return to their former homelands. The recorded return from exile bears little resemblance to the return as portrayed in the impassioned poetry of the prophet. There was no visible manifestation of the Lord, no highway across the desert, no transformation of nature, no vast throng of liberated exiles to repeople the former 'waste places'. Led by Sheshbazzar, Zerubbabel and others, small groups of exiles returned, not all together on one occasion, but over several decades of time.[1] The period following their return was one of difficulty and disillusionment. Drought and bad harvests, poverty and the hostility of the surrounding peoples, apathy and cynicism long delayed the rebuilding of the Temple

[1] See pages 189–190.

and the walls of the city of Jerusalem. The kingdom of God was not established, the land was not populous and fertile, the heathen were not converted. The great expectations of the prophet were not fulfilled in the events immediately following his ministry. His announcement of the decisive intervention of God for the emancipation of his people was a deferred hope. Events seen in timeless sequence in the exalted visions of the prophet were, in world history, separated by long tracts of time.

The coming of God the Redeemer, heralded by Second Isaiah, is recorded in the New Testament. All the gospel accounts of the ministry of Jesus Christ begin with quotations from this prophecy (Matthew 3: 3; Mark 1: 3; Luke 3: 4–6; John 1: 23). John the Baptist, the voice in the wilderness, prepared the way for the coming of the Lord, and in the ministry, death, and resurrection of Christ, the decisive intervention of God for the emancipation of his people took place. At the baptism of Jesus, the descent of the Spirit was accompanied by a voice, 'Thou art my beloved Son; with thee I am well pleased' (Mark 1: 11). The second part of the quotation is from the first Servant Song (42: 1). Jesus was the Spirit-endowed Servant of the Lord, who in his ministry of healing 'took our infirmities and bore our diseases' (Matthew 8: 17 citing Isaiah 53: 4). He came 'to give his life as a ransom for many', to pour out his blood of the new covenant 'for many' (Mark 10: 45; 14: 24). In both sayings, the word 'many' is a reference back to the fourth Song, in accordance with which Jesus interpreted his own sufferings and death on the cross (53: 11, 12).

The sequence of thought in the four Songs is reproduced in the ministry, death, and resurrection of Jesus.[1] Like the gentle Servant of the first Song, he began his ministry as a preacher of good news. In the second Song, the Servant's mission to Israel precedes his mission to the world. The ministry of Jesus was at first confined to 'the lost sheep of the house of Israel'; after the resurrection, his ministry was extended, his disciples were sent out 'into all the world'. The suffering of the Servant is first portrayed in the third Song, and from the time of Peter's confession at Caesarea Philippi, Jesus began to predict his passion and death. The shadow of the Cross lies on the latter part of his ministry. In the fourth Song, the sufferings of the Servant are depicted in the context of his triumph, and it was through his

[1] I am indebted to H. H. Rowley, *The Servant of the Lord*, 54, 55, for this insight.

vicarious sufferings that Christ won the victory over sin and death, manifested in his resurrection and exaltation.

He was the Servant of the Lord, and his apostles and evangelists interpreted his work in the light of the four Songs. 'In the preaching of the early Church, as recorded in the Acts, the conception of the "Servant" becomes one of the chief categories under which the Person of Christ is presented.'[1] (See Acts 3: 13, 26; 4: 27, 30.) The preaching of evangelist Philip may be taken as typical. An Ethiopian, returning from Jerusalem in his chariot, was reading the fourth Song. Invited to explain to him the meaning of the passage 'Philip opened his mouth, and beginning with this scripture he told him the good news of Jesus' (Acts 8: 26–35). The work of the Servant was realised in Jesus. He alone offered the sacrifice of perfect obedience, voluntarily surrendering his holy life for the benefit and salvation of all mankind. Through his sufferings and triumph men are accounted righteous and made whole, are moved to penitence and to the grateful acknowledgement that he suffered on their behalf. He it is who has entered into his glory, through his sufferings; and before him, highly exalted, 'kings shall shut their mouths'. The vocation of the Servant was fulfilled in 'that one man Jesus Christ'.

On the other hand, the Servant is Israel; in his saving work Christ is the Representative, he is the One who includes the many. Christians are 'in Christ' the Founder of the new Israel, branches in the heavenly Vine, members of the body of which he is the Head. The Servant of the Lord is Christ and the Church, and the unique benefits of his passion are mediated to mankind through those who have entered 'the fellowship of his sufferings' and who 'complete what is lacking in Christ's afflictions for the sake of his body, that is, the church' (Colossians 1: 24). That which he alone could do *for* mankind (a finished work) is made available *to* mankind (an unfinished work) through the service and suffering of the members of the body of which he is the Head. Once again, the conception of the Servant oscillates between the One and the many. Under the old covenant, the movement is from the many to the One, from Israel to the Remnant to the Christ; under the new covenant the movement is from the One to the many, from the Christ to the Remnant to the Church. Through the Church the risen and exalted One now ministers in all the world. As foreseen by Isaiah of Babylon,

[1] H. Wheeler-Robinson, *The Cross in the Old Testament*, 103.

the mission of Israel is now universal. Through his Servant, God's light now shines in all the world and his salvation reaches to the end of the earth. But not yet are the expectations and predictions of the prophet *completely* fulfilled. Only when the Lord Jesus Christ returns in power and glory will all the hopes of the prophet 'be emptied in delight'. Then, with the arrival of 'the last things', the redeemed of the Lord will return to Zion with ever-lasting joy, and the whole creation will 'be set free from its bondage to decay and obtain the glorious liberty of the children of God' (Romans 8: 21). Then the divine purpose revealed to the prophet will be fulfilled. 'To me every knee shall bow, every tongue shall swear' (45: 23; Philippians 2: 9–11).

XII

Haggai

When Cyrus of Persia overthrew the neo-Babylonian empire in the year 539 B.C., he reversed the policy of his Assyrian and Chaldean predecessors. The deported peoples were permitted to return to the homelands from which they had been uprooted, and were encouraged to revive their traditional ways of worship. The decree of Cyrus, issued a year after the fall of Babylon, permitting the return of the Jewish exiles, is preserved in both the Hebrew and the Aramaic languages (Ezra 1: 1–4; 6: 3–5). Some exiles took advantage of this decree and returned from Babylonia to Jerusalem. They were led by Sheshbazzar, son of the exiled King Jehoiachin,[1] who took back the sacred vessels of the Temple. He was appointed by Cyrus as governor of Judah, which was probably not a separate province, but an annex to that of Samaria. On reaching Jerusalem, the returned exiles rebuilt the altar of sacrifice and laid the foundation-stone of the second Temple.

This information is derived from the Chronicler—the name given to the author of I and II Chronicles, Ezra, and Nehemiah. Writing long after the return from exile, the Chronicler made use of the books of Samuel and Kings, of the memoirs of Nehemiah and Ezra, and of other written sources, and reinterprets the history of Israel from the ecclesiastical point of view. After this beginning described by the Chronicler, the work of rebuilding the Temple was interrupted for eighteen years. Several reasons can be advanced for this long delay. Judah had been devastated by the Babylonian invasion, and Jerusalem and many of the other cities were still in ruins. The best citizens and the soldiers had been deported, and the land had been subject to invasion by hostile neighbours. In the territory of the former Northern Kingdom, the native Israelites had married and intermingled with the foreign colonists introduced by the Assyrian conqueror. This mixed race, the Samaritans, viewed with suspicion any

[1] See page 135.

attempt to restore the economic prosperity, the political power, or the religious influence of Judah. Both economically and socially, the inhabitants were in a wretched condition. Prolonged drought and a succession of bad harvests had resulted in a shortage of food and clothing, and money had little purchasing power (1 : 6). Preoccupied with the struggle for survival, the people had neither the inclination nor the energy to undertake the formidable task of rebuilding the Temple. In any case, they were not disposed to regard the reconstruction of the sanctuary as a matter of urgency, for the destruction of Solomon's Temple by the Chaldeans had not brought about the cessation of worship. During the exile worshippers had continued to assemble in the courts around the fire-gutted ruins, to offer, to praise, and to pray. (Jeremiah 41 : 4, 5). For these various reasons no further progress was made on the work of reconstruction during the reign of Cyrus (538–530 B.C.) and of his son and successor Cambyses II (530–522 B.C.)

The latter monarch, who subjected Egypt to the Persian rule, died without a son, and was succeeded by Darius I Hystaspis. For a whole year Darius had to fight many battles in various places against a usurper called Gautama and his supporters, and the following year against a certain Nebuchadnezzar who had stirred up a rebellion in Babylonia. The vast Persian dominion was convulsed and appeared to be in process of dissolution. 'The shock that went through the great empire in that year revived in Israel the expectation of the last decisive crisis in history which the prophets had foretold.'[1] The preaching of the two prophets Haggai and Zechariah must be set in the context of this crisis. Sheshbazzar, governor of Judah, had been succeeded by his nephew Zerubbabel, a Babylonian Jew who had returned to Palestine during the reign of Darius. He was a descendant of David, being a grandson of the exiled King Jehoiachin. Following the disturbances in the Persian empire, the two prophets hoped for the restoration of the Davidic kingship in the person of Zerubbabel. Since the Lord was about to restore the kingdom and return to Jerusalem, it was imperative that the Temple should be rebuilt.

The messages of Haggai were addressed to Zerubbabel the governor and Joshua the high priest and, through them, to all the people. He began to preach towards the end of the year 520 B.C., and as a result of his impassioned words, the work of

[1] Martin Noth, *The History of Israel*, 311.

rebuilding the Temple was then resumed. The Samaritans offered to help, but the offer was rejected by Zerubbabel. 'So the hand of friendship curled into a fist.'[1] Some of the Samaritan leaders stirred up trouble; they incited the Persian officials to question the authority of the Judeans to rebuild the Temple. 'Who gave you a decree to build this house and to finish this structure?' (Ezra 5: 3). When the matter was referred to Darius the king, he confirmed the original decree of Cyrus, and authorized the Jews to continue the work (Ezra 6: 1–15). Completed in four years (520–516 B.C.) the rebuilding was a combined operation in which the inspired preaching of Haggai and Zechariah, the leadership of Zerubbabel the governor and Joshua the priest, and the manual labour of the people, all played a necessary part. This second Temple was destined to be the centre of the devotion and worship of the Jewish people for five centuries—until it was replaced by Herod the Great in the year 20 B.C.

THE FOUR MESSAGES

Apart from the information given in this brief prophecy, and a couple of references in the Book of Ezra (5: 1; 6: 14) nothing is known of the personal life of Haggai—a name derived from the word for 'a festival'. He may have been an exile who returned from Babylonia under the leadership of Zerubbabel. If he belonged to that small minority who 'saw this house in its former glory', he must have been very old, for the Temple had then been in ruins for sixty-six years; but the reference in 2: 3 does not necessarily carry that implication. Haggai was a man of indomitable faith, and was aflame with zeal for the restoration of the Temple and its worship. He could not only stir men to action, but also inspire them to continue a difficult work in the face of discouragement. His four oracles, dated in the year 520 B.C. and all delivered within four months, were collected and edited by an unknown disciple. This compiler, who refers to the prophet in the third person, provides the dates and framework, and records not only the messages, but also the effect they had on the people. As regards the months, these are numbered by the Babylonian calendar, according to which the year began in the spring—in March/April, for our calendar months do not exactly correspond.

The first of the four oracles, delivered in August/September,

[1] Bernhard W. Anderson, *The Living World of the Old Testament*, 440.

was addressed to the leaders Zerubbabel and Joshua and, through them, to the whole community. The people, some of whom are dwelling in panelled houses (or in houses which, unlike the gutted sanctuary, have roofs) are rebuked for their procrastination in rebuilding the Temple. The disasters which have come upon them, drought, bad harvests, shortage of food and clothing, inflation, are the judgment of God upon their apathy and neglect (1: 1–11). They are urged to go up into the hills, and bring back wood for the repair of the Temple, that the Lord may return in glory to his reconstructed house. Recognizing with awe that the words of the prophet were inspired by God, the people responded with obedience. About three weeks after he began to preach, led by Zerubbabel and Joshua they started to rebuild the Temple (1: 12–15).

After working for about a month, the builders were disheartened, for the structure they were erecting was so obviously inferior to its predecessor. The old men who remembered the magnificent Temple of Solomon were inclined to scoff at its modest successor. The despondent leaders and workers were then encouraged by the prophet with a two-fold assurance. The spirit of the living God who delivered Israel from Egypt is with his people. Soon he will shake the earth and all the nations upon it, and establish the messianic kingdom. The treasures of all nations will then be brought to enrich his house; it will far surpass the first Temple in splendour (2: 1–9).

A third oracle was delivered some two months later. The prophet consults the priests, and secures a directive on a matter of ritual. They enunciate the principle that the holy is less contagious than the unclean, for whereas holiness cannot spread from object to object, uncleanness can. Haggai then brings his charge of uncleanness by contagion. This may be the sin of apathy; the indifference of the people to the state of the ruined Temple has corrupted their worship and tainted the life of the whole community. It is possible, however, that Haggai intends the principle to be applied to the Samaritans ('this people') who had volunteered to help rebuild the Temple. The offer of the mixed race is to be rejected, lest the Jewish community be polluted. The Judeans cannot sanctify the Samaritans, but the Samaritans can corrupt the Judeans (2: 10–14). (See II Corinthians 6: 14 to 7: 1.) The message ends with a promise of economic prosperity. Before they began to rebuild the Temple, the yield from field and vineyard had been disappointing. Now that the foundation stone is laid, in a little while the earth will yield its increase and the Lord will bless them with prosperity (2: 15–19).

The fourth oracle, uttered on the same day as the third, was addressed to Zerubbabel. This prince of the house of David is encouraged with the assurance that the Lord is about to intervene in the affairs of men and break the power of the heathen nations. 'On that day, says the Lord of hosts, I will take you, O Zerubbabel my servant . . . and make you like a signet ring.' A signet ring was used for impressing its owner's signature on the seals of documents. It was a symbol of authority and royalty (2: 20–23). Did Haggai believe that the Persian empire, so recently convulsed at the accession of Darius I, was about to collapse, and that the Davidic monarchy was soon to be restored in the person of Zerubbabel, grandson of royal Jehoiachin? There seems little doubt that the prophet's hope of the restoration of the Davidic kingship, through divine intervention in history, was focussed on the person of Zerubbabel. The vision of Haggai was telescoped, or foreshortened; the far distant was seen as near. The hope he cherished in his own heart and inspired in others, was long deferred. 'The throne of kingdoms' was not immediately overthrown, and Zerubbabel was not the promised messiah. Yet in the fullness of time the long-deferred hope was realised. He who bears the very stamp of the divine nature and authority reigns from the throne of David, and the treasures of all nations are brought to enrich and beautify his holy Temple.

GETTING OUR PRIORITIES RIGHT

The message of Haggai is very easy to grasp and very difficult to accept. Judah was 'a depressed area' within the vast Persian empire, and many of the Jewish people were living in poverty. Haggai maintained that there was a direct relationship between that poverty and the sinful negligence of the people in rebuilding the Temple. The national economy was in a depressed state because, as a people, they were not giving priority to the worship of God. Some had found pleasure in building and panelling their own houses, but had long ignored the silent yet eloquent appeal of the gutted and ruined house of God. They had been preoccupied with their own 'standard of living', but had not been mindful to give to the Lord the glory due his name. Having failed to put first things first, they had also failed to

N

acquire the secondary things on which they had set their hearts. 'Consider how you have fared' (1: 7). Harvests had been poor and goods scarce. Due to inflation, the hard-earned wages of the worker had little purchasing power; he was like a man attempting to carry money in a bag with holes (1: 6). The poverty of the community was a judgment on their neglect of God.

It is extremely difficult for contemporary man to believe that there is a direct relationship of this kind between piety and prosperity, between the acknowledgment of God in worship and the condition of the economy. For we are not in the habit of interpreting natural calamities or adversities as judgments of God. We account for things in terms of 'secondary causes'. If there is a drought, we turn for explanation to the meteorological experts, and if the land fails to yield good crops, we buy fertilizers or seek to improve our agricultural techniques. Are we then to dismiss the message of Haggai as credible only in a pre-scientific age? By no means—for there is indeed a fundamental relationship between obedience to God and the fertility of the earth, between the acknowledgment of God in worship and the economic prosperity of mankind. Whenever man turns away from his chief end (the worship and the service of God) the consequences of his rebellion are manifested in three directions—the corruption of his own nature, the destruction of community, the perversion of his relationship to the earth into one of exploitation and domination. 'This technical civilization, the pride of mankind, has brought about a tremendous devastation of original nature, of the land, of animals, of plants . . . it has occupied everything for domination and ruthless exploitation.'[1] As a result of the fall of man, of racial sin, Nature is subjected to frustration (Genesis 3: 17–19; Romans 8: 19–21). As man is liberated by God, Nature shares in the deliverance, and at the consummation paradise is restored. For Nature and man are closely interrelated, and when man is right with God, Nature shares the blessing. 'The sympathy of a shared life between land and people, will bring such a removal of the evils suffered by Nature as to make a land fit for the heroes of God. This unity of land and people for weal and woe derives from their common dependence on God as their creator, upholder and future transformer.'[2]

As is evident from the book of Job, there is no necessary link

[1] Paul Tillich, *The Shaking of the Foundations*, 79.
[2] H. Wheeler-Robinson, *Inspiration and Revelation in the Old Testament*, 32.

between *individual* piety and material prosperity. That is not to say that there is no connection. It has often been observed, and rightly, that some of the virtues of the godly man, such as integrity and industry, do militate in the direction of material prosperity. The relationship, however, is not invariable—some excellent people do not prosper, and many prosperous people are far from excellent. Haggai is addressing, not individuals, but the community. A prosperous economy has a moral basis, and the earth approximates to paradise as the inhabitants thereof acknowledge the supreme worth of God. Irreligion is the root cause of social decay and economic disaster. In this twentieth century nations and communities have all the scientific and technical knowledge necessary to bring untold benefits to all mankind. Yet, in fact, multitudes are living in conditions of abject poverty, deprived of many of the good things of life, and many millions suffer from malnutrition and hunger. There is abundant evidence to prove that when men give absolute priority to the satisfaction of *their own* material needs and desires, the result is not health, happiness, and prosperity for all. For in an age obsessed as never before with the material, the economic, there is widespread poverty and desperate need.

Get your priorities right—that is the timeless truth proclaimed by Haggai. Put first things first, and other things also necessary to man will follow as a result. Priority number one in human life is God, for to trust and to love, to revere and to worship, to obey and to serve him, is the chief end of man. For Haggai, the rebuilding of the Temple was the outward and visible sign of the desire and determination of the leaders and people to put God first. He would have endorsed the precept of St. Benedict—'nothing must come before the worship of God'. The message of the prophet was taken up into the teaching of the Lord Jesus. Food, drink, and clothing have their importance, and our heavenly Father knows that we need these things. They will be ours—if we get our priorities right. 'Seek *first* his kingdom and his righteousness, and all these things shall be yours as well' (Matthew 6: 33).

XIII

Zechariah

'Through the prophesying of Haggai the prophet and Zechariah the son of Iddo' the Jews were inspired to rebuild the Temple (Ezra 6: 14). As the two prophets were contemporaries, what is written in the previous chapter on the historical background of Haggai applies also to the ministry of Zechariah. He began to prophesy 'in the eight month, in the second year of Darius', i.e. in October/November 520 B.C. (1: 1). That was one month before Haggai delivered his last oracle. The final messages of Zechariah are dated November/December 518 B.C. (7: 1). This means that whereas the oracles of Haggai were all delivered within four months, those of Zechariah cover a period of two years. Since the activity of the two prophets overlapped for one month only, most of the preaching of Zechariah followed that of Haggai. He was either the son or the grandson of Iddo, who is probably to be identified with the priest of that name who returned from exile with Zerubbabel (Nehemiah 12: 4). In which case, Zechariah was a priest as well as a prophet, and we have an additional reason for his concern for the immediate rebuilding of the Temple. We have already seen that it was at the instigation of Haggai that the people began the work of restoration, and he it was a month later who encouraged the workers to continue to build when their initial enthusiasm had waned. Then Zechariah began to preach, and by means of his visions and oracles gave impetus to a work already under way. He did not, like Haggai, offer the reward of material prosperity as an incentive for rebuilding the Temple, but endeavoured rather to rekindle hope and strengthen the hands of the people by announcing the advent of the messianic kingdom. This hope, which included a contemporary figure, Zerubbabel the governor, is the theme of the book.

The authentic prophecies of Zechariah are all to be found in chapters 1 to 8, and were probably collected and edited by a disciple soon after the time of their delivery. There are several weighty reasons for assigning the material in chapters 9 to 14 to different authors and a later age.[1] We are not now concerned with this latter part of the book commonly known as Second Zechariah.[2]

First Zechariah (chapters 1 to 8) stands at the beginning of the period of transition from prophecy to apocalyptic, and has some of the characteristics of the latter. The apocalyptic writers are largely concerned with 'the last things', with the consummation of history and the final victory of God. Likewise, the main preoccupation of Zechariah is with the establishment of the messianic kingdom. Another feature this prophecy has in common with apocalyptic is the use of picture language with a hidden meaning. While strange visions and fantastic symbolism are found earlier in Ezekiel, they are the outstanding characteristic of Zechariah. The secrets of God are revealed to the prophet in visions of the night. Their cryptic language and bizarre imagery imparts an atmosphere of mystery to the whole prophecy. The appearance of angelic mediators and interpreters is another feature common to Zechariah and the apocalyptic writers. Yet, in spite of these similarities, there is one fundamental difference between the visions of this prophet and those of the apocalyptists. Zechariah is concerned with history—with the Persian empire, with Zerubbabel the governor and Joshua the priest, with a kingdom to be established on earth at Jerusalem, with the activity of God in the present and the immediate future. This emphasis upon the activity of God in history and through human agents he shares with all the prophets.

THE EIGHT VISIONS AND THE MESSIANIC KINGDOM

Zechariah was inspired with the hope that God would establish at Jerusalem a kingdom, over which he would set his anointed one, the messiah-king of the house of David. This expectation that the messianic kingdom was about to be set up, a hope which included Zerubbabel the governor and Joshua the priest, is the clue to the interpretation of the eight visions, given to the prophet in a single night three months after his call (1: 7).

In the first vision, four angelic horsemen sent out by God to patrol the earth report that all is quiet. The widespread disturbances in various parts of the Persian dominion which had followed the accession of Darius I, had been interpreted by

[1] The reasons are given on page 242.   [2] See chapter xix of this book.

Haggai as a sign of the dawning of the messianic age. But the revolts had been suppressed and the fire of hope was dying down. In spite of the report of the horsemen, the prophet is assured through an angelic interpreter that the judgment of God upon the heathen will not be delayed indefinitely. For the Lord loves his people and will return to Jerusalem; the Temple will be rebuilt and the prosperity of Judah restored (1: 7–17).

In the Bible the horn of the ox is often used as a symbol of strength and aggression, and the four horns in the second vision represent the powerful nations hostile to Israel. The four smiths stand for the powers which God will employ to destroy those wicked nations as a prelude to the coming of his kingdom (1: 18–21).

The prophet then sees a young angel going forth to measure Jerusalem, with a view to rebuilding it in accordance with its former dimensions. He is intercepted by another angel, for his plans are too restricted. Jerusalem is to be rebuilt without walls, for in the new age her population will overflow the old limits, and God himself will be her defence (2: 1–5).

Joshua the high priest is then seen standing in the heavenly court, clothed in filthy rags, the symbol of mourning for acknowledged sin. He is accused by Satan, the adversary of mankind. The angel of the Lord who presides over the trial rebukes the accuser and dismisses the charge against Joshua. His filthy garments are then taken away and he is clothed in rich apparel. In this scene the high priest stands as the representative of the people who, having been saved from exile like 'a brand plucked from the fire', are now forgiven, cleansed, and accepted by God. Joshua is given authority over the Temple and its sacrificial worship and, if he is obedient, the privilege of free access with the heavenly beings into the presence of God. The restored priesthood is a sign that the messiah-king, 'my servant, the Branch' (cf. Isaiah 11: 1; Jeremiah 33: 15), is on the way (3: 1–10).

In the fifth vision (4: 1–5; 10b–14),[1] Zechariah sees a seven-branched candelabrum. 'The upper part of the lamp-stand was a bowl with a broad rim on which were seven lamps of clay or metal, each with seven protuberances ('lips') where wicks rested.'[2] On each side of this candelabrum stood two olive trees.

---

[1] The three sayings about Zerubbabel, verses 6b to 10a, are displaced, and are not part of the fifth vision.
[2] *The Jerusalem Bible*, 1533, footnote.

The lamp-stand with its forty-nine lights is a symbol of the omniscient God who is watchful over all the earth. The two olive trees are Zerubbabel and Joshua, the anointed servants of the Lord endowed with his authority. 'Zechariah thus sees—and this is unique in prophecy—the new Israel constituted as a dyarchy; the representative of the priestly office stands with equal rank next to the representative of the royal office.'[1]

The prophet now sees an immense scroll, on which a curse is written, flying over the land. This power-laden curse, entering the houses of liars and perjurers, destroys them (5: 1–4). Not only these social evils, but all sin is to be removed from the Holy Land in preparation for the coming of the kingdom.

In the seventh vision wickedness, personified as a woman sitting in a barrel, is carried out of Palestine and deposited in Babylon (5: 5–11).

The imagery of the last vision is like that of the first. Four chariots, drawn by horses of different colour, are sent out east, north, west, and south, to patrol the earth. The angelic horsemen symbolize the spirit of God whose power controls the nations. Attention is focussed on 'those who go toward the north country', the traditional home of Israel's enemies. There in Babylonia the spirit of God, his power in operation, executes judgment upon the enemy, and stirs up the exiles to return and rebuild the Temple (6: 1–8).

Through the picture language of these eight visions, significant truths about the coming and character of the kingdom of God were revealed to Zechariah. The purposeful activity of the all-seeing and all-powerful God in the affairs of men and nations is vigorously affirmed. It is revealed that, as a prelude to the last things, all the organized powers of evil will be crushed and moral evil and apostasy taken away. The new Jerusalem, surrounded with no walls except the walls of salvation, will contain a great multitude of people which no man can number. God in his mercy will forgive his sinful people. In the person of their representative, the high priest, they will be cleansed and accepted on the ground of God's loyal love. Zechariah foreshadows the great evangelical truth, proclaimed in the stories and deeds of the Lord Jesus and expounded in the letters of the apostle Paul, that we are justified by faith. Through him who was made to be sin for us our sins, our filthy rags, are taken away, and we are accepted by God and clothed in the robes of

[1] G. von Rad, *Old Testament Theology*, II, 287.

righteousness. Through Christ our great high priest we have access into the presence of God. Finally it is revealed that two men, one a priest and one a king, are to be used by God in the establishment of his kingdom. Joshua had already been anointed high priest. With gold and silver brought back by exiles returned from Babylon, the prophet was ordered to make a crown and place it on the head of Zerubbabel.[1] Between the Davidic king and the high priest there would be perfect cooperation and harmony (6: 9–14). The deferred hope of the prophet, focussed upon Joshua and Zerubbabel, was in the fullness of time realized in the anointed One, the Messiah, who combines the offices of priest and king. Through human agency, through 'the man Christ Jesus', the kingdom was established with power.

THE CHARACTER OF GOD

In this prophecy, the eternal God is revealed as transcendent, righteous, and omnipotent. During and after the exile there was an increasing awareness of the transcendence of God. Exalted above the earth, enthroned in the heavens, he was regarded as 'a God afar off', away beyond the reach of mankind. So great was the distance which separated him from sinful men, that not even the prophets were regarded as having direct access to him. He who had spoken directly to Amos and Jeremiah now communicates with Zechariah indirectly through the mediation of angels. These celestial beings, intermediaries between the transcendant God and his servant, are prominent in this prophecy. They act as messengers of God to the prophet, as interpreters of his visions, as reporters of the affairs on earth to God, as instruments of divine purpose in the heathen world, as intercessors for Israel, and as 'ministering spirits sent forth to serve, for the sake of those who are to obtain salvation' (Hebrews 1: 14). One of them, the Satan, the adversary, appears here for the first time in the Old Testament. As in a later book (Job 1: 6–12), this superhuman being is not represented *at this stage* as inherently evil, as the antagonist of God. Subject to God, he acts as the accuser of mankind, the prosecuting attorney at the heavenly court (3: 1, 2).

The transcendent God is also righteous, and requires righteousness of life from his people. Zechariah was commanded at the

[1] 6: 9–14. It is clear from verses 12–14 that the crown was intended for Zerubbabel the Branch. This was altered later to 'Joshua, the son of Jehozadak, the high priest'.

outset to call them to repentance. Judgment had come upon
their ancestors, because they had disregarded the persistent
warnings of 'the former prophets' and had refused to repent.
Taught by disaster, their descendants must not repeat that
mistake. 'Return to me, says the Lord of hosts, and I will return
to you' (1 : 1–6). It will be seen that Zechariah was not only concerned with the rebuilding of the Temple and the full restoration
of the sacrificial worship. Like the former prophets, he knows that
God will not accept rite and ceremony as a substitute for moral
obedience and right personal relationships. In November/Dec-
ember 518 B.C., a deputation from Bethel came to Jerusalem, to
enquire of the priests and prophets whether or not they should
continue to observe the fast commemorating the destruction of
the Temple—since it was now being rebuilt. In his reply
Zechariah widened the scope of the enquiry, and dealt with all
four fasts associated with the fall of Jerusalem. He declared that
the fasts of the people had been self-regarding, and were of no
value to God. What the Lord required was justice, kindness, and
mercy in personal relationships, concern and care for the needy
members of society, and a loving heart free of evil intentions. It
was because the former generation had disregarded these
ethical demands that they had been exiled and scattered among
the nations (7: 1–14). As for the four fasts, in the happy days
ahead when truth and justice, love and peace were enthroned,
they would all be transformed into joyful feasts (8: 14–19).

The transcendent and righteous God is also omnipotent,
supreme not only in heaven, but also upon earth, where he is
actively engaged in the furtherance and fulfilment of his purpose. What he has already decided in heaven, he will accomplish on earth—in spite of great obstacles, of the frailty of the
human agents, and of the seeming insignificance of their
achievements. Haggai and Zechariah did not believe that the
messianic kingdom would be established through mere human
effort or as the result of political rebellion against Persia. 'Not
by might, nor by power, but by my Spirit, says the Lord of
hosts.' Through the purposive activity and hidden power of
God, the great mountain of difficulty which confronted Zerubbabel would become a plain—the formidable task of rebuilding
the Temple would be carried through to completion and the top
stone would be laid with shouts of joy (4: 6–9). Because it was
smaller than its predecessor, the new Temple was not to be
despised, for with God size has nothing to do with significance,

and tiny beginnings may have a momentous outcome (4: 10; cf. Mark 4: 30–32). The people are to have confidence in the strategy and the methods, in the activity and the purpose of the all-powerful God.

Finally, he who is transcendent, righteous, and omnipotent, is the God of hope, who is working to fulfil his promises and to save and bless his people. He will return to Jerusalem and dwell within her. The inhabitants of the faithful city will live to a ripe old age and throngs of happy boys and girls will play in her streets. The dispersed exiles will all return to Zion and live henceforth in covenant relationship with their God (8: 1–8). The Gentiles also will come to Jerusalem to worship the Lord and to learn of him from the people made holy by his presence among them (8: 20–23). The blessings of the messianic age are summed up in the words which end the prophecy—'God is with you'. In the age of salvation the transcendent God would be immanent, dwelling in the midst of his people in the New Jerusalem.

XIV

Third Isaiah

Third Isaiah, the last part of the book of that name (chapters 56 to 66) is a miscellaneous collection of oracles. It contains the messages of a number of authors who were in the tradition of Second Isaiah, and lived in the period following the return from exile. Some scholars make no distinction between Second and Third Isaiah, and attribute all the material in chapters 40 to 66 to the anonymous prophet who preached to the exiles in Babylonia. It is true that some of the passages in Third Isaiah, (e.g. chapters 60 to 62) closely resemble the poems of Second Isaiah, and the two parts have several subjects in common (e.g. the return of all the exiles, the rebuilding of Jerusalem). But there are important differences. The background is no longer Babylonia but Palestine. There are allusions, not to Cyrus of Persia, but to native leaders. It is evident that some of the former exiles have returned, and the Temple has been rebuilt. The moral and religious conditions are like those presupposed in the books of Haggai and Zechariah. As to the date, several references to the Temple point to a time later than 516 B.C., when it was rebuilt (56: 7; 60: 7). On the other hand, it is implied that the walls of Jerusalem are still in ruins. They were rebuilt by Nehemiah in 444 B.C., and so the messages must be earlier than that date (58: 12; 60: 10). It is doubtful, however, if all the material in Third Isaiah is from one period or from one author. Yet while it is possible that a few oracles are exilic or pre-exilic, it is evident that most of them are the product of authors deeply influenced by the poems of Second Isaiah. The prophecy as a whole probably belongs to the period shortly after the time of Haggai and Zechariah.

It supplies valuable information about the conditions existing in Jerusalem and Judah towards the end of the sixth century. The Jewish community at that time was like a field of wheat and tares, and that is why in Third Isaiah there are both words of judgment and words of consolation. 'In the post-exilic period the division of the Jewish people into two different groups, the faithful and the apostates, became even more marked than before.'[1] There are 'the rebellious people, who walk in a way that is not good' and there are the pious faithful 'who tremble at' the word of the Lord (65: 2; 66: 5). The former group had failed to learn the hard lesson of the exile, and was condemned for its idolatry and immorality. In particular, the degenerate spiritual leaders, the prophets and the priests, are rebuked in language of extreme severity. They are blind watchmen and dumb dogs, indolent and greedy, shepherds who care for themselves and not for the flock, drunken and dissolute (56: 9–12). The people are idolatrous and licentious. They mock the faithful, participate in heathen fertility rites, practice child-sacrifice, and send envoys to the shrines of foreign gods (57: 3–13). No wonder the true God seems to be remote, and in response to their prayers does not intervene to save. 'Your iniquities have made a separation between you and your God, and your sins have hid his face from you so that he does not hear' (59: 1, 2). They are guilty of murder, lying, injustice, dishonesty and wicked schemes. 'Their feet run to evil, and they make haste to shed innocent blood; their thoughts are thoughts of iniquity, desolation and destruction are in their highways' (59: 3–7). Since no human champion can possibly overcome all these evils, God himself will intervene. Like a mighty warrior, he will put on righteousness as a breastplate, salvation as a helmet, vengeance for a garment, fury for a mantle (59: 15b–17). (See I Thessalonians 5: 8 and Ephesians 6: 10–17.) According to their deeds he will deal with his foes in Judah and in all the world, breaking forth in judgment upon them like a rushing stream driven by a strong wind (59: 18, 19).

'And he will come to Zion as Redeemer, to those in Jacob who turn from transgression, says the Lord' (59: 20). He comes to save as well as to judge. Messages of consolation are addressed to the faithful, who are despondent about the moral and religious condition of the community. The prophet who speaks in the passage best known to Christians is entrusted with a message of encouragement and hope. He announces that the Lord God has anointed him with the Spirit and appointed him to bring good news to the afflicted and healing to the broken-hearted. He has been sent to proclaim liberty to the captives, and to announce the Day of the Lord. His mission is to comfort all who

[1] J. Lindblom, *Prophecy in Ancient Israel*, 406.

mourn and to transform their sorrow into joy and praise (61: 1–3). The prophet-evangelist is conscious of his call and endowment to bring good news and healing to the despondent people who have returned from exile with high hopes which have not been realized. His mission is to give new strength and hope to those imprisoned within the distressing circumstances of the post-exilic period, by announcing the approach of God's day of salvation for the faithful, which is also a day of judgment for the oppressors. The first two verses of this passage were read by Jesus in the synagogue at Nazareth at the outset of his ministry. His comment on the reading was—'Today this scripture has been fulfilled in your hearing.' For him, the words of the prophet were a perfect description of the ministry he had come to fulfil (Luke 4: 16–21).

RELIGIOUS OBSERVANCES

Third Isaiah has valuable teaching on the Temple, fasting, the sabbath, and prayer. The post-exilic prophets believed that the Temple and its sacrificial worship was ordained by God. Haggai and Zechariah initiated and encouraged the movement to rebuild it. Haggai insisted that the prosperity of the community and the return of the Lord were related to the rebuilding of the Temple; and Malachi was zealous for the due performance and purity of its sacrificial worship. This emphasis upon Temple and cult is challenged by the prophet who speaks in Isaiah 66: 1, 2. 'Thus says the Lord: "Heaven is my throne and the earth is my footstool; what is the house which you would build for me, and what is the place of my rest?" ' The God who created all things and who fills the universe, cannot be localized or contained in a building erected by men. He whose throne is in the heavens and whose footstool is the whole earth, requires no temple. He looks to the man who is aware of his own unworthiness and who waits with reverence and expectation for the divine word (66: 2). In his marvellous grace, the transcendent God, 'the high and lofty One who inhabits eternity' who dwells 'in the high and holy place', is also present with the man 'who is of a contrite and humble spirit' (57: 15). 'For the disciples of Second Isaiah, the emphasis on the importance of getting the Temple rebuilt is misplaced. God wants the inner reform which goes with the humble spirit.'[1] In the verses which follow, the offering of corrupt sacrifices is condemned (66: 3).

[1] G. E. Wright, Isaiah, 157.

It is not the Temple, but exaggerated emphasis on its importance, it is not sacrifices as such, but the substitution of these for
obedience (66: 4) that the prophet opposes and condemns.

This same attitude is found in another passage, in which the
fasts of the people are criticized. In addition to the Day of
Atonement, four fasts commemorating the fall of Jerusalem
were observed during and after the exile (Zechariah 8: 19).
Aware that God takes no notice of their fasts, the people ask why
they should continue them. The prophet replies that their fasts
are made ineffectual by immoral conduct and callous indifference to the needs of others. The fast days are profaned, because
on these days they pursue their own business, oppress their
workers, quarrel and fight. The mere external acts of bowing
down like a rush or spreading sackcloth and ashes are futile.
The fast God chooses is to let all the oppressed go free, and to
care for the hungry and the naked, the poor and the defenceless;
to put away contempt and slander and to have compassion on
those in need. Such a fast would bring rich rewards—light,
healing, answers to prayer, the presence and guidance of God,
inner spiritual sustenance, and the outward restoration of Jerusalem (58: 1–12). In his demand for social righteousness and
loving kindness, the prophet is not rejecting outward observances in principle. He is insisting that ritual fasting is unacceptable to God if divorced from 'true fasting'—righteousness and
helpfulness, kindness and charity.

Along with fasting, the observance of the Sabbath received
new emphasis during the exile and is the subject of the next
paragraph. The Sabbath is God's day, not to be desecrated by
business, pleasure seeking, or idle talk, but to be received as
honourable, joyful, and holy. It was probably during the exile
that the synagogue with its services came into being, and the
day of rest affords the opportunity to 'take delight in the Lord'
(58: 13, 14). Not only Jews, but also proselytes who keep the
Sabbath, will be made joyful in the house of prayer, which is
for all nations (56: 1–8). The observance of the weekly day of
rest, which became the mark of the true Israelite exiled in a
heathen land, is not a matter of trivial importance; for it is
those who keep holy the special time who are thereby enabled
to be devoted to the Lord and to walk in his ways all the time.

Great importance is also attached in this prophecy to the
habit of prayer, which is efficacious in the context of charity
(58: 9). If the prayers of the people go unanswered, it is not

because God is deaf, but because the petitioners are separated from him by disobedience (59: 1, 2). God is far more ready to hear than we to pray, and waits eagerly to be found by those who do not seek him (65: 1, 2). Third Isaiah contains prayers of confession and penitence, of intercession and praise, and several of the poems are liturgical in form. Like the eucharistic prayers of the Christian Church, one of these is a thankful recital, a solemn commemoration of the saving deeds of the Lord in the history of his people. 'In all their affliction he was afflicted, and the angel of his presence saved them.' Addressing God as 'Our Father', the climax of this sublime prayer is an urgent appeal that the Redeemer God of the past will reveal himself afresh to his people in the present (63: 7 to 64: 12).

The emphasis placed in this prophecy on humility and penitence, obedience and charity, reverence and prayer, should not be set in false antithesis to external observances. 'The Bible does not recognize our distinction between the outward and the inward ... the "heart" in the biblical sense is not the inner life, but the whole man in relation to God.'[1] The prophets were closely associated with the cult they criticized, and were not the advocates of a 'purely spiritual' religion. Temple and sacrifice, ritual fasting and Sabbath observance can be valuable and even necessary ways of expressing devotion to God. They were instituted to be channels of his grace. But the disciples of Second Isaiah, like their predecessors the great prophets, give priority to a reverent and humble walk with God and to justice and loyal love to men.

THE NEW JERUSALEM

The prophet whose words were read and appropriated by Jesus, announces that he is empowered by the Spirit and sent by God to proclaim the coming of the day of salvation and vindication (61: 1, 2). He is determined that he will not cease to preach and to pray until the promise of salvation is fulfilled. 'For Zion's sake I will not keep silent, and for Jerusalem's sake I will not rest, until her vindication goes forth as brightness, and her salvation as a burning torch' (62: 1). All God's watchmen, the prophets, are to pray without ceasing for the coming of the Day of the Lord (62: 6, 7). The fervent desire of their hearts finds expression in a prayer for the advent of God and the manifestation of his glory to all nations. 'O that thou wouldest rend the

[1] D. Bonhoeffer, *Letters and Papers from Prison.*

heavens and come down . . . that the nations might tremble at thy presence' (64: 1, 2).

This self-manifestation of God, the dawning of his glory, is like the rising of the sun upon Jerusalem. 'The Lord will arise upon you, and his glory will be seen upon you.' The surrounding world lies in thick darkness, but God sheds forth his light upon Zion, who is commanded to rise and reflect it (60: 1, 2). On that day, there will be no need of sun or moon, for the Lord himself will be the everlasting light of his people (60: 19). This glorious and abiding manifestation of God will transfigure the old Jerusalem, making all things new. Both the outward and the inward life of the community will be transformed. Surpassing Solomon's Jerusalem in splendour, her walls will be called Salvation and her gates Praise, and the violence and destruction of former days will give way to perpetual security and peace (60: 17, 18). The city will be given a new name, i.e. the character of the community will be changed, and the people will be called 'The holy people, the redeemed of the Lord' (62: 2, 12).

From all parts of the Diaspora, the exiles will be drawn back to this holy city. When mother Zion sees her scattered children gathering together, and returning to her from afar, she will be radiant with joy (60: 4, 5). The nations will expedite their triumphant return to Zion (66: 18–20). So also, when they hear of her splendour, the Gentiles and their kings from all parts of the world will stream to the holy city (60: 3). They will not come empty-handed, but will bring the wealth of the earth with them (60: 5). The ships of the Mediterranean will bring, not only exiles, but also silver and gold, and the gates of Jerusalem will be open continually for the wealth of the nations to be brought into her (60: 8, 9, 11). From Arabia camels will bear treasures, gold and frankincense, for the worship of the Temple, and flocks will come up to offer themselves for the altar (60: 6, 7). From the forests of Lebanon precious wood will be brought to beautify the sanctuary (60: 13). The Gentiles will serve the citizens of the New Jerusalem who are destined to be a priesthood in the world, declaring God's word, interceding for mankind (60: 10, 14; 61: 5, 6). The new community will have a new environment. Here, as elsewhere in the prophets, nature is transformed at the advent of the Lord. 'For behold, I create new heavens and a new earth' (65: 17). 'The meaning is not that the present world will be completely destroyed and a new world created, but rather that the present world will be completely transformed.'[1]

Yet there is darkness as well as light in the prophetic portrait of the future. The year of the Lord's favour is also the day of vengeance (61 : 2). He who announces vindication and is mighty to save, is seen returning from Edom,[2] the symbol of a world hostile to God. Like one who has trod a winepress, his garments are red with the blood of his enemies. The Day of the Lord is the day of universal judgment, the day of the manifestation of his holy indignation, the day of his unaided victory over all sin (63: 1–6). There is another terrible picture of the judgment in the last verse of the book. The Valley of Hinnom (Gehenna) to the south of Jerusalem, the refuse-dump of the city, was a foul place where worms bred on the carcases and the fires smouldered perpetually. It became a symbol of the realm of punishment and final ruin (66: 24; Mark 9: 43–48).

The portrayal of the New Jerusalem in this prophecy raises some basic questions. Is the language to be understood literally or symbolically? Is the New Jerusalem material or spiritual? Is it to be established here on earth or is this a picture of heaven? The disciples of Second Isaiah were not conscious of these contrasts. 'There is no more tiresome error in the history of thought than to try to sort our ancestors on to this or that side of a distinction which was not in their minds at all.'[3] The language is both literal and metaphorical, the New Jerusalem is both material and spiritual. The new order is to be established on earth—yet upon the earth transformed by the presence and power of God. Having in mind *our* distinction between this world and the world to come, it would be an oversimplification to regard the prophetic vision as applicable to the latter only. 'May we not look forward to a city of God on earth, in which the will of God will be done? This is the hope which Christian men have always kept before their eyes. It has been the inspiration of all effort for social welfare, of all sacrifices in the cause of liberty, justice, right government.'[4] We are to hope, pray, and work for the coming of the kingdom of God on earth.

On the other hand, the New Jerusalem is the symbol of a reality which transcends history, of a community which is eternal, of a new age beyond the end of this world. Some of

[1] J. Muilenburg, *The Interpreter's Bible*, Vol. V, 755.
[2] See page 213.   [3] C. S. Lewis.
[4] E. F. Scott, *The Book of Revelation*, 96.

those things which no human eye has seen are revealed to us by the Spirit in this vision of the New Jerusalem. It is the city of the epiphany, the sphere of the self-manifestation of God. Here God is present, and, bringing their choicest gifts, men worship him whose glory transforms all things. It is the holy city; the hearts of its citizens have been renewed and evil has no place within it. The holy community is also catholic; men of all nations, drawn by the glory of God, enter through the ever-open gates. It is a realm of beauty, joy, and love. 'You shall be a crown of beauty in the hand of the Lord . . . and as the bride-groom rejoices over the bride, so shall your God rejoice over you' (62: 3, 5). It has stability and permanence; the city, like God, is eternal. 'For as the new heaven and the new earth which I will make shall remain before me, says the Lord; so shall your descendants and your name remain' (66: 22).

XV

Obadiah

Obadiah, the shortest book in the Old Testament, is a prophecy directed against Edom, the neighbour of Judah to the south-east. The Edomites, whose reputed ancestor was Esau, occupied the territory south of the Dead Sea and north of the Gulf of Aqabah, bounded on the west by the depression of the Arabah and on the east by the Arabian Desert. In the central region, extending about seventy miles from north to south and fifteen from east to west, the Edomite plateau is well over 5,000 feet above sea level, and is divided into two unequal parts. Bozrah in the smaller northern region, and Sela in the higher southern region, were ancient strongholds. In the Bible, Edom is also known as Mount Seir, the name of its chief mountain range (e.g. Ezekiel 35: 1–9), and as Mount Esau, after the ancestor of the Edomites (9). The word *Edom* means 'the red region', and has reference to the colour of the rocks and the soil. It was the land of mystery, 'the wide areas of sandstone creating a bizarre world of dark, gigantic cliffs, and deep, terrifying gorges'. The Edomites 'could not hope to get their wealth by farming ... but, like the Phoenicians, they were taught by the stern land in which they lived to find their fortune in trade'.[1] The Red Sea port of Ezion-geber lay to the south, and the iron and copper mines of the Arabah to the west. Camels laden with the products of Arabia and Africa passed along 'the King's Highway' (Numbers 20: 17) which traversed the land from south to north. 'This trade brought them into contact with the almost legendary world of the East, which other people knew only by hearsay, and so they acquired among the Israelites a reputation for wisdom and strange knowledge.'[2] (See 8; Jeremiah 49: 7.)

There was bitter hostility of long standing between Esau and Jacob, Edom and Israel. After the Exodus, the king of Edom had churlishly refused to allow Moses to lead the Hebrews through his territory (Numbers 20: 14–21). Conquered by

[1] Denis Baly, *The Geography of the Bible*, 241, 245.　　[2] Ibid., 245.

David, the Edomites continued in subjection to Solomon and his successors, but revolted during the reign of Joram. Although reconquered by Amaziah and Uzziah of Judah, Edom quickly regained her independence. Later on the Edomites took mean advantage of the Babylonian conquest of Judea. When Jerusalem was besieged by the army of Nebuchadrezzar, they sided with the enemies of Judah. A psalmist remembered with bitterness how they egged on the Chaldean soldiers to make a thorough job of destroying the holy city. 'Raze it, raze it! Down to its foundations!' (Psalm 137: 7). They raided the country and annexed Judean territory. They gloated over the tragic misfortune of God's people, plundered their goods, cut off the fugitives or handed them back to the enemy (10–14). This violation of the ties of kinship (Esau and Jacob were brothers) was bitterly resented and never forgotten by patriotic Judeans.

During and after the exile, the Edomites were subjected to a series of raids, and to growing pressure from the Nabateans, an Arab tribe from the desert to the south-east. In response to this pressure, Edomite refugees occupied the southern region of Judea which, after them, came to be known as Idumea. By the fourth century B.C., whether by armed conflict or by gradual infiltration, the Nabateans had occupied the whole territory of Edom (7). They built their capital city, Petra, round an ancient Edomite settlement, probably Sela, a name which like Petra means 'rock' (3). This place is visited now by large numbers of tourists in the Kingdom of Jordan. Ascending the Wadi Musa on horseback, and passing through the narrow gorge called the Siq, the visitor to his astonishment finds himself in a plain surrounded by massive cliffs. Among the wonders to be seen are the ruins of temples, a Roman basilica and theatre, and many finely-carved monuments hewn out of the rock.

The prophecy of Obadiah is dated some time after the fall of Jerusalem in 587 B.C. and before the Nabatean conquest of Edom. Obadiah interprets the Arab raids which have taken place and the final conquest still to come, as the judgment of God upon Edom for her despicable treatment of Judah at the time of the Babylonian conquest (1–14). The second part of the book, assigned by some scholars to a later period, has reference to the *ultimate* fate of Edom and other heathen nations on 'the day of the Lord' (15–21). Some verses of the oracle against Edom in the book of Jeremiah (49: 7–22) bear a close resemblance to the words used in Obadiah (1–9). While it is possible that both prophets made use of an earlier prophecy against Edom, it is more likely that the oracle in Jeremiah is later than the time of that prophet, and is dependent upon the original in Obadiah (1–9). Beyond the fact that he was a patriotic Judean moved with indignation against Edom, nothing is otherwise known about Obadiah himself. His name means 'servant of the Lord'.

THE LAW OF RETRIBUTION

The subject of this little book is the just judgment of God, who does not overlook the wrongs done by evil men or nations, but visits them with retribution. First, the prophet speaks of God's judgment upon arrogance. He hears a report that a human messenger has gone forth to stir up the nations against Edom. In the formation of this military alliance, Obadiah sees the Lord of history at work. His purpose, which he is determined to carry out, is to humiliate the sinful nation. But Edom is defiant. He believes that his mountain fortress is inaccessible, his strongholds secure, his capital Sela, surrounded by high cliffs, invincible. Yet Esau is but self-deceived. True, he lives on high where the eagle builds its nest; but even if he could soar as high as the eagle and build his dwelling in the sky, God would bring him down (1–4). Obadiah, in common with other Hebrew prophets, declared the judgment of God upon human arrogance and self-sufficiency.[1] 'Pride goes before destruction, and a haughty spirit before a fall' (Proverbs 16: 18). Jesus quoted a number of times what may have been a popular proverb. 'Whoever exalts himself will be humbled.' In the moral order, humiliation follows arrogance as night follows day, for 'God opposes the proud, but gives grace to the humble' (I Peter 5: 5).

The law of retribution is clearly stated at the conclusion of the next and principal oracle of the book. 'As you have done, it shall be done to you, your deeds shall return on your own head' (15). What Edom had done is outlined in verses 10–14; what would be done to Edom is described in verses 5–9. When the Babylonians captured Jerusalem in 587 B.C., the conduct of the Edomites was heartless, cruel, and treacherous. By standing aloof in the hour of Judah's need, they violated the ties of kinship. 'On that day' they gloated over the sufferings of God's people, and shared in the looting; they cut off the fugitives or handed them over to slavery. What they did then would now in

[1] See pages 77, 81, 104, 119, 164–165.

turn be done to them. Robbers by night do not steal everything, and grape-gatherers leave some gleanings—but the destruction of Edom, already begun, would be complete. As Esau had despoiled his brother Jacob, annexing his territory, so with poetic justice, the Edomites would be dispossessed ('driven . . . to the border') by their former friends and confederates, the Nabatean Arabs. Her wise men and her warriors would alike be destroyed. The Bible provides many illustrations, positive and negative, of the principle, 'as you have done, it shall be done to you'. Ruth showed great kindness to Naomi, and later on at Bethlehem was the recipient of great kindness from Boaz (Ruth 2: 8–13). Jacob deceived his father Isaac, and was himself deceived by his own sons (Genesis 27: 1–29; 37: 29–36). Haman erected a gallows for Mordecai, and was himself hanged upon the gallows he had erected (Esther 7: 9, 10). For good or ill, life gives back what we put into it; as we treat others, so they will treat us. The principle, which applies to nations as well as to individuals, has an important qualification. No farmer ever reaps immediately after sowing; the despicable deed of Edom did not return *at once* upon his own head. The judgments of God in history are manifested only in the long run.

The book ends with a description of the Day of the Lord, of the *ultimate* judgment upon Edom and all the heathen nations. Judah has already experienced the judgment of the Lord at the hand of the Chaldeans; the time was near when the other nations would also drink the cup of his indignation. The Jews who escaped that judgment, the remnant, would dwell without fear on Mount Zion, and would dispossess their dispossessors. Israel and Judah would then combine to destroy Edom as a flame destroys stubble, and all the territory lost in the Holy Land would be regained. Led by Saviours, Israel would gain the victory over Edom and the kingdom of God would be established (15–21). This insight was taken up by the Apostle Paul. On the Day of the Lord there would be a complete reversal of fortunes; things would be turned upside down—or rather, the right way up. The oppressors of this age would be punished in the age to come, and those who were now oppressed would find rest and security (II Thessalonians 1: 5–10).

The message of Obadiah as a whole is a corrective both to the sentimentality and to the individualism of this present age. Like Nahum, who is also concerned with a foreign nation, Obadiah reveals the severity rather than the kindness of the Lord, the austere God of indignation and retribution rather than the gracious God of compassion and salvation. This insight is necessary if the popular but distorted image of the divine love, which ignores the elements of demand and judgment, is to be corrected. Furthermore, since the message of Obadiah has to do with communities, races, nations, it is a valuable complement to our modern tendency to think of the dealings of the Lord with men too exclusively in terms of the individual. In a hidden manner, God is at work in history, and no nation—however strong and secure—can escape his judgment. It is through the instrumentality of other nations that the law of retribution operates. That is how we today might express it, but Obadiah did not think in such an abstract and impersonal manner. He saw the hand of the living God in the rise and fall of nations. It was the purpose of 'the Judge of all the earth' at work in history, not only to deliver a purified remnant, but also to establish his rule over all nations. 'The kingdom shall be the Lord's' (21).

XVI

Malachi

Prophet and priest unite in the person of Malachi. It was once the fashion to contrast prophecy and cult, and to represent Amos, Hosea, Micah, Isaiah, and Jeremiah as hostile to the latter. The prophets of the Persian period did not thus interpret the message of their predecessors. Haggai and Zechariah were zealous for the rebuilding of the Temple and Malachi for the offering of unblemished sacrifices upon its altar. While the ethical teaching of the former prophets is not absent from this prophecy, Malachi is predominantly concerned with the Temple and with the maintenance and quality of its worship. He is a prophet in the service of the Temple.

It is a distinctive feature of this prophecy that the six oracles are cast in the form of a conversation with question and answer. These dialogues may well be the literary counterpart of the verbal arguments between the prophet and his opponents. It was an approach well suited to the rationalism and scepticism of the age.

Malachi is not a personal name; taken from chapter 3, verse 1, the Hebrew word means 'my messenger'. It is convenient to use it as a designation for the anonymous author about whom, apart from these oracles, nothing is known. His ministry cannot be accurately dated. It is implied that Judah has a Persian governor (1 : 8), that the Temple has been rebuilt, and that the cult has been restored—long enough for the priests to be thoroughly bored with it. Some of the men of Judah have married foreign women. Nehemiah dealt with this problem of mixed marriages when he became governor of Jerusalem for the second time. Malachi belongs to the period between the rebuilding of the Temple (516 B.C.) and the governorship of Nehemiah (444 B.C.) The latter part of that period, about 450 B.C., is the more likely date. It was a time of discouragement and disillusionment. The hopes kindled by the fall of Babylon and the return from exile had not been realized. The number of

returned exiles was small and the Jewish community was confined to Jerusalem and its immediate environs. The soil was
unproductive, the rainfall scanty and unreliable, the harvests
poor. In addition to many human adversaries, the people had
to contend with swarms of locusts and blight, with drought and
famine. The enthusiasm and hope engendered by the return
from exile had been followed by depression and despair. Many
became sceptical and cynical, and even the pious were bewil-
dered and tempted to doubt. There was a growth of rationalism
and a tendency to question the traditional dogmas. Some of
these questions and doubts the prophet records. 'How hast thou
loved us?' (1:2). 'Where is the God of justice?' (2:17). 'It is vain
to serve God. What is the good of our keeping his charge?' (3:14).
To these related questions, the prophet gives three answers.

First, he answers those who question the love of God for
Israel. Does not the miserable plight of the community disprove
the prophetic doctrine that Israel is an elect race, the special
object of God's love? In reply, the prophet draws attention to a
disaster which has recently befallen Edom, Judah's neighbour
to the south-east. The ancestors of Israel and Edom, Jacob and
Esau, were twin brothers. Yet in spite of the close racial affinity,
the Edomites had gloated over the destruction of Jerusalem by
the Chaldeans in 587 B.C., and had taken advantage of the
collapse of Judah to annex some of her territory. Shortly before
the ministry of Malachi, the Edomites had been invaded by the
Nabatean Arabs, who in the course of time were destined to
dispossess them of their land. Like Obadiah,[1] Malachi interprets the Nabatean invasion as a divine judgment upon Edom
for her treachery and inhumanity, and as a proof that the Lord
does care for the people he has chosen (1:2–5).

Secondly, Malachi answers those who have made the hardships and disappointments of the time a reason for calling into
question the justice of God. He says that in some ways the priests
and the people are simply getting what they deserve. The careless priests are insulting God with blemished sacrifices and, by
neglecting to teach the Law, are failing to enlighten and guide
the people. The mean laymen are selecting inferior animals for
the altar and withholding the full payment of tithes for the maintenance of the ministry. Faithful wives are divorced, labourers
are defrauded, widows and orphans are oppressed. How can
people, guilty of these gross sins of omission and commission,

[1] See page 212.

complain that they are not being dealt with by God in strict accordance with their deserts (2: 2, 9, 12, 13, 14; 3: 9)?

Thirdly, in his teaching on the Day of the Lord, the prophet has a message for the sceptics who deny God's justice and for the faithful who are tempted to question his love. God is coming to right the wrongs of this present age. He will send a messenger in advance to prepare his way by purifying the Temple and the priesthood. Then, when his own house has been set in order (cf. I Peter 4: 17), God the Judge will come suddenly and rid the land of evil-doers. The sins listed by the prophet, which merit the swift judgment of God, are mostly social evils, and include the oppression of the weak and helpless. Malachi was not only concerned with ritual offences, but also with man's inhumanity to man (3: 1–5).

Meanwhile, those who fear the Lord are not forgotten, even if the wicked do seem to prosper, and prayer goes unanswered and piety unrewarded. For God has in heaven a book of remembrance in which the names and deeds of the righteous are recorded, and on the day of his coming he will separate them from the wicked and take them as his own treasured possession. To the wicked, that day will be like a raging destructive fire, but to the faithful it will be like the rising of the sun with its healing, life-giving rays (3: 13 to 4: 3). For Christians, the rising sun is the symbol of Christ the true 'Sun of Righteousness', who by his advent and epiphany has brought illumination and healing to all who revere him.

Malachi's portrait of the Day of the Lord includes a feature not found in any of the other prophets.[1] In order to prepare people for his coming, a messenger will be sent in advance of the Lord. For Malachi himself, the forerunner was an angel of the Lord, but later on, a scribe who wrote the appendix to the Book of the Twelve (4: 4, 5), identified the messenger with Elijah the prophet. Commenting on this later scribal interpretation, Jesus identified Elijah the forerunner with John the Baptist (Matthew 17: 9–13). 'The spirit and the power of Elijah' (Luke 1: 17) rested upon John, and by preaching and baptizing he prepared the way for the mission of Jesus Christ.

Malachi, in his attempt to 'justify the ways of God to men',[2] provides three valuable insights for the guidance of all those who

---

[1] For the preparation of the *way*, as distinct from the preparation of the *people* of the Lord, see Isaiah 40: 3.

[2] John Milton, *Paradise Lost*, Book I.

are perplexed by the injustices of this life. Even within the limits of observed or recorded events, we can often see the operation of the principle of retribution in the lives of men and nations. In the long-run the wicked nation (Edom) does not escape judgment, and it is not true to the observed facts to say 'everyone who does evil is good in the sight of the Lord, and he delights in them' (2: 17). That men often do *not* get what they deserve in this life does not cancel out the truth that men often do get what they deserve in this life. Because of the danger of over-simplification and misapplication, we must not deny the large element of truth in Malachi's second answer. *Some* of the suffering in human life is manifestly due to the sin of society, and we may ourselves be to blame for the very disappointments and frustrations of which we complain. Lastly, only on the Day of the Lord will justice be fully done and be seen to be done. The present life does not make sense, unless we look beyond it to the life of the world to come. Although Malachi looked for the dawning of the Day of the Lord on this earth, yet in his conception of 'the book of life' in which the names of the faithful are indelibly written, he foreshadows the Christian hope of eternal life.

UNACCEPTABLE WORSHIP

The longest oracle of the book (1: 6 to 2: 9) is a denunciation of the priests, the ministers of God appointed to offer sacrifice and to interpret his will to men. Honour is due to a father from his son, respect to a master from his servant, but the priests have witheld both alike from God. The law required that the animal victims offered to God in sacrifice should be without blemish (Leviticus 22: 20–22; Deuteromony 15: 21; 17: 1). Only the best was to be offered. But the priests were accepting from the people and presenting to God blind, lame, and sick animals. By their casual and careless performance of the ritual, they were despising the altar-table and showing contempt for God. They would not dare to insult the Persian governor by offering to him such cheap, second-rate gifts. How then, by such gifts can they hope to secure the favour of God? Far better shut the doors of the Temple altogether, than to continue to insult the Lord with such shabby gifts! Better the sincere worship offered in all parts of the world by the heathen, than this insulting parody offered by the priests at Jerusalem. They show their contempt for God by regarding the service of his sanctuary as a dull and boring routine. The curse of God will fall upon any layman who discharges a vow by offering a blemished victim; and, unless they mend their ways, upon the priests who encourage such practices. He will take away all their blessings and benefits and they will be utterly degraded and rejected.

This warning has been given because of the covenant made by God with their ancestor Levi and his tribe. According to that solemn agreement, God gave to the Levites, the priestly tribe, life and peace, and they in turn were put under obligation to serve him with reverence and awe. In former times, the priests had faithfully discharged these obligations. Men of integrity, they had given true instruction and direction to the people, and had thereby saved many from committing acts of sin. For a priest is called to be a teacher of the people, a messenger of the Lord of hosts. Unlike these faithful priests of a former generation, the contemporaries of Malachi have led many astray by their false teaching and have destroyed the covenant of Levi. Guilty of partiality, they will become objects of universal contempt (2: 1–9).

The words of Malachi to the Levitical priesthood apply to the 'royal priesthood', the Christian Church, and to all those within it who have been ordained to the sacred ministry. God requires unblemished offerings. He is worthy of the best that we can give. We have been 'built into a spiritual house, to be a holy priesthood, to offer spiritual sacrifices acceptable to God through Jesus Christ' (I Peter 2: 5). What about our blemished spiritual sacrifices—sentimental, subjective hymns badly sung; listless, half-hearted praise; insincere, rambling prayers; gifts which cost us little or nothing; poor sermons and formal sacraments; the outward performance of rites and ceremonies with coldness of heart, wanderings of mind, and weariness of spirit? 'Not for our sins alone, thy mercy, Lord, we sue; let fall thy pitying glance, on our devotions too.'[1] We are not called to penitence for our imperfect, but for our blemished spiritual sacrifices. The best we can offer to God is always imperfect, but if it is our best, it will be acceptable to God through the one and only perfect sacrifice of Jesus Christ.

It is also of great significance that, according to Malachi, the *primary* function of a priest is to be 'the messenger of the Lord of hosts'. An ancient description of the dual task of the Levitical priesthood puts the teaching of the word of God before the offering of sacrifice. 'They shall teach Jacob thy ordinances,

[1] From the hymn by Henry Twells.

and Israel thy law; they shall put incense before thee, and whole burnt offering upon thy altar' (Deuteronomy 33: 10). Nothing could show more clearly the error of creating a false antithesis between prophet and priest in the Old Testament, for both alike, in different ways, are servants of the word. Under the New Covenant, those who are appointed to lead the People of God in offering the spiritual sacrifices of praise and prayer must give priority to the ministry of the word, for they are messengers of the Lord of hosts. Bunyan's description of the Christian Minister in *Pilgrim's Progress* owes something to Malachi's portrait of the ideal priest. 'Christian saw the picture of a very grave person hung up against the wall; and this was the fashion of it. It had eyes lifted up to heaven, the best of books in his hand, the law of truth was written upon his lips, the world was behind his back. It stood as if it pleaded with men.'

FOUR NOTABLE INSIGHTS

In the course of his denunciation of two contemporary sins, Malachi sets forth four cardinal truths which anticipate the teaching and mind of Christ. The first of these sins is the subject of the third oracle (2: 10–16). Some of the men of Judah were breaking covenant, disregarding solemn obligations. Many foreigners had settled in Palestine during and after the exile, and the existence of this mixed population constituted a serious threat to the integrity of the Jewish community. Some of the men had put away their Jewish wives and had married foreign women. Such were guilty of violating the covenant which bound Israel to God. 'Have we not all one father? Has not one God created us? Why then are we faithless to one another, profaning the covenant of our fathers?' Having in God a common Father and Creator, the members of the covenant community were brothers and sisters in one family. Marriages between men of the Jewish faith and women who were worshippers of foreign gods, were a treacherous breach of the covenant relationship. The very presence of the heathen women in Jerusalem and its environs was a profanation of the sanctuary (2: 10–12). When the prophet asks 'have we not all one father?', he is referring to the Jewish community. It cannot therefore be maintained that he is here affirming 'the brotherhood of man' under 'the Fatherhood of God'. Yet, freed by Christ from this limitation to Israel, this insight of the prophet continues to influence and disturb men and nations. All men have been created by one God and through faith in Jesus Christ all men can become sons of one Father. For this reason we are under obligation to live and deal with all men in loyal love.

The prophet goes on to say that these men of Judah who have broken covenant with the Lord and with one another, have also violated the covenant of marriage. Divorce is treachery to the wife who is put away; it is an act of disloyalty, a callous disregard of the obligations freely accepted. Witnessed by God, the marriage covenant between a man and the wife of his youth is not to be set aside for frivolous or selfish reasons. Just because her husband is attracted by some young foreign girl, a wife married in youth, who has fulfilled God's purpose by bearing children, is not to be set aside because she has grown old. For God hates divorce and the cruelty involved ('covering one's garment with violence'), and requires fidelity of all his people (2: 13–16). In his hatred of cruelty, his sympathy for woman, his insight into the purpose of God, Malachi anticipated the teaching of Christ on marriage and divorce. While it was permitted in the Mosaic law (Deuteronomy 24: 1–4), Jesus taught that divorce was a concession to human weakness and sinfulness. 'From the beginning of creation' when God instituted marriage, he intended the relationship of one man and one woman to be permanent, the union of the two to be indissoluble. 'What therefore God has joined together, let no man put asunder' (Mark 10: 2–12).

In his condemnation of the sin of meanness, Malachi also enunciates two truths of fundamental importance. In the fifth oracle (3: 6–12) he contrasts the faithful God with Israel, who is and always has been faithless. He then calls upon the people to repent of the sin of robbing God by witholding, wholly or in part, the payment of the tithes required by the law for the support of the Temple priesthood (Numbers 18: 21). The people, no doubt, made the hardness of the times an excuse for this laxness, but the prophet interprets it as the outward sign of an inner contempt for God. Like Haggai, he believes that there is a relationship between this failure to give priority to God and the economic plight of the community. If they will but obey the law and discharge in full all their debts to God, he in turn will send down the blessing of abundant rain, forbid the locusts ('the devourer') to destroy the vegetation, and cause the earth to bring forth abundantly. The principle that we reap what we sow, that those who in meanness withhold what they should give are themselves thereby inevitably impoverished, and that those who give abundantly are themselves thereby inevitably enriched, finds expression in Hebrew wisdom (Proverbs 11: 24, 25) and in the teaching of Christ (Matthew 7: 2) and the apostle Paul (II Corinthians 9: 6). As Christians we do not have laws about giving, but guiding principles. We are to give every Lord's Day in proportion to our income—to maintain the Christian ministry, to relieve the needs of others, to advance the mission of the Church in the world—out of sheer gratitude for the gift which is beyond words, Jesus Christ.

In condemning the meanness of the priests, Malachi sounds the note of universalism in a manner almost without precedent in the Old Testament (1: 11). In God's name, the prophet makes a contrast: although the worship offered at the Jewish Temple in Jerusalem, where careless priests present blemished victims, is unacceptable to God, yet 'in every place' the Gentiles are honouring him with incense and a 'pure offering'. Ancient commentators usually read this statement as a prediction (cf. A.V. 'my name *shall be* great among the Gentiles') fulfilled or to be fulfilled in the world-wide worship of the Christian Church, especially in the eucharistic sacrifice (e.g. The Didache 14: 2, 3). But Malachi is referring to the contemporary situation. Some scholars maintain that the prophet is speaking of the worship of the Jewish dispersion; but that worship was neither world-wide ('from the rising of the sun to its setting') nor sacrificial. At the time of Malachi, the cult of the supreme God, 'the God of heaven', was widespread throughout the Persian empire. The prophet is referring to the sacrificial worship offered in all parts of the world by the heathen. All sincere and noble worship, in whatever name, to whatever god it is offered, is really worship of the one true God, and is accepted as such by him. (See also Acts 10: 34, 35.) This truth, that men may be worshipping 'the only true God' even when they do not know his name, has far-reaching implications. It should not be regarded as a contradiction of the complementary truth that worship is acceptable to God only through Jesus Christ. For 'all that is noble in the non-Christian systems of thought, or conduct, or worship is the work of Christ upon them and within them',[1] and the worship of men, whether offered B.C. or A.D., is acceptable to God only in view of the sacrifice of Christ the Saviour of the world.

[1] W. Temple, *Readings in St. John's Gospel*, 10.

XVII

Joel

The Book of Joel belongs to the period of transition from prophecy to apocalyptic. The best examples in the Bible of the latter type of literature are the Books of Daniel and Revelation. Although the former is placed in our English Bible between Ezekiel and the Twelve Prophets, in the Hebrew Bible it is included in the third and last division of the Old Testament known as the Hagiographa or Writings. For Daniel is not prophecy, it is apocalyptic. By reference to that example of fully developed apocalyptic literature, it will be seen that the book of Joel has some of the characteristics of apocalyptic in rudimentary form.[1] The occasion of the prophecy was a locust plague of unprecedented severity. Joel interpreted that visitation as a judgment of God upon his people, and as a sign and warning of the coming of the Day of the Lord. As the interpreter of a contemporary historical event, Joel belongs to 'the goodly fellowship of the prophets'. On the other hand, the prophecy has some of the features of later apocalyptic literature, e.g. Joel is concerned with the advent of God in judgment at the end of the age, and makes use of visionary symbolism to portray that supernatural intervention. The book may be described as prophecy on the way to becoming apocalyptic.

From internal evidence, it may be inferred that Joel, son of Pethuel, was a native of Judah and probably a resident in Jerusalem. It is possible that he was a cult-prophet, for he was familiar with the Temple, and held the priests, 'the ministers of the Lord', in high esteem. He greatly valued the regular services of worship and was distressed when the daily sacrifice could no longer be offered (1: 9). Joel was also 'a well-read man'; there are numerous quotations in his messages, especially from the writings of his prophetic predecessors (e.g. 2: 2 from Zephaniah 1: 15; 2: 6 from Nahum 2: 10; 2: 32 from Obadiah 17; 3: 18 from Amos 9: 13). He was a gifted poet of great

[1] See page 197.

imaginative power, as may be seen in his graphic descriptions of the devastation of the countryside by the invading army of locusts, or their irresistible attack like disciplined warriors on the walled city of Jerusalem (1: 4–12; 2: 4–9). His clear and forcible style, his vivid and concrete language, his skilful use of rhythm, repetition, and contrast, his choice of image, metaphor, and simile, entitle Joel to a place of honour among the great poets of the Old Testament.

It is not possible to determine the date of the prophecy with any assurance, for there is no external evidence, and the internal evidence is not conclusive. There are some clues. The people of Judah have been scattered among the nations and the land has been divided up by foreigners (3: 2). There is no mention of a king, but, as in the post-exilic period, the priests and the elders are the leaders of the community (1: 13, 14). Jews have been sold as slaves to the Greeks (3: 6). The Temple and the walls of Jerusalem have been rebuilt (1: 14; 2: 9). As already mentioned, there are quotations from the prophets, including Obadiah and Malachi. The descriptions of the Day of the Lord show some of the features of apocalyptic literature. These various clues taken together point to a date later than the middle of the fifth century, i.e. between 440 and 400 B.C.

The prophecy has two main divisions, in the second of which the apocalyptic features are much more prominent. This fact has led some scholars to question the unity of the book, and to assign the second part to an author or authors who lived later than the time of Joel. However, since the style, the historical background, the habit of quoting from earlier prophets, and the references to the Day of the Lord are features common to both parts of the book, there is no compelling reason for attributing the prophecy to two authors. In the first section, the prophet describes a locust plague and a drought, calls the people to fasting and penitence, and records God's answer to their prayers (1: 2 to 2: 27). Then, turning from the present to the future, he describes events which precede and accompany the Day of the Lord, i.e. the outpouring of the Spirit upon all his people, the judgment of the nations, and the final blessedness of Israel (2: 28 to 3: 21).

THE PLAGUE OF LOCUSTS

The locust plague was an evil to which the people of Bible lands were periodically subject. Under certain climatic conditions these insects increase to immense numbers and, driven

P

by a strong wandering instinct, may make their way to far distant lands. Such a visitation could be a disaster, for the myriads of locusts often denuded the land of almost all vegetation. 'Still today such an event in the East is a catastrophe: when the swarms of these insects, which form clouds able to hide the sun, settle on the ground, all is lost; after half an hour of their passage these innumerable, voracious creatures leave trees completely robbed of foliage and crops entirely destroyed.'[1] A disaster of that magnitude was the occasion of Joel's prophecy.

He begins by saying that the visitation, which is of such unprecedented severity that the old men can recall nothing like it, is to be recounted from generation to generation (1: 2, 3). Using four different Hebrew words for the locust, which probably indicate four stages of growth in the life of the insect, the prophet describes the total destruction of the crops and vegetation (1: 4). Let the drunkards lament, for the vineyards are destroyed (1: 5)! 'Powerful and without number', organized like an army, armed with teeth like lions, they have stripped vine and fig tree of leaves and bark (1: 6, 7). Let the nation lament like a girl bereaved of her bethrothed, for owing to the shortage of cereals, oil, and wine, the daily sacrifice can no longer be offered; and the priests and the desolate fields are in mourning (1: 8–10). Let the farmers lament, for crops and vintage are destroyed, the fruit trees are denuded, and all human joy has vanished (1: 11, 12).

Having portrayed the devastation caused in the countryside, in a second passage Joel describes the locusts themselves and their assault upon the city. From Jerusalem the priests are to sound the alarm, warning the people of the approach of the Day of the Lord, of which the present visitation is the harbinger. The myriads of locusts which darken the mountains are like a destructive fire; they turn a land fair as Eden into a wilderness (2: 1–3). In appearance and speed, they are like horses, and the sound of their wings is like the rumbling of chariots or the crackling of blazing stubble (2: 4, 5). The people shrink back in terror as, like a disciplined army, they advance in perfect order, storming the city walls which are powerless to hold them back, and entering the dwelling houses like thieves (2: 6–9).

The locust plague is accompanied by severe drought, which has shrivelled the seeds in the ground so that the garners are empty and desolate. The burning heat has scorched the pastures

[1] W. Corsant, *A Dictionary of Life in Bible Times*, 135.

and dried up the brooks; the flocks and herds wander in search of food and the wild beasts pant for water (1: 17–20).

Joel sees in both locust plague and drought the judgment of God. It is difficult for us today to accept the view that a natural calamity is an act of God. We tend to regard the universe as an impersonal law-abiding realm, a morally neutral order in which the unbroken sequences of cause and effect operate without any reference to the virtues and vices of men. We account for a locust plague or a drought in terms of secondary causes, and then accept such a description of natural processes as an explanation of the event. Three things may be said of Joel's interpretation of natural evil or catastrophe.

First, the truth revealed to the prophet that one specific natural calamity is a judgment of God, does not mean that all disasters in all circumstances are to be interpreted as visitations of God. Secondly, according to the biblical view of the world, animate and inanimate nature shares in the disastrous consequences of the fall of man; in particular, the plants and the creatures are involved in the disorder created by man's sin. Nature is not morally neutral, and the disordered relationship between man and the creatures can operate for harm in both directions. The creatures may suffer because of man (1: 18, 20), man may suffer because of the creatures. Seen in this way, some of the suffering inflicted by the creatures on man may be a just judgment, a sign of God's moral order. Thirdly, it should be noted that Joel interprets the locust plague primarily as *a warning* of the approach of the Day of Judgment, and as a challenge to the people to repent. Although the two are closely intertwined in some passages (1: 15, 16; 2: 1, 2, 10, 11) they are not identified; the plague is the harbinger of the Day, the visitation is the herald warning of the approaching judgment. Christ set his seal on this interpretation of present calamity as a warning of future judgment. The eighteen men who were crushed to death by the sudden collapse of a tower in Siloam were not 'worse offenders than all the others who dwelt in Jerusalem'. But the disaster should serve as a salutary warning to all survivors. 'Unless you repent you will all likewise perish' (Luke 13: 4, 5).

Such a call to repentance Joel sounds with a voice like a trumpet. The priests are commanded to 'gird on sackcloth', the sign of mourning, go into the sanctuary and spend the night in prayer (1: 13). They are to institute a fast for the whole nation as an outward sign of corporate penitence (1 : 14). For in spite of the magnitude of the disaster, there is still hope if the people, grieving for sin, return to God with sincerity of heart. They will find that the Lord, who is gracious and merciful, is ready to forgive their sins, to deliver them from the locust plague, and to restore the prosperity of the land (2: 12–14). No one is to be excluded, no age group from the old men to the infants, not even the newly wedded, from this urgent call to repentance (2: 15, 16). Between the porch and the altar, the priests are to weep and intercede—'spare thy people, O Lord' (2: 17). For when men turn to God in true repentance, he turns to men in pardoning love, and in response to sincere prayer reverses the fortunes of his people.

Through the prophet, God promises—the people being penitent—to restore the fertility of the land and to drive away the locusts into the southern desert, the Dead Sea and the Mediterranean. The land, the animals, and the people will all rejoice, for the rain will fall at the appropriate seasons and the earth yield bountiful harvests. The damage done by the locusts will be made good and the people will know with assurance that the Lord is in their midst (2: 18–27). From this repeated call to national penitence, it is evident that the outward and formal observances of religion were of importance to Joel. Sackcloth is to be worn, fasts are to be proclaimed. Days of prayer and night vigils are to be observed. Restored prosperity is welcomed because it makes possible the restoration of the daily sacrifice. The priesthood is held in honour and the Temple is regarded as the centre of the communal life. Yet this emphasis on religious observances is counter-balanced by the demand for genuine repentance and deep contrition of heart. In memorable words, often used in Churches as a call to penitence, especially during the Lenten season, God tells us through the lips of his prophet that his primary requirement is the conversion of the will. The sacrifice he desires is the broken and contrite heart. 'Return to me with all your heart, with fasting, with weeping, and with mourning; and rend your hearts and not your garments' (2: 12, 13).

THE LAST DAYS

In the first part of the book we see Joel preoccupied with a contemporary event, the locust plague—yet a contemporary event seen as a warning and foretaste of the coming Day of the

Lord. We turn now to the second part of the prophecy, which contains several visions of the end-time, descriptions of the events which precede and accompany the Day of the Lord. First of all, in the new age of fulfilment, there will be an out-pouring of the Spirit of God upon his people, endowing them one and all with the gift of prophecy. In former times the Spirit of the Lord had rested on leaders and judges, kings and prophets. A few only had been chosen from among the people by God, and endowed with the Spirit for the discharge of some special vocation. Among those so chosen were the prophets, who by the inspiration of the Spirit were able both to discern and to declare the purpose of God. On one occasion Moses had expressed the desire that the gift bestowed upon the few might become the possession of all. 'Would that all the Lord's people were prophets, that the Lord would put his spirit upon them' (Numbers 11 : 29). Joel foresaw that in the messianic age God would bring to realization that which Moses had desired. The Spirit would be poured out upon all God's people without distinction, without exception, upon men and women, upon old and young, upon master and servant. As a result, each one would be a prophet, receiving revelation through dream and vision, discerning and declaring the mind and purpose of God (2 : 27–29).

These words of Joel were cited by Peter on the day of Pente-cost, for in that outpouring of the Holy Spirit the predictions of the prophet were fulfilled in a four-fold manner. Through the death and resurrection of Jesus Christ and the pentecostal effusion of the Spirit, the last days arrived, the messianic age dawned. 'This is what was spoken by the prophet Joel.' Further-more, the Christian fellowship, like the prophets of old, was given insight into the mind of God. Illumination was available for all, through the Spirit who communicates God's true wisdom. ,

With the insight into the nature and purpose of God, went the responsibility of declaring the revelation to others. The Holy Spirit imparted the power of utterance to the disciples, 'giving them both the gift of tongues, and also boldness with fervent zeal constantly to preach the Gospel unto all nations'.[1] Joel foresaw that the gift of the Spirit would be extended from the chosen few to all *Israel*—'your sons . . . your daughters . . .

[1] Preface to the eucharistic prayer for Pentecost, *The Book of Common Prayer*.

your old men . . . your young men'. In the New Testament the promise is extended still further to embrace all mankind; it is universalized (Acts 2: 16–18).

The approach of the Day of the Lord will be heralded not only by these manifestations of the Spirit, but also by other extraordinary signs. On earth will be seen the accompaniments of war—blood, fire, and the smoke of burning cities—and in the heavens, solar eclipse and blood-red moon. From the dread, impending judgment, every faithful Israelite who invokes the Lord in worship will be saved. For as God has already declared through his prophet Obadiah, a faithful remnant will escape (2: 30–32, quoting Obadiah 17). The apostles Peter and Paul, citing Joel 2: 32, extend the principle of salvation through faith to all mankind (Acts 2: 21; Romans 10: 13).

Over against the salvation of the faithful the prophet sets the condemnation of the nations. When the Lord restores the fortunes of Judah and Jerusalem, he will summon all the heathen into the Valley of Jehoshaphat and excute judgment upon them. They will be charged with crimes against Israel—with scattering her people, occupying her territory, and, for a mere pittance, selling her sons and daughters into slavery (3: 1–3). The Judge will be especially severe on those notorious slave traders, the Phoenicians and the Philistines, who have plundered Israel and sold some of her people as slaves to the Greeks. He is about to stir up and bring back those scattered captives, and hand over to them their former oppressors, who will in turn be sold into slavery to a people in far-off South Arabia (3: 4–8). God then commands his heralds to summon all nations to arms. When they are assembled in the Valley of Jehoshaphat for the final conflict, the warriors of the Lord, the angels, receive the order to cut down the ripe grain, to crush the grapes in the wine-press (3: 9–13). There is no direct description of the ensuing battle between the angelic host and the multitude of the heathen; owing to the veiling of the sun, moon, and stars, the conflict takes place in darkness. In the valley there is tumult and shouting, and from Zion, like the roar of a lion, the Judge utters his verdict of condemnation (3: 14–16a).

Ever since the fourth century A.D. the Valley of Jehoshaphat has been identified with the Valley of the Kidron just beyond the eastern wall of Jerusalem. Both in Christian and Moslem tradition, the Kidron with its monuments and countless tombstones has been regarded by many as the place of final judgment. It is unlikely, however, that Joel had in mind a particular location, a literal valley; he was not concerned with geography but with symbolism. For the word *Jehoshaphat* means 'the Lord judges' or 'has judged'. It is the place where God announces and executes *his* decision (not the place where we make ours), *his* verdict upon the nations. The Last Judgment is an essential feature of the prophetic interpretation of history and the world. Judgment does not begin on the Last Day, for it is an activity of God within history. In the present, except to those endowed with prophetic insight, the judgment is partly or entirely hidden; in the end-time, it will be fully manifested to all. The nations are sitting now for the examination; at the consummation of history the results will be announced to the whole universe.

From Joel's description we may learn three things. The Last Judgment will be universal in range; all the nations of the world will be summoned to the valley of decision. True, Israel is excluded; but that is because she has been under judgment already within history, and a few only have escaped (2: 32; compare John 5: 24). There is a standard of judgment: the nations are judged according to their treatment of Israel. This same criterion is accepted and extended by Christ in his Parable of the Last Judgment. Some are accepted for eternal life and some are rejected, according to their treatment of 'one of the least of these my brethren' (3: 2; Matthew 25: 31–46). The prophet also affirms the complete and final victory, won by the Lord himself, over all the organized powers of evil; his cause is vindicated, his purpose for mankind is triumphant (see Revelation 14: 14–20).

The prophecy ends with a figurative description of the blessings of the new age beyond the final judgment. Land and city alike are to be transformed. Judah will be amazingly fertile, and life-giving waters will flow forth from the Temple.[1] Jerusalem, no longer violated by the heathen, will be the holy city, the eternal city, the dwelling place of God (3: 18–21). Judah and Jerusalem, the land and the city, creation and community, the life of the countryside and the life of the town, all that is of value in man's natural and social environment, will be transformed and conserved in the new age.

[1] See page 163.

XVIII

Jonah

THE PURPOSE

The Book of Jonah is the best known of all the books of the prophets. There is a reason for this. Unlike all the other prophecies, it is a story and not a collection of oracles. Folk who know little about the Bible have heard about Jonah and the whale—although in fact there is no mention of a whale in this book! In popular speech, a person who by his presence brings misfortune or calamity, is still known as 'a Jonah'. The book gained notoriety in the controversies of the nineteenth century. The story of the man swallowed by a large fish and coming out alive three days later, was ridiculed by sceptics and enemies of the faith. As to a banner on the field of battle, believers rallied to the defence of this tale, the literal acceptance of which became a test of orthodoxy. Thus the book became well known—for the wrong reasons. It deserves to be well known, because the truth and spirit of the gospel is embodied in this tale.

We begin by asking when and why the story was written. It was composed in the period after the return of the Jews from exile in Babylon. At that time Judah was a tiny province in the vast Persian Empire. A crucial question had to be faced during this Persian period—that of the relationship between the Jewish community and the Gentile world. Israel could adopt one of two attitudes to the heathen. There was the way of segregation and exclusion, of zealously guarding the precious heritage of faith and life behind the hedge of the law. On the other hand, Israel could be the missionary servant, seeking to share her unique knowledge of the true God with other races and nations. In the work of Haggai and Zechariah the prophets, of Nehemiah the patriot, and of Ezra the scribe, the emphasis fell upon separation and exclusion. Priority was given to those things which distinguished the People of God from the heathen—the Temple cult, the strict observance of the law, the rite of circumcision, the keeping of the Sabbath. There was opposition to mixed marriages, hostility to the Samaritans, bitterness toward foreign powers. The outcome of this policy was a steady growth of that rigid exclusiveness, narrow nationalism, and religious bigotry which were to become the characteristics of Judaism.

Yet not all were in sympathy with these powerful trends, and the Book of Jonah is a vigorous protest against such narrowness, prejudice, and exclusiveness. The author has the missionary spirit and universal outlook of Second Isaiah. The ugly spirit of bitterness and hatred towards foreign nations is personified in Jonah. Set over against the universal concern and compassion of the Lord, contrasted with the tenderness of his love and the wideness of his mercy, the narrow and vengeful attitude of the Jewish community to the heathen is exposed and condemned. The author is otherwise unknown, and it is not possible to assign an exact date to his tract. It was probably written *after* the work of Nehemiah and Ezra (397 B.C.) and *before* the Book of Ecclesiasticus (190 B.C.), whose author refers to 'the twelve prophets'. It could have been written any time between 400 and 200 B.C. The main purpose of the author is to challenge Israel to fulfil her missionary vocation.

THE STORY

Jonah, the son of Amittai, was commanded by God to go to Nineveh, the capital of Assyria. He was summoned to announce that the judgment of God was about to fall upon the inhabitants of that wicked city. For reasons which emerge later in the story, the prophet was unwilling to go. So he went down to Joppa (the modern Jaffa) and, having paid his fare, boarded a ship bound for Tarshish—probably the city of Tartessos in the south of Spain. This was in the opposite direction to Nineveh, on the extreme western edge of the world as then known. His purpose was to escape from the Lord, whose presence, he supposed, was confined to the territory of Israel. Having gone down into the hold of the ship, he fell asleep. Then the Lord 'hurled a great wind upon the sea', and the ship was threatened with destruction by the huge waves. In dire peril, the heathen mariners at once resorted to prayer and, being from many lands, each called upon his own god for deliverance. Then they threw overboard some of the tackle and cargo in order to lighten the ship.

Meanwhile, the captain came upon Jonah asleep. Astonished and indignant, he roused the prophet, and with sharp words urged him to call on his god. When, in spite of their frantic prayers, the storm persisted, the sailors came to the conclusion that someone on board had offended one of the gods, and this offended god was the cause of the storm. So they cast lots, and thereby discovered that Jonah was the culprit. In response to their questions, the runaway prophet disclosed that he was the servant of the Creator and Ruler of the world—a revelation which greatly increased the dread of the mariners. They then enquired of Jonah what must be done to quieten the storm, which was increasing in fury. On being told that they must throw him into the sea, they shrank from such a deed and, instead, tried to bring the ship to land. Failing in this attempt, they were compelled, with great reluctance, to do what Jonah had advised. First, they prayed to God that he would not hold them responsible, and then they cast his disobedient servant into the sea. The storm subsided, the mariners offered a sacrifice of thanksgiving and made vows.

Meanwhile, at the command of the inescapable God, a great fish swallowed up Jonah, and he remained within it for three days and nights. By this monster he was taken safely to land, and, after a prayer for deliverance, was disgorged on the sea-shore. Jonah was now commanded for the second time to go to Nineveh. Sobered by his terrible experience, yet with profound reluctance, he obeyed. On reaching the vast city, he walked for a whole day into it, and then began to announce the impending doom. The response was instantaneous. 'The men of Nineveh ... repented at the preaching of Jonah' (Luke 11: 32). Discarding his robe and donning sackcloth, the king himself issued a proclamation. All were to fast, wear sackcloth, and 'cry mightily to God', in the hope that he would change his mind and spare the city. Seeing their sincere repentance, God decided not to destroy them.

This decision provoked Jonah to an outburst of anger, in which he revealed why, from the beginning, he had been unwilling to go as missionary to Nineveh. For he had known all along that the God of the covenant was merciful and compassionate, and would be only too willing to pardon the heathen if they repented. His worst fears had been realized, and he would now prefer to die rather than live to see God's favour extended to the heathen. Going a little way out of the city to the east, the petulant prophet constructed a shelter, and waited to see what would happen. God then caused a large plant to spring up overnight. It could have provided shelter from the fierce heat of the sun, but at dawn God sent a worm to destroy it. The plant had become precious to Jonah, and he was deeply grieved at its destruction. Exposed to the scorching desert wind, he told himself that he would be better off dead. God then chided his sulking servant. Jonah had felt grief and pity at the destruction of a plant he did not create and which lasted but for a day. Then should the Lord not have compassion on Nineveh, the great city, with its 120,000 children and all its cattle?

HISTORY, ALLEGORY, OR PARABLE?

What are we to make of this story? What kind of literature is this? According to the traditional view, still widely accepted, the book is an historical narrative. It is maintained that the story gives the impression of being a record of actual events, and it was accepted as such by almost all biblical scholars and readers until comparatively recent times. Also we know from the Second Book of Kings, that there *was* a prophet called Jonah, son of Amittai, who in the reign of Jeroboam II (783–743 B.C.) predicted that Israel would recover her lost territories (II Kings 14: 25). Furthermore, the Lord Jesus refers to the mission of Jonah in Nineveh. He then goes on to speak of the visit of the Queen of Sheba to Solomon (Luke 11: 29–32; Matthew 12: 39–42). Why accept the latter as history and not the former?

There are, however, several cogent reasons for rejecting this interpretation of the book as biography. The chief of these is the highly miraculous nature of the story. He who believes in the God who raised his Son from the dead does not doubt the possibility of miracles. But is it in accordance with all that we otherwise know of God, that he should act as described in this story? A great tempest subsides suddenly; a man is swallowed by a fish; within the gullet of this sea-monster he composes and utters a psalm of deliverance; he emerges unharmed seventy-two hours later; Jonah, a Hebrew, preaches in a language understood by the people of Nineveh; the whole population of a vast heathen city repents; in a single night a plant grows higher than a man. The evidence of archaeology is also against the acceptance of the book as history. In the story, the city of Nineveh is so vast that it takes three days to walk across it (3: 3). It would take far less time to walk across Greater London. Excavations have revealed that the walls of

Nineveh were rather less than eight miles in circumference. Furthermore, there are several indications that the book was written centuries after the fall of Nineveh in 612 B.C. That city is spoken of in the past tense—'Nineveh *was* an exceedingly great city' (3: 3). The Aramaisms in the language, and the dependence of the author on Jeremiah and Joel, also point to a period long after the collapse of the Assyrian empire.

This book, then, is not history, but a 'made-up' story, in which a prophet who did actually live in the distant past, and about whom virtually nothing is known, appears as the villain. Our Lord could use the story of Jonah as an illustration, just as a speaker today can enforce a point by quoting the words of Hamlet from Shakespeare's play or by recounting the deeds of Giant Despair in *Pilgrim's Progress*. Like the latter, the Book of Jonah may be regarded as an allegory—'narrative description of a subject under guise of another suggestively similar'.[1] 'Jonah' means 'dove', a traditional symbol of Israel, and Nineveh stands for the heathen world. Israel was summoned by God to bear the knowledge of himself to the heathen nations. She shrank from this task. Jonah's flight to Tarshish depicts the refusal of Israel to be the missionary people in the period before the exile. For her disobedience she was 'swallowed up' alive by Babylon. 'Nebuchadrezzar the king of Babylon has devoured me . . . he has swallowed me like a monster' (Jeremiah 51: 34). Then, like Jonah in the fish, Israel in exile turned to the Lord, and after over half a century in captivity, was released from her imprisonment. In the period following the return from exile, Israel was commanded for the second time to carry out her mission. At this point in the allegory we reach the time of the author. In the response of the Ninevites to the message, he suggests the readiness of the heathen to repent. In the bitter, malicious Jonah, he portrays the narrow and intolerant spirit, the hatred of the Gentiles characteristic of his own time.

While this interpretation is true in its broad outlines, it would be misleading to regard this book as a sustained allegory after the fashion of *Pilgrim's Progress*, and to attempt to find a parallel at every point between the story of Jonah and the history of Israel. In the Bible, no hard and fast lines can be drawn between allegory and parable—a fictitious story which embodies *one* main truth. This book is like a parable of Jesus. The author, a superb story-teller, paints the portrait of a man who

[1] *The Oxford Dictionary.*

bears some resemblance to the elder brother in the parable of the Prodigal Son (Luke 15: 25–32). It is a single ugly picture of a narrow, intolerant Hebrew, who hates the heathen. David, listening to the parable of Nathan, was led to pass judgment on himself (II Samuel 12: 1–7). This parable, also, is like the thrust of a sword. The purpose of the author is to hurt, to convict, to condemn the selfishness of his contemporaries, who are withholding the saving knowledge of the true God from the other nations of the world.

THE MESSAGE

'The Church exists for those who are not yet members of it.'[1] When God called Abraham, the ancestor of the chosen race, he made the promise—'in you all the families of the earth will be blessed; (Genesis 12: 3 margin). The privileges enjoyed by Abraham and his descendents were, in due time, to be extended to the Gentiles. The purpose of the Lord was to benefit the many through the one, to enlighten all nations through one holy nation, to save the human race through one chosen race. He did not choose his servant, Israel, for privilege divorced from responsibility. From the beginning his purpose was universal. 'I will give you as a light to the nations, that my salvation may reach to the end of the earth' (Isaiah 49: 6). Hitherto, Israel had failed to carry out this missionary task. Now, as with the sound of a trumpet, the author calls the People of God to world mission.

Through the Book of Jonah God continues, in all ages, to challenge the new Israel, the Christian Church. Like Jonah, the Christian can be narrow-minded and hard-hearted. Like the people of Israel, the members of the Church can withdraw into a comfortable ecclesiastical ghetto, instead of venturing forth to give service and to bear witness to mankind. We can hide the light of the gospel under a pail, clutch to our bosoms the faith entrusted to us for others, and selfishly keep within the Church of our own land the salvation intended for all mankind. Who then is Jonah? The book is effective as the reader or listener sees himself portrayed in the chief character. And yet the purpose of the author is not only to convict of sin; he also gives us two powerful incentives for sharing the message with others.

The first of these has to do with the heathen; the second

[1] William Temple.

with the nature of God. The author does not soft-pedal the sinfulness of men. Nineveh is a wicked city, and unless the inhabitants repent, they will all perish. Yet the book also represents the heathen in a favourable light. In the storm, the sailors resort at once to prayer, and even when he advises it, are most reluctant to throw Jonah into the sea. When the storm subsides, they stand in awe of the living God now revealed, and in gratitude offer sacrifice to him and make vows. The heathen men of Nineveh believe in God. They hear and accept the message, truly repent, fast, and pray fervently for deliverance. In the story all the heathen, sailors and citizens, *respond* to the revelation and word of the true God. That was an aspect of the life of the world which the exclusives in the Jewish community had ignored. Admirable qualities of character are to be found in some of the heathen. The Book of Ruth, written at about the same time, has the same message. The heroine, the embodiment of loyal love, the ancestress of David, is a Moabitess, a pagan. In society today, Christians have no monopoly of virtue. There are many good, kind, helpful people outside the Church. In social and political life much service, responsible, voluntary, and costly, is given by those who do not call on the name of the Lord. There are also many worthy people in the world who, if given the opportunity, would respond to the gospel. Even bad people are not hopeless, and wicked cities are not outside the pale. True, all alike—the virtuous and the wicked—need the call to repentance; and, hearing it, some will respond. Through the work of the Spirit of God, unbelievers can respond to the Word of God. This conviction can give a mighty impetus to witness and evangelism.

Yet there is a still greater incentive. God *loves* the heathen. It was because he already knew that perfectly well, that Jonah refused his initial assignment (4: 2). He was afraid at the outset that, given their repentance, God in his great mercy and compassion would abandon his plan to destroy, and would gladly spare the Ninevites. And so, alongside his ugly portrait of a Jonah whose heart was full of bitterness and hatred, the author hangs his lovely portrait of 'a gracious God and merciful, slow to anger, and abounding in steadfast love' (4: 2). The restricted sympathy of Jonah is contrasted with the boundless mercy of God. In his warm and tender compassion, God longs to deliver the people, the infants, and even the cattle of

Nineveh. His love embraces the whole human race, and his tender mercies are over all his works. He loves without limit and wills all men to be saved. That is why each Christian, constrained by the love of Christ, must bear witness, and the whole Church be the missionary servant of God in the world.

XIX

Second Zechariah

'Behold, a he-goat came from the west across the face of the whole earth, without touching the ground; and the goat had a conspicuous horn between his eyes. He came to the ram with the two horns, which I had seen standing on the bank of the river, and he ran at him in his mighty wrath . . . and the ram had no power to stand before him, but he cast him down to the ground and trampled upon him' (Daniel 8: 5–7). Looking back over the centuries, the author of the book of Daniel used this picture language to describe the head-on clash between the Macedonian-Greek empire of Alexander the Great and the Medo-Persian empire of Darius III Codomanus. Cyrus of Persia, greeted by Second Isaiah as the shepherd and anointed of the Lord, established an empire which lasted for two centuries (538–333 B.C.). Haggai, Zechariah, Third Isaiah, Obadiah, Malachi, Joel, and Jonah all belong to the period when the Jews were subject to the Persian yoke. Apart from these prophecies and the information given in the books of Nehemiah and Ezra, very little is known about the Jews during the Persian period. As one tiny province within a vast empire which extended from India to the Aegean Sea, from the steppes of Central Asia to the pyramids of Egypt, Judah had no influence upon the political and military events of the age.

The westward expansion of Persia brought her into conflict with Greece. During the reign of Darius the Great (522–486 B.C.), the Persian army was defeated by the Greeks at the battle of Marathon (490 B.C.). The son and successor of Darius, Xerxes I (486–465 B.C.), crossed the Hellespont with a vast army, and waged war against continental Greece. Overwhelming the heroic Spartan King Leonidas and his 300 soldiers at the pass of Thermopylae (480 B.C.), Xerxes succeeded in occupying Attica; but after his defeat in a naval battle in the Bay of Salamis, the Persian armies withdrew from Greece. With the rise of Alexander of Macedon, the military roles of

Greece and Persia were reversed; it was the turn of the he-goat to attack the ram. Born in 356 B.C., son of Philip II of Macedon, a pupil of the philosopher Aristotle, a king at twenty years of age, Alexander was resolved to end the Persian threat to Greece. Having defeated the armies of the Persian emperor Darius III at Granicus in Asia Minor (334 B.C.) and at Issus in Upper Syria (333 B.C.), he besieged and captured Tyre, and passed through Palestine to the conquest of Egypt. According to the Jewish historian Josephus, Alexander visited Jerusalem and offered sacrifice in the Temple. The story may be fanciful, but the victorious general did include Palestine in his dominion, as part of a province known as Coele-Syria. From Egypt, where he founded the city which bore his name, Alexandria, he passed into Mesopotamia and inflicted a decisive defeat upon the Persians at the great battle of Gaugamela near Arbela (331 B.C.). Pressing on as far as the river Indus, he had established in a military campaign of only eight years duration, a dominion greater than the empires of Assyria, Babylon, or Persia.

In process of time the culture of Hellas (Greece), known as Hellenism, followed the conquests of Alexander. The thought and philosophy of Greece, mediated through her language and literature, began to leaven the civilizations of the Near East. Things Greek—laws and institutions, art and architecture, gymnasiums and theatres, dress and customs—came into fashion throughout the vast empire. Through the spread of the language, the *koine* Greek, Alexander and his successors were used by God to prepare the world for the coming of Christ. Alongside the native dialects, there was one common language, used and understood throughout the world, in which the apostles, evangelists, and missionaries of Christ could write and preach the gospel.

The death of Alexander from fever at the age of thirty-three was followed by a period of confusion and strife, during which his empire was divided into several kingdoms. Eventually four of his generals gained positions of supremacy. 'The great horn was broken, and instead of it there came up four conspicuous horns toward the four winds of heaven' (Daniel 8: 8). One of these four generals, Ptolemy Lagi, governor in Egypt, took possession of Palestine. Although not without many a struggle, Ptolemy and his successors (the Ptolemies) ruled the Holy Land for over a century until 198 B.C. During the Ptolemaic period, while subject to tribute, the Jews were allowed a

Q

measure of self-government. Many of them settled in the capital city, Alexandria, where the Septuagint (the Greek version of the Hebrew scriptures) originated.

The collection of prophetic oracles known as Second Zechariah (chapters 9 to 14) probably belongs to this period when the Jews were subject to the Ptolemies. It is not possible to date these messages with any assurance, for the historical references are indefinite and ambiguous, and among scholars there is no general agreement on questions of authorship, occasion, and interpretation. Zechariah 11: 12–13 is quoted in Matthew 27: 9 and attributed to Jeremiah. This fact, taken together with references to the Northern Kingdom and to Egypt and Assyria as prominent powers, led some biblical commentators of former times to date these oracles in the period before the Babylonian exile. This view has few supporters today.

The Book of the Twelve Prophets concludes with three collections of anonymous oracles, all introduced by the same title—'the burden of the word of the Lord' (9: 1; 12: 1; Malachi 1: 1). The third of these collections obviously bears the stamp of a single personality and became known as the book of Malachi. To make the sacred number twelve, the other two anonymous collections were simply added to the book which preceded them—Zechariah. There is almost complete agreement among scholars that the material in chapters 9 to 14 cannot be attributed to the prophet Zechariah. In the authentic messages of that prophet (chapters 1 to 8) there are definite dates, allusions to the recent exile and the rebuilding of the Temple, and references to certain individuals—Zechariah, Zerubbabel, Joshua, Darius. All these features, together with the night visions and the angelic mediators, are absent from chapters 9 to 14.

It is unlikely that the two anonymous collections are themselves the work of a single author, for there are significant differences between them. The first collection is historical (chapters 9 to 11). Some of the history is in the form of allegory, and it is often not at all clear who are the persons or what are the events to which reference is made. Nevertheless, the oracles are about definite nations and specific historical events. The second collection is apocalyptic (chapters 12 to 14). These passages are concerned with the distant future, with the last days, with the final destiny of the nations as a whole. Even within these two collections, there is evidence that the material has more than one author. There are, for example, within the second collection two different accounts of the last great assault of the heathen on Jerusalem. They can hardly have come from the same author (12: 1–14: 6; 14: 1–21). It seems likely, therefore, that the seven oracles in the first collection and the three in the second came from a number of different writers, all of whom lived after the conquests of Alexander, during the period of the Ptolemaic rule in Palestine. The book is frequently quoted in the New Testament, especially in connection with the passion of Christ (Matthew 21: 5; 26: 15; 26: 31; 27: 9; Mark 14: 27; John 12: 15; 19: 37; Revelation 1: 7).

HISTORY AND ALLEGORY

In the defeat of the forces of Darius the Persian in the battles of Granicus and Issus and the victorious advance of the armies of Alexander of Macedon, the prophet sees the activity of the Lord. Through the instrumentality of the Greeks his judgment is about to fall on the cities of Syria (Hadrach, Damascus, Hamath), Phoenicia (Tyre, Sidon), and Philistia (Ashkelon, Gaza, Ekron, Ashdod), which lie on Alexander's line of advance. They too belong to the Lord and he will incorporate them in his land. Even self-confident Tyre on her rocky island will not escape. (In the event, Alexander built a mole about half a mile long, from the mainland to the island on which Tyre stood, and the city was compelled to surrender after a siege of seven months.) The cities of the Philistine confederation will be overthrown, and the remaining inhabitants, cleansed from idolatry, and observing the Jewish food laws, will eventually be incorporated in Judah. The prophet looks forward not to the extermination of these agelong enemies of Israel, but to their conversion and incorporation (9: 1–7).

The victories of Alexander precede the advent of the messianic king, who will enter Jerusalem in triumph and inaugurate a reign of universal peace. Departing from the tradition of the kings of the earth, the messiah will not enter the holy city on a horse, the symbol of power and war, but like the princes of primitive times (Genesis 49: 10, 11; Judges 5: 10; 12: 14) he will ride upon an ass, the symbol of royalty and peace. Triumphant and victorious, i.e. vindicated and delivered by God, he will be gentle and humble in heart. The Prince of Peace, he will abolish armaments from Ephraim (the former

Northern Kingdom) and Judah, and unite these two kingdoms, so long disunited. Restoring the ancient kingdom of David, from the Mediterranean to the Dead Sea, from the Euphrates to the southern desert, he will proclaim and secure peace among all nations (9: 9–10). Christ had this prophecy in mind when he entered Jerusalem riding on an ass, amid the waving palm branches and the glad acclamations of his disciples. He is the king in the form of a servant, regal and humble, establishing peace through the cross, vindicated through the resurrection, uniting and reigning over his people, destined to win the allegiance of the whole reconciled race. Some of the hopes of the prophet have been realized and all will be fulfilled in him (Matthew 21: 1–9). 'Blessed be he that hath come and is to come in the name of the Lord, Hosanna in the highest'.[1]

The oracle which follows probably comes from a somewhat later period. The hopes inspired by the victories of Alexander have been disappointed. The yoke of Greece has replaced that of Persia. Yet in the heart of the prophet hope springs eternal: God will himself restore the scattered exiles, he will mobilize Ephraim and Judah and lead them forth to victory over the oppressor. 'I will brandish your sons, O Zion, over your sons, O Greece.' Although the day of deliverance has been deferred, yet it will surely come (9: 13–17). 'The belief in the coming of the kingdom, constantly disappointed in particular secular situations, remains an indestructible element in biblical faith.'[2]

In another oracle, God declares that he is angry with the shepherds, the foreign rulers and their Jewish agents, the mercenary priests, and he will raise up strong and aggressive leaders from within Israel (cornerstone, tent peg, battle bow) who with his aid will wage war successfully against these tyrants. God will then bring back his exiles from Assyria and Egypt (i.e. from the two neighbouring Greek kingdoms, the Seleucid to the north and the Ptolemaic to the south of Judah); they will come in such vast numbers, occupying and filling all the territory formerly ruled over by David, that the return will seem like a second Exodus (10: 3–12). A mock lament is uttered over the foreign tyrants, who are likened to the cedars of Lebanon and to the oaks of Bashan (11: 1–3).

Then follows the allegory of the shepherd and the flock.

[1] Liturgy of the Church of South India.
[2] R. C. Denton, *The Interpreter's Bible*, Vol. VI, 1098.

The prophet is commanded by God to take charge of a flock destined for slaughter at the hands of pitiless shepherds. He accepts the oversight, taking with him two rods called Grace and Union. The flock is worthless and detests the shepherd; in revulsion, he breaks the rod called Grace and leaves them to their fate. When he asks for his wages, the owners pay him a paltry sum, thirty shekels of silver, the price of a slave. Casting this into the Temple treasury, the shepherd then breaks the second rod, Union. Finally, in order that the worthless sheep may get what they deserve, the prophet is commanded to assume the role of a worthless shepherd. The interpretation is blended with the allegory. God's people, exploited by foreign rulers and their Jewish agents, are unworthy of the beneficent rule of God. Because of persistent disobedience, God's relationship with Judah has been ruptured; the people are no longer the objects of his grace and favour. God has annulled his covenant with the surrounding nations by which they were restrained from attacking his people. He will no longer protect them. Because the covenant has been broken, the bond uniting the people has also been broken. 'This passage may be the earliest evidence we have of the Samaritan schism. According to Josephus, it was in about the year 328 that the Samaritans built a rival temple on Mount Gerizim.'[1] Having rejected God's representative, a cruel tyrant will arise; he will be killed and a small part only of the nation will be saved (11: 4-17).

The breaking in succession of the two rods is a dramatic parable, disclosing to us the relationship between covenant and unity, between the grace of God and human harmony. To reject the loyal love of God is to rupture the bonds of fellowship between men. Conversely, whenever and wherever men respond in faith and obedience to the unmerited love and favour of God, they discover that the barriers which formerly kept them apart have been broken down (Ephesians 2: 14). Grace and Union belong together. The insult done to God by the rulers, who weigh out thirty shekels of silver—a paltry amount—as wages to his representative, is seen by the Christian evangelist as a prefiguration of the contemptuous attitude to God of the Jewish hierarchy, who for the purchase of his only beloved Son, pay the same amount to Judas the traitor (Matthew 26: 15; 27: 3-10).

[1] Note from *The Jerusalem Bible*, 1541.

THE FINAL CONFLICT

The oracles in the second collection (chapters 12 to 14) describe the last great assault of the nations upon Jerusalem. We have already looked at some aspects of this final conflict in the books of Isaiah (chapters 24 to 27), Ezekiel (chapters 38 and 39), and Joel (chapter 3).[1] Apocalyptic in character, these messages are concerned with the end-time, the destruction of the heathen nations, the deliverance of Jerusalem, the coming of the kingdom of God. Jerusalem, assaulted by the nations of the earth, will be to them like an intoxicating cup. They will be made to reel like drunkards, they will be crushed as with a heavy stone. God himself will rout the heathen hordes. At first the men of Judah will stand aloof, but when they see the intervention of God, they will join with vigour and zeal in the fight against the enemy. The Lord will use this victory won by the men of Judah to humiliate the arrogant citizens and nobility of Jerusalem; but having achieved that purpose he will then protect Jerusalem, make her citizens strong and valiant, and restore the Davidic dynasty (12: 1–9).

This decisive victory over the heathen powers will be followed by a national act of mourning. For the Lord will pour out upon his people a spirit of generosity and supplication, 'so that, when they look on him whom they have pierced, they shall mourn for him, as one mourns for an only child.' In this mourning, which will resemble in intensity the lamentations of the heathen over their dying gods, the nobility, the prophets, the priests, the people—every family of the land will share (12: 10–14). Who is this mysterious person who is murdered and whose death is subsequently repented of by those guilty of it? He is clearly someone of great importance, for his martyrdom elicits a national response. It is noteworthy that this national mourning follows the final victory of God and precedes the opening of a cleansing fountain in Jerusalem. Numerous attempts have been made to identify this martyr with some historic personage. It is much more likely that the prophet has been influenced by the portrait of the Suffering Servant of the Lord (Isaiah 52: 13 to 53: 12). It is significant that the death of an innocent victim at the hands of the representatives of the nation, is the necessary prelude to the messianic age. John the apostle interprets the verse as a prediction of the passion of

[1] See pages 95, 165, 230.

Christ, and John of Patmos looks to his Second Advent for the fulfilment of the prophecy (John 19: 37; Revelation 1: 7).

At the time of the deliverance and the repentance, a fountain will be opened in Jerusalem for cleansing from sin and impurity, from idolatry and prophecy. The inclusion of prophecy is significant. At this late date in the Hellenistic period, fanatics and imposters had so discredited the institution that this prophet (cf. Joel 2: 28, 29) can envisage no place for prophecy in the messianic age. Parents would then put to death a son who claimed to be a prophet, and a prophet having incisions on his body made during ecstasy (cf. I Kings 18: 28) would seek to escape death by claiming that the scars had been received during a drunken brawl (13: 1–6). Linking Zechariah 13: 1 with Revelation 7: 14, William Cowper wrote the well-known evangelical hymn—'There is a fountain filled with blood'. The citizens of Jerusalem are cleansed from all sin through the sacrifice of the Pierced One. There follows a description of the woes which are to precede the messianic age. The shepherd will be struck down and the flock scattered; the leaderless people will be left defenceless. Passing through the fiery ordeal, most of them will be destroyed; a purified remnant will survive (13: 7–9). This oracle was quoted by Christ just before his arrest in the Garden of Gethsemane (Matthew 26:31).

There is a second and different account in chapter 14 of the final assault on Jerusalem. The nations gathered to fight, capture the city and deport half the population, but this disaster is turned into victory by the intervention of God and the angelic hosts (14: 1–3). The conquest of the heathen will be followed by the transformation of nature. Winter and night will be abolished; there will be perpetual spring and never-ending day. Jerusalem will remain exalted, but all the rest of Judah will be depressed to the level of the Jordan Valley. The Mount of Olives will be divided, and through the valley so formed, a stream will flow eastwards from Jerusalem to the Dead Sea. The valley to the south of the city (Gehinnom) will be filled in, and another perennial stream will flow westwards from Jerusalem to the Mediterranean Sea. These accounts of vast geological changes are not to be taken literally; they are figurative descriptions of the spiritual exaltation of Jerusalem, from which 'streams of living water' will flow for the refreshment of mankind.[1] Jerusalem will be supreme; Jerusalem will

[1] See page 163.

be the source of spiritual life. On that day all nations will acknowledge the one, true God, and he will reign over all the earth (14: 4–11). The enemies of Jerusalem, together with all their animals, will be consumed by plague, and the city will be enriched by their wealth (14: 12–15).

The survivors among the nations will go year by year to Jerusalem to celebrate the festival of the enthronement of the Lord as King (14: 16–19). Not the Temple only, but the whole city will be holy to the Lord. Even the horses, formerly used for war, will be consecrated to the service of the Lord. The contagious holiness will consecrate the common pots and pans, so that worshippers thronging to Jerusalem may use them with impunity for sacrificial purposes. The ordinary will be sanctified, the secular become sacred, the common be transformed into the holy (14: 20, 21). When John of Patmos looked through an open door into heaven, he saw no temple in the New Jerusalem. The entire city was holy of holies. So it is to be in the end-time.

These various visions, set forth in the traditional language and imagery of apocalyptic, were born of despair. For the hope of the coming of the kingdom of God inspired by the former prophets had not been realized. Assyria—Babylon—Persia—Greece, one oppressive yoke had been replaced by another, and the promised Day of the Lord had not yet dawned. Taught by these painful lessons of history, with hearts made heavy by deferred hope, the authors of these oracles do not look for the coming of God within history through the agency of men and nations. They have set their hope upon the supernatural intervention of God for the deliverance of his people from heathen oppression. Hope deferred was not extinguished, but took a new direction. With the confidence of a sure faith in the sovereignty of God, they never relinquished the hope of the advent and triumph of his kingdom. Faced with delays and disappointments, they hoped against hope.

* * *

There is a phrase in Zechariah 9: 12 which may be taken as a description of the outlook of the prophets as a whole. Calling upon the scattered exiles to return to Zion, the prophet addresses them as 'prisoners of hope'. The life of Israel is characterized by hope; she is the Church expectant. Her prophets look forward to the advent of God, to the complete vindication of his purpose, to the final triumph of his kingdom. What is said of the heroes of faith applies to them—'And all these, though well attested by their faith, did not receive what was promised' (Hebrews 11: 39). They were 'hopeful captives' awaiting the day of emancipation. Jesus began his ministry by announcing that the kingdom, foreseen by the prophets, was very near. 'The time is fulfilled, and the kingdom of God is at hand; repent, and believe in the gospel' (Mark 1: 15). In the person and mission of Jesus Christ, through his ministry mighty in deed and word, through his saving death and glorious resurrection, through his exaltation and the gift of the Holy Spirit, the eternal God came to earth in judgment and salvation. The kingdom which was then established with power will be completed at his advent in glory. 'Then comes the end, when he delivers the kingdom to God the Father' (I Corinthians 15: 24).

Index